The Do-Gooders

The Do-Gooders

A History of the Calgary Local Council of Women, 1895–1975

Lillian MacLennan
Marjorie Barron Norris

DETSELIG
ENTERPRISES LTD

Calgary, Alberta, Canada

The Do-Gooders: A History of the Calgary Local Council of Women, 1985–1975
© 2011 Marjorie Barron Norris

Library and Archives Canada Cataloguing in Publication

MacLennan, Lillian, 1900–1997
      The do-gooders : a history of the Calgary Local Council of Women, 1895–1975 / Lillian MacLennan, Marjorie Barron Norris.

Includes bibliographical references.
ISBN 978-1-55059-418-8

      1. Local Council of Women of Calgary--History.
2. Women--Alberta--Calgary--History. I. Norris, Marjorie, 1923– II. Title.

HQ1910.C35M33 2011   305.4206'0712338   C2011-904385-8

Detselig Enterprises, Ltd.
210-1220 Kensington Rd NW
Calgary, Alberta T2N 3P5
www.temerondetselig.com
temeron@telusplanet.net
Phone: 403-283-0900
Fax: 403-283-6947

Detselig Enterprises, Ltd., recognizes the financial support of the government of Canada through the Canada Books Program.

Also acknowledged is the financial assistance of the Government of Alberta, Alberta Multimedia Development fund.

SAN 113-0234
ISBN 978-1-55059-409-6
Printed in Canada.
Cover design by James Dangerous.

A cautionary word regarding "Do-Gooders." *Partridge's Concise Dictionary of Slang and Unconventional English* notes the word is applied to people who interest themselves in social work. The *Paperback Oxford Canadian Dictionary* defines a do-gooder as a person who actively tries to help others, especially one considered unrealistic or officious. It's a matter of choice.

Contents

November 1895 founding of short-lived first Local Council by Lady Aberdeen. Madame Alvina Rouleau President. Countess Aberdeen's December 1896 Calgary address. Founding of 1912 Local council by Calgary's leading ladies. Alice Jamieson first President. Annie Foote Calgary's first woman trustee. Appointment of first police matrons. Formation of Canada's first Consumer League by Local Council's Georgina Newhall. Introduction of Copper coinage. Alice Jamieson's role in the 1916 franchise petition. Council's formation of Wartime Emergency Committee, a Labor Bureau and Woman's Exchange, and a Wartime Nursing committee.

Mothering concerns: Introduction of community playgrounds, special schools for mentally handicapped children, a pre-school health clinic, monitoring of dance halls, theatres, and impure literature. Introduction of Scripture reading in schools.

During the Great Depression the focus was on those suffering economic hardship. Local Council supported the YWCA's club for unemployed girls and distributed food, clothing, and literature to city camps for the unemployed. Council argued that removal of domestic science and manual training courses and closing of Commercial and Technical High Schools would lessen employment opportunities for youth. Council asked for contributary unemployment inusrance and health insurance. Their 1931 "Made in Calgary and Alberta" project was a success, but their 1933 resolution asking for birth control clinics in Alberta resulted in the withdrawal of the Catholic affiliates. Alice Grevett's January 1939 President's address highlighted the 26-year heritage of Local Council's organized service to the community.

During World War II, patriotic causes prevailed. The 1941 exhibit of the Princess dolls raised almost $2000 for European refugee
relief. Local Council formed a Soldiers, Sailors, and Airmen
Committee chaired by Millicent McElroy to welcome and support
veterans. The war years changed society, but not for the better.
Council women saw food wastage, malnutrition, illegitimacy, and
spread of venereal disease as concerns. Their lobby for surplus
food warehouses and a Food Conservation board failed. When
their lobby for a day nursery in Calgary went nowhere, they set up
one in the James Short School. Finally, after years of lobbying, two
women were appointed to the Police Force, and hospital maternity care was free.

Despite Council's waning in the early fifties, meetings were now
held in City Council chambers. Under the 1951 presidency of
Alberta Clark, their first project, the formation of The Council of
Christians and Jews, proved a triumph. Alberta Clark's 1955
President's Report also revealed how she viewed her long service
as President. As the decade ended, Local Council investigated
prison conditions and lack of rehabilitation programs for women
at the Fort Saskatchewan jail. They endorsed the formation of an
Elizabeth Fry Society in Calgary. On behalf of consumers, they
opposed price increases for whole milk, the required coloring of
margarine, and urged the Province to outlaw trading stamps.

Success during the halcyon years included a successful early sixties
lobby against the C.P.R. relocating its tracks along the south bank
of the Bow River. With environmental protection in mind, they
organized a December 1968 symposium on strip mining on public
lands titled "This Land is Your Land – Beautiful or Scarred." A
panel of experts from industry and environment argued the issue
of environmental ravage. Their continued preoccupation with the
neglect of women's prisoners, 70% of whom were Aboriginal,
resulted in possibly their greatest achievement: the Indian
Friendship Centre, which opened in October of 1964. In the
mothering category, resolutions related to the battered child,
kindergartens, day care centres, and sex offenders.

1970–1975   103

1970 critique of the Calgary Local Council of Women set the stage for the coming decade. The feminist movement reached Calgary in 1972 with the release of the Federal Government's Status of Women Commission's Report. On the recommendation of the National Council, Calgary formed its own committee, and out of that grew a "flourishing" Status of Women Action Committee. In 1975, International Women's Year, the Federal Minister of Health and Welfare, the Honorable Marc Lalonde, addressed a Calgary public meeting where he promised continued federal support beyond 1975. Efforts to save Rundle Lodge, Calgary's early hospital, from demolition failed; however, Nose Hill Park, Canada's largest urban park, did become a reality. Additional measures to protect the battered child and the handicapped were approved. In the seventies, the Calgary Local Council of Women initiated the Irene Murdoch Fund to pay legal costs of the farm wife's appeal against a court decision that ruled she was not entitled to a share of the farm assets upon divorce. It was a high-profile case.

ADDENDA

Foreword

THE *DO-GOODERS* by Lillian MacLennan is an amazing account of the world of women in Calgary and Canada from 1893 to the 1970s. It is important and necessary information, compiled and written clearly and thoughtfully. It is also history, not bedtime reading. (Although it has its moments!) It's more like a treasure trove of names, initiatives, attitudes, legislation, and memories for historians and researchers. This is "the way we were," we women in Calgary and Canada.

History must thank MacLennan for assembling such a careful outline of the work undertaken by the Council of Women between 1895 and 1975. And in turn, history must thank Marjorie Norris of Calgary for recognizing the importance of *The Do-Gooders*, for revising it and bringing it up-to-date, and for adding information to help us understand the larger picture. Between MacLennan and Norris, every name and date, every issue and argument, is as accurately presented as possible.

—Nancy Millar

Preface

Ifirst read Lillian MacLennan's typewritten manuscript *A History of the Calgary Local Council of Women* in 1990. Her lively chronicle of Calgary's once-dominant women's lobby of affiliated societies proved an invaluable guide for me during my preparation of *A Leaven of Ladies* – a history of the Calgary Local Council of Women (hereafter referred to simply as the Local Council) written to commemorate the city's centennial year in 1994.

Lillian's manuscript had also been prepared as a commemorative gift, but in recognition of an earlier civic milestone: Century Calgary 1975 – the 100th anniversary of the North West Mounted Police fort at the junction of the Bow and Elbow Rivers. The scope of the Local Council's "Historical Book" project, begun in 1972 during my presidency, was described three years later at the Local Council Annual Meeting in a progress report by Margaret Buckmaster, Secretary of the Editorial Committee. It read:

Report of Editorial Committee, Historical Book, Calgary Local Council of Women

The committee consists of Dr. Ruth Gorman, Editor, Mrs. Joni Chorny, Mrs. Grace Johnson, Mrs. Frances Roessingh, Mrs. Grace Stonewall, Mrs. Mary Winspear, Mrs. Lillian MacLennan, Mrs. Alberta Clark, Mrs. Aileen Fish, Mrs. Marjorie Norris, and Mrs. Margaret Buckmaster, Secretary.

The preparation of a manuscript giving the history of the Local Council of Women, and outstanding women of Calgary, is indeed an exciting, stimulating, and interesting experience for this committee.

We received a $3600 grant from the Government of Alberta to finance the research and manuscript preparation portion of this project. It is hoped we will be able to publish two versions, a limited edition in a hard cover coffee-table format and a low cost paper-back edition provided we can obtain financial support for publication of our manuscript.

We are grateful to have received the pen-sketch histories of our affiliates as well as their contribution of biographical sketches of their group's historic members.

Mrs. MacLennan and Mrs. Stonewall are collecting material on the Local Council of Women. Our history is recorded in newspaper clippings, minutes, and in the minds of its former members. We need your help to reconstruct our early years so would welcome any information you can remember. Mrs. MacLennan will write this history when all the material is collected.

Authors are busy writing under ten chapter headings which are – Role of the Volunteer, Citizenship, Health and Nursing, Education, Women in Politics, Laws and Changing Laws, Women in Business, Authors and Artists, Drama and Music, and Sports. The two title manuscripts finished are excellent.

Mrs. Fish is compiling the anecdotes. She would also welcome any funny stories you can contribute.

We intend to approach the Government of Alberta for further financial support to permit the publication of our manuscript. They have indicated verbally that they will provide the necessary financial support. We will endeavour to have this verbal assurance confirmed in writing in the near future.

Hopefully we will be able to celebrate the successful launching of our book at our next annual meeting.

—Margaret Buckmaster

Clearly, our aspirations knew no bounds. At that 1975 Annual Meeting, a reference to Lillian MacLennan's brief report read:

"Mrs. MacLennan, speaking in light of her experience as researcher for the L.C.W. History, stressed how important it was that each Chairman pass all records to her successor." Years later, Dr. Ruth Gorman attributed the failure of the Local Council's magnum opus to the large scope of the endeavour, limited funds, attrition of able researchers and authors, and the loss of all but four of the editorial committee due to death and moving.

Lillian MacLennan was well qualified for her contribution to the undertaking. She was a journalist by training and a free-lance writer for the *Albertan*. More importantly, she knew whereof she wrote. In the halcyon years of the sixties, while serving as the affiliate representative of the Calgary branch of the Canadian Association of Consumers, Lillian chaired the Local Council's Economics Committee and served as Corresponding Secretary, Courtesy Secretary, Vice-President, President (1963–1965), and Past President.

In 1987 she and her husband retired to Victoria where she died, a decade later, on July 21, 1997, at 97 years of age. Her obituary, which was published in the *Times Colonist, Victoria, Calgary Herald, Calgary Sun*, the *Gladstone, Manitoba*, local paper, *The Toronto Star*, and *The Globe and Mail*, read:

> MacLennan, Lillian Marguerite (née Broadhead), born in London, England on April 5, 1900 – died peacefully at Mt. Tolmie Hospital, Victoria, B.C., on July 21st, 1997. Beloved wife of the late Kenneth MacLennan, dear sister of Marie Cumber, Dorothy Elson, Hilda Good and her brothers Edwin and John Broadhead, all of Toronto. She was predeceased by her brother Norman. For many years Lillian worked in the oil industry in Alberta and the North West Territories, and later as a freelance writer for the Calgary Albertan. She was a Past President and Honorary Life Member of the Calgary Local Council of Women, and active in the First Baptist Church, Calgary.

She and her husband were avid gardeners and naturalists.
A private memorial service will be held at a later date. In
lieu of flowers, a donation may be made to the church or
a charity of your choice.

Lillian's manuscript *A History of the Calgary Local Council of
Women 1895–1975* never became a book. In 2009, I happened
to loan a copy to historian Stephan Guevremont who had a special interest in Dr. Ruth Gorman's role within the Local
Council of Women. Shortly afterwards, I also loaned a copy to
Donna Livingstone, Director of the University of Calgary
Press, who had a special interest in one of the affiliated societies. Both suggested I arrange to have the history published.
With their encouragement, and because I never could put a
well-written manuscript out of my mind, I decided to edit it for
publication.

There was one problem – because *A History of the Calgary
Local Council of Women 1895–1975* was intended to be a com-
ponent, albeit an important one, of the Historical Book project, it was not book length. Moreover, few of the women and
affiliates were identified in this condensed narrative which
focused on their lobbying efforts. Therefore an addendum that
identified the executive and affiliated societies at the outset of
each decade seemed requisite. The secretary and convenor
reports were selected to represent a range of views. Among
these the Laws and Resolutions Committee reports verify
Local Council's lobbying role – its raison d'être. Annual meeting addresses and autobiographies reveal how the members
interacted with one another, while the tributes tell us how they
were remembered by their peers.

This book is therefore divided into two parts. The first is
Lillian's text, minimally edited to preserve her voice. The second contains the addenda, which provide numerous original
source documents helpful to understanding the Local Council
of Women.

The unfailing help of Assistant Chief Archivist Doug Cass and his staff at the Glenbow Archives, the recollection of events by Margaret Buckmaster, a survivor of the 70s, and the encouragement of historian Nancy Millar sustained me. My grandson, Matthew O'Connor, who helped me search the Glenbow archives, recorded the sources with absolute accuracy and edited the archival pictures. His wife, Shylah, salvaged my ongoing format entanglements. Debby Stevens undertook the exacting editing of my final drafts. I am also grateful to my publisher, Detselig Enterprises, and to Aaron Dalton for his efforts editing and designing the book. I decided that the title should be *The Do-Gooders*. I rather think that Lillian would have approved.

—Marjorie Baron Norris

Marjorie Norris's Council of Women Record

Calgary Local Council of Women: Membership Committee 1970–71, President 1972–73, Citizenship Committee 1975, Vice-President 1976–78. Chair of Local Council's host committee for the 1978 National Council Convention held at the Banff Springs Hotel. I was awarded an Honorary Life Membership in the Calgary Local Council of Women, a Life Membership in the National Council of Women of Canada, and in 1978, I was awarded the Queen Elizabeth Jubilee Medal on the recommendation of the National Council of Women of Canada.

I have authored two women's histories: *A Leaven of Ladies: A History of the Calgary Local Council of Women* (1995) and *Sister Heroines: The Roseate Glow of Wartime Nursing, 1914–1918* (2002). Following these endeavors, I edited the World War I memoir of Captain Harold W. McGill, Medical Officer, 31st Battalion C.E.F., enitled *Medicine and Duty*; it was published in 2007.

Presidents: 1895–1975

Madame Charles Rouleau, 1895–98
Mrs. R.R. Jamieson, 1912–16
Mrs. George Kerby, 1917
Mrs. Charles Fenkell, 1918–19
Mrs. P.S. Woodhall, 1920–21
Mrs. H.G.H. Glass, 1922–23
Mrs. W.A. Geddes, 1924–25
Mrs. A. MacWilliams, 1926–27
Mrs. H.J. Akitt, 1928–29
Mrs. H.J. Robbie, 1930
Mrs. Guy Johnson, 1931–32
Mrs. F.G. Grevett, 1933–34
Mrs. R.L. Freeman, 1935
Mrs. A. Blight, 1936–37
Mrs. F.G. Grevett, 1938
Mrs. Ervin Hirst, 1939–41
Mrs. F.S. Ditto, 1942–43
Mrs. Wallace Neale, 1944–45
Mrs. L.G. Fisher, 1946–47
Mrs. H.F. Clarke, 1948–50
Mrs. Russell Clark, 1951–55
Miss Una MacLean, 1955/58
Mrs. A. Russell Hutchison, 1958–59
Mrs. O. Stonewall, 1959–63
Mrs. K.F. MacLennan, 1963–65
Mrs. A.D. Winspear, 1965–67
Mrs. H.G. McCullough, 1967–68
Mrs. A.C. Luft, 1968–69
Mrs. Barbara Langridge, 1970–71
Mrs. Marjorie Norris, 1972–73
Mrs. Joni Chorny, 1973–74
Mrs. Gwen Thorssen, 1975–77

Madame Charles Rouleau,
1895–98

Mrs. R.R. Jamieson, 1912–16

Mrs. George Kerby, 1917

Mrs. Charles Fenkell, 1918–19

Mrs. P.S. Woodhall, 1920–21

Mrs. H.G.H. Glass, 1922–23

Mrs. W.A. Geddes, 1924–25

Mrs. A. MacWilliams, 1926–27

Mrs. H.J. Akitt, 1928–29

Mrs. H.J. Robbie, 1930

Mrs. Guy Johnson, 1931–32

Mrs. F.G. Grevett, 1933–34

Mrs. R.L. Freeman, 1935

Mrs. A. Blight, 1936–37

Mrs. F.G. Grevett, 1938

Mrs. Ervin Hirst, 1939–41

Mrs. F.S. Ditto, 1942–43

Mrs. Wallace Neale, 1944–45

Mrs. L.G. Fisher, 1946–47

Mrs. H.F. Clarke, 1948–50

Mrs. Russell Clark, 1951–55

Miss Una MacLean, 1955/58

Mrs. A. Russell Hutchinson,
1958–59

Mrs. O. Stonewall, 1959–63

Mrs. K.F. MacLennan, 1963–65

Mrs. A.D. Winspear, 1965–67

Mrs. H.G. McCullough, 1967–68

Mrs. A.C. Luft, 1968–69

Mrs. Barbara Langridge, 1970–71   Mrs. Marjorie Norris, 1972–73

Mrs. Joni Chorny, 1973–74   Mrs. Gwen Thorssen, 1975–77

1972 L.C.W. Diamond Jubilee Greetings

Office of the Lieutenant Governor

Many thanks for informing me of the 60th Anniversary of the Calgary Local Council of Women to be celebrated on April 26th.

I would wish to convey to all your members, through you, my greetings and best wishes on this notable Anniversary occasion. It is indeed a mark of maturity when organizations such as yours can mark sixty years of public service and you and your friends in the organization will find much to bring them pride.

Alberta, as a province would be only seven years old when the Calgary Local was formed, and the Western Canadian economy was based almost entirely upon wheat and cattle. Most Albertans lived on farms and were without cars, tractors, electricity, telephone and the numerous inventions which have changed life so completely. In point of change it is indeed a far cry from 1912 to 1972 and notable as it has been, it is no more distinctive than the magnitude of public service rendered by groups such as yours.

As I congratulate the Calgary Local Council of Women on their 60 years of performance, I express the hope that the next 60 will be no less fruitful in work and influence.

—Grant McEwan

Office of the Premier, Calgary, Alberta

On behalf of the Province of Alberta I am pleased to be able to congratulate the Calgary Local Council of Women on their Sixtieth Anniversary.

I know that the Council has done a great deal in many fields such as reform of women's prisons, the advancement of equal rights for women in our society and other areas such as the establishment of the Indian Friendship Centre in Calgary.

There are still important areas of work to be done concerning women in our society and I am pleased to see the current activity of the Calgary Council of Women.

Please accept my best wishes for continued success in the future.

—Premier Peter Lougheed

Office of the Mayor, Calgary, Alberta

On behalf of the citizens of Calgary I am pleased to have the opportunity to extend congratulations to the Local Council of Women on the occasion of its 60th Anniversary.

The contributions of the Local Council of Women to the quality of life in Calgary are well known and most sincerely appreciated in the community. The role that women play in our society has changed drastically in the last few years and I am pleased with that change. I am delighted that women are becoming more involved and making a constructive effort to improve the communities in which they live.

Congratulations on 60 years of service. It is my hope that Calgarians will benefit from your organization for many years to come.

—Rod Sykes

The National Council of Women of Canada

Thank you so much for your kind letter informing me of the Diamond Jubilee of the Calgary Council of Women. I was also delighted to learn that your Council is proposing two of your members for National Life Memberships. Your generous response to our request is most heart warming.

The National Council of Women join me in extending sincere congratulations to your Council. A Diamond Anniversary is truly a momentous occasion. It is the culmination of many years of resourceful and indomitable effort on the part of the women in your Council to contribute in a very significant way to the well being of their fellowmen.

The National Council of Women would like to express its deep appreciation to the many dedicated members, who throughout the sixty years have worked with perseverance and devotion to promote understanding and goodwill in your community. We wish you continued success in the future.

May I add my personal good wishes to each member of your Council. I shall be thinking of you on April 26th.

—Helen Hnatyshn

Part One

Lillian's History of the Local Council of Women

Chapter One

First Years: Before 1920

WHAT IS COUNCIL OF WOMEN? It has been called many things: a bunch of do-gooders, busybodies, McKenzie King called it "the most powerful lobbying group in Canada," Mr. Diefenbaker's description was "The Women's Parliament," and a Calgary newspaper editorialized about "The National Council of Old-fashioned Sensible Women."[1]

There is probably some truth in all of them. But when in 1893 Lady Aberdeen, wife of the then Governor General of Canada and President of the International Council of Women, was elected as the first president of the newly formed National Council of Women of Canada, she made it clear that she wanted the members' overriding activity to be "mothering." "Not all women are called upon to be mothers of little children," she told an audience, "but all women are called upon in some way or another to mother."

Mothering was much needed in those days. Boatloads of young girls from Britain and Europe were arriving frequently at Canada's shores to fill the never-satisfied plea for domestic help, and the stories of exploitation of some of these girls are almost unbelievable.

In 1895, Lady Aberdeen brought her enthusiasms and her mothering ideas to Calgary. It was a terrific meeting. The gaily-decorated Opera House was crowded, with many standees; the Governor General was on the platform, supporting his wife, along with many prominent Calgary women; the Calgary Fire Department band played ("scrambled through the National Anthem" was what the reporter said); applause was spontaneous and frequent; and the newspapers were generous with coverage. When the Countess left Calgary, she was able to write on the November 26th page of her notebook: "Calgary Council formed . . . Mdme. Rouleau President . . . good meeting." The vote to form a Local Council was unanimous, we are told. The 1895 Local Council only functioned for a short time, though.

The December 11, 1896, edition of *The Calgary Herald*, on its front page, reported this special meeting with Lady Aberdeen while on her brief visit to Calgary:

COUNTESS ABERDEEN ADDRESSES THE NATIONAL COUNCIL OF WOMEN

Lady Aberdeen's address in the courthouse on Wednesday afternoon to the local branch of the National Woman's Council was one of congratulation and encouragement.

The work of the first year was reviewed and proved so suggestive a budget that night came long before the meeting was ready to disperse. Those who represented the local council in the relief committee were especially congratulated upon their success. Her Excellency dwelt upon the importance of inquiring into cases, of giving in such a manner as not to pauperize, and of organization to prevent the overlapping of charity.

It was a surprise to many present to learn that over 30 families have been helped to help themselves and are now self supporting; that a home has been established where the poor who are out of work may be housed until employment is found for them, and that the whole expense has been defrayed by voluntary offerings from the townspeople and ranchers.

Lady Aberdeen reminded the ladies that though their effort to establish a curfew in Calgary had thus far failed, their desire might yet be attained, as the Legislative

Assembly had passed a law giving town councils authority in the matter. The other subjects that have occupied the local council were touched upon briefly: The advisability of teaching sewing in public schools, the inquiries concerning the circulation of impure literature and the selling of cigarettes to children, the donation to the Armenian fund, the establishment of home reading circles, and the opening of classes in cookery.

Lady Aberdeen assured the ladies they would find in Miss Livingstone, who is expected to give lessons in cookery here in January, not only a thoroughly competent but a keenly interested and most interesting teacher.

Her Excellency had with her a number of Mr. Stead's penny books, among which are 50 standard novels and 40 of the best poets. Mr. Stead has replaced the "penny dreadful" by the penny delightful.

In closing, the council was urged to earnestly consider means whereby medical aid and nursing may be brought nearer the settlers in outlying districts. In British Columbia the Government gives a grant to physicians settling in such places. Some such plan might be adopted with regard to nurses, and might be extended to the Territories.

A vote of thanks was given to Lady Aberdeen for the kindness she had shown in responding so readily and with such warm and womanly sympathy to the invitation to address the Calgary council, and the meeting closed with the singing of the national anthem.

Beginnings

Seventeen years after that initial false start, some civic-minded women from various like-minded organizations, seeking strength in unity, sponsored a mass meeting in Paget Hall.

Actually their purpose was to form a Women's Civic League, but they allowed themselves to be persuaded that a branch of the National Council of Women might have a much wider scope and be more representative. They appointed a committee to bring in a recommendation, and, as a result, on October 26th, 1912, "a small but extremely animated meeting," chaired by Mrs. O.C. Edwards of Medicine Hat (a vice-president and Alberta representative of the National Council of Women), voted to form the Calgary Local Council of Women, with Mrs. R.R. Jamieson as its first president.[2]

Mrs. Jamieson was one of the most active of the fine group of women who made up that first executive. She has gone down in history as the first woman police magistrate and the first judge of a juvenile court in the British Empire. Other members of that original executive were Mrs. G.W. Kerby, wife of the principal of Mount Royal College, Mrs. E.A. Cruikshank, Mrs. William Pearce, and Mrs. P.J. Nolan, wife of one of Calgary's most famous lawyers.

It is regrettable that the records covering the first six years cannot be found; however, from retrospective resumés made in later years by members who apparently had access to those lost papers, from the 1915 Calgary Club Women's Blue Book, and from tidbits here and there it is plain that the charter members lost no time in getting to work. Indeed, they were off and running from the moment of organization. At that very first meeting the suggestion was made that a woman candidate for School Board Trustee be nominated. It "met with tumultuous applause." That this would require an amendment to the city charter did not deter them one bit. They *did* have an ace up their collective sleeve, though – it was a male school board member who had whispered the idea into the receptive ear of one of the ladies! That was all they needed to spur them to action. On June 18, 1913, the city charter was amended and Miss Annie Foote was elected to the School Board in 1915, the first female to be elected to any civic office in Calgary. Within a few days, the Local Council's first regular general meeting was held, and a letter urging affiliation was sent to the presidents of every women's organization in the city.

The constitution adopted naturally, and of necessity it followed that of the National Council. The aims and objects as set out then have changed only in superficial wording throughout the years. They were: "To bring the various associations of women in Calgary into closer relationship through an organized union. But no society entering Local Council should thereby lose independence in aim or object, or be committed to any principle or methods of procedure of any other society in the Council. The object of our Council is to serve as a medium of communication between women's organizations, and as a means of prosecuting any work of common interest. The Local Council of Women is a confederation of societies and ideas rather than of individuals."

The preamble to the constitution then, as now, is practically the same as Lady Aberdeen presented it in 1895, and is the foundation of all Council action: "We, women of Canada, sincerely believing that the best good of our homes and nation will be advanced by our greater unity of thought, sympathy and purpose; and that an organized movement of women will best conserve the highest good of family and state, do hereby band together to further the application of the Golden Rule to society, custom and law." The Golden Rule remains the Local Council's motto.

Before a month had passed, committees were appointed to work for "the betterment of conditions in jails for women; the enlargement and support of hospitals; improvement in laws concerning women's property rights, better schools, and supervised playgrounds." It is interesting to note that the plight of women in jails was an intensive concern in 1959–1960 and that women's property rights is still a top priority on the Local Council's agenda.

There was no excuse for any woman who could read to be ignorant of what the Council of Women was all about. The *Calgary Albertan* was very cooperative, and prior to the organizational meeting it had published a series of articles giving detailed information about all aspects of National and Local Councils in Canada "for the convenience of several hundred members of women's clubs in Calgary which will probably affiliate." The *Albertan* also published, in full, the lengthy and comprehensive invitational letter sent out by the first corresponding secretary, Mrs. Eva Jacobs, following the first meeting.

All this publicity brought quick results. Soon forty-three societies had affiliated, including such prestigious organizations as the Women's Christian Temperance Union, Young Women's Christian Association, Women's Canadian Club, American Women's Club, and Women's Press Club. Each organization was allowed one delegate for every 25 members up to 100, and for every 50 thereafter. The fee was $1 a year for each delegate. Presumably, each paying delegate was a voting one, and evidently each delegate was a working one, for the accomplishments of the first few years are impressive.

By the end of the decade they had obtained, or were building the groundwork for, city or provincial regulations regarding the wrapping of bread, protection behind glass of meats and baked products for sale, chairs to be provided behind counters for female store clerks, separate toilet facilities for girls employed in offices and stores, a pure water supply (filtration plant), marriage licenses to be issued only by a government official (until then a license could be obtained from any jeweler), registration and strict inspection of boarding houses for young people, suppression of the red-light district (jail, not fines, for prostitution), government supervision of stock yards and storage plants, and legislation to ensure proper weights and measures. With women's lot in mind, they got copper coinage introduced into Calgary; before then it took fifteen cents to pay for a twelve cent item. In reporting the copper coinage success, a

Local Council member remarked, "the merchants may consider this a curse, but to the housewife it is a blessing." They asked that a police matron and police women be appointed. Mrs. Mathieson was sworn in as the first police matron in 1914, but it took much urging and thirty years more before police women were a reality. Promised by the provincial government was a home for mentally ill children and destitute old people, a detention home or reformatory for women criminals, and industrial schools – one for boys and one for girls. Success crowned their efforts to have the school board make special provision for the sub-normal child, with a specially-trained teacher in charge. One of the earliest concerns of the new Calgary Local Council of Women was a safe and clean milk supply. Tuberculosis was rife, and milk was blamed. Pressure by the National Council of Women had produced a federal order-in-council in 1914, giving cities and towns the right to demand that their milk come from T.B. tested herds. Calgary L.C.W. lost no time in seeking to have the order implemented in their city, and Calgary was one of the first cities to avail itself of the new measure. Several years later, however, the Calgary Local Council refused to endorse a National Council resolution calling for pasteurization of milk. Pasteurization does not take care of "dirty" milk, they contended.

One project in which they took particular pride was the organization of a Consumers' League following two mass meetings which were sponsored by L.C.W. and arranged by its Home Economics chairman Mrs. Newhall. They were commended by one and all for the successful farmers' market that grew out of it and flourished for many years.[3]

The range of this new organization's interests is amazing. Out of their meager funds they erected a shelter outside the general hospital for the convenience of hospital visitors waiting for street cars. It is sad to note from subsequent reports that vandalism was a problem even then.

Another program begun by L.C.W. in 1914, and which grew like Topsy, was the Vacant Lot Garden club. With economy and beautification its two-pronged purpose, citizens were asked to plant vegetables and flowers in vacant lots around the city. It was a tremendous success from the start: 250 signed up the first year, 950 the second. The city itself later took over management of the project, keeping close track in Depression years of welfare recipients who did not take advantage of the good cost savings it provided.

Threaded through all of the Calgary Local Council's early history is a continued attempt to alleviate the situation that domestic workers found themselves in, and to upgrade the profession. In this they worked hand-in-glove with the Housekeepers' Association and the Women's Labor League. That these immigrant girls were exploited there is no doubt. This is surprising when reports intimate that very few immigrant domestics reached the West where the demand was tremendous. Council women complained that the government provided fare only to port, and waiting lines of women at Halifax, Montreal, and Quebec snapped up the girls as soon as the boat hit the dock. The law of supply and demand was apparently not working, for when L.C.W.'s Mrs. Margaret Lewis called a meeting of employers of girls to discuss the situation, not one of them showed up. However, they never gave up on this, and, as conditions improved, part of the credit should go to the Council of Women.

Probably not many of today's Calgarians know that the beauty of tree-lined Memorial Drive was originally the idea of Calgary L.C.W. Here is the original resolution from the Local Council's minutes of June 13, 1919: "In view of the fact that the City is trying to acquire a strip of land running along the waterside, it is suggested that a suitable memorial to the memory of our brave heroes in the late war would be a memorial war garden of the Local Council of Women of Calgary; each large organization or group of smaller ones undertaking charge of a large strip; thus taking the first step to beautify our city." Later discussions designated "the strip of land between Memorial Drive and the river, and from Hillhurst Bridge to St. George's Island" as the possible memorial area; and a tree Planting Committee was appointed to sell to organizations and individuals the idea of buying one tree or several – each to bear a plate with the name of a fallen soldier.

Details of what happened after that are sparse. But we do know that the project was taken over by local service clubs, and Local Council became a member of a broader-based community committee. Progress, though sure, was slow.[4] In 1923 the L.C.W. records show a payment of $14 for seven Memorial Drive trees, from proceeds of a tea held for that purpose. It is believed that at least some plates were purchased but never affixed. A 1968 newspaper clipping indicates that they were "gathering dust in a military museum."

Having been sidetracked from their original plans, Local Council selected an untidy riverbank spot, Elbow Park, and decided to beautify it as their memorial instead. However, before they got around to taking action, the land was purchased from the city by a civic-minded citizen and is now a small green playground known as Woods Park.

The Franchise

Probably the most outstanding activity during the first years of Calgary Local Council was the part they played in obtaining the franchise for women. After organizing, it didn't take them long to realize that their efforts at reform would always be handicapped unless women sat on boards and in legislatures where decisions were made. This is what those politically minded charter members had in mind when they met in Paget Hall. Besides, many of them were also members of the W.C.T.U., and a referendum on prohibition was in the offing. They had no faith in the judgments of men in a caucus minus female influence. As a matter of fact, W.C.T.U. had a suffrage committee at the time of its affiliation with Local Council, and the subject had been smoldering within its ranks for some time. There was also an Equal Suffrage League in Edmonton at the time. It is documented history that the Calgary Local Council shared with other Alberta organizations the work and honor of eventually securing the franchise for women in Alberta. What is perhaps not well known is that Mrs. R.R. Jamieson, the first president of the Calgary L.C.W., was the spark that lit the flame, and that a man – her husband (a two-term mayor of Calgary) – spurred her on. In an interview she told a reporter "I am not a feminist, but my husband told me it was my place to help women obtain the franchise."

Mrs. Jamieson spearheaded a canvass for signatures on a petition, and in the fall of 1912, with L.C.W. Laws Convener Mrs. Harold Riley accompanying her, she journeyed to Edmonton to present the petition to the Premier, the Honorable Arthur Sifton. Mr. Sifton squirmed out of making a decision by noting that only the city had been canvassed. Farm women must be included, he said. Disappointed but not daunted, the ladies scurried around, added more city names, and, with help from United Farmers (who were strongly behind them) and Women's Institutes, secured 4000 rural names. The delegates taking this surprise package for Mr. Sifton to Edmonton in the fall of 1913 included Mrs. Jamieson, Mrs. G.W. Kerby (an L.C.W. vice president), Mrs. Fred Langford (vice president of the W.C.T.U.), and members of the Edmonton Equal Franchise League. The result of that meeting was a vague promise that something would be done and an invitation to return when the legislature sat again. But then war was declared, and for a while the women concentrated their efforts on war work. They had not forgotten, only postponed, the franchise question. But now they had fantastic support; and when the next delegation descended on the provincial legislature on February 26, 1915, it was composed of about one thousand community leaders – male and female – from all over the province, carrying a petition containing between forty thousand and fifty thousand names, over six thousand of them rural. The delegation represented not only the Local Councils of Calgary and Edmonton, but also the United Farmers of Alberta, the Edmonton Equal Franchise League, and W.C.T.U. Many prominent men, including R.B. Bennett, openly supported the movement.

Among the handful of women allowed to speak to the bill on the floor of the legislature were Mrs. Alice Jamieson, Mrs. Nellie McClung (she had just come to Alberta to make her home), and Mrs. Emily Murphy (Janey Canuck). The bill received assent on April 19, 1916, and these three ladies nearly went wild. One reporter paints a word-picture of them weaving arm-in-arm along Edmonton's Jasper Avenue on their way to a photographer as though drunk – and they all stout supporters of the W.C.T.U.!

Alberta was the first province to promise the franchise to its women through legislation, but because of the many parliamentary delays, it lost the distinction of being the first province to implement enfranchisement. Manitoba's bill was passed in January 1916.

An amusing sidelight is the fact that the bill carried unanimously except for one vote. The holdout was a man who said he "didn't want the women to get the franchise too easy."

Two wars interrupted Local Council's progress during the years covered by this history, and Calgary Local Council of Women can be justifiably proud of its contributions to both.

At the outset of the Great War, an Emergency Committee was set up, its mandate: to be part of the war effort wherever and whenever the need arose. This committee performed many useful services. One they considered most important was the establishment in 1914 of a Labour Bureau and Woman's Exchange, through which, after diligent checking and matching, suitable homes were found for girls and women wishing to work in the country. A Wartime Nursing Committee channeled volunteers into nursing services and looked after the needs of convalescents. Council women – individually and collectively – gave time to manning government booths, handling ration cards, and selling war stamps, as well as assisting at provincial government registration centers where women were invited to register for the kind of war work they were willing and able to do. A Calgary L.C.W. executive member, Mrs. Margaret Lewis, was appointed organizer of this work for the province. Local Council also undertook to be responsible for providing field comforts for "The Boys," relieving the Red Cross of this function. Talk to any early L.C.W. member and she will recall Mrs. Millicent McElroy's devoted service to returning soldiers and their families through both wars. As L.C.W.'s representative, she welcomed the boys at the station, lifting their spirits with tunes on her cornet, and followed up with sympathetic and practical help, beyond the call of duty, for them and their families. Both during and after the war, Local Council initiated or supported other organizations in a variety of Canadian and overseas relief programs.

Until well into the 1930s, presidents of Calgary L.C.W. were invited and honored participants in the city's Armistice Day ceremonies, and yearly laid wreaths – most often homemade ones – on the graves of soldiers on Decoration Day.

Chapter Two

The 1920s

WITH THE FRANCHISE WON and the war over, the Council of Women entered the 1920s with more time to give to local needs and to follow up on unfinished business from the previous disrupted decade.

It will be remembered that community playgrounds was mentioned as a major priority at L.C.W.'s first meeting. From then on the records are sprinkled with pleas and confrontations on the subject with city fathers. But success did not come until 1921. In that year the city appropriated $1500 of its budget for the establishment of two playgrounds. The next year, asking for another $1500, and perhaps not expecting too much, the women decided to hold a tag day to augment the amount the city might allot to playgrounds. They were probably surprised when city council voted $1500 for two playgrounds and $1500 for swimming pools in Riley Park and St. George's Island. In 1923, the city budgeted $1000 for playground supervision and equipment, and a L.C.W. tag day boosted the amount by $400. By 1926 there were seven playgrounds.

Tag days became a sure-fire way to raise money when it was needed. Sometimes it was for their own purposes, but they were just as ready to tag in support of worthwhile causes of other organizations, particularly their affiliates. That not all members were in favor of that method of fundraising is clear. A resolution presented by a member for consideration at one meeting deplored the use of tag days: It accused they were "not conducive to the well-being of citizens, particularly children." It asked that Local Council go on record as opposing the "begging for money on the streets." But necessity triumphed over high principles when, later in the same meeting, the treasurer's report, having revealed that there was insufficient money in the kitty to pay all outstanding bills, a motion to hold a tag day on a certain date was adopted.

By the middle of the 1920s another early project had come to fruition. Two special schools for mentally handicapped children were in operation, and a special Mental Hygiene committee was working for institutional care for the lower-grade retarded, together with a program to help their mothers. They didn't hide the fact that they favored sterilization, or, as they phrased it, "checking the reproduction of the subnormal," when noting an increasing birth rate among mentally defective persons. In 1923, the Health Convener reported there were 3000 mentally defective persons in Alberta. The women also talked the C.P.R. into providing privacy and special care for mental patients being transported from Calgary to Ponoka.

The need for psychiatric facilities in hospitals is an accepted fact today, and such facilities are available in old and new hospitals. Calgary L.C.W. saw this need back in the 1920s and began exerting continuing pressure to fulfill this need. Rehabilitation help for patients between a stay in mental institutions and their return to normal living has also been a long-standing active concern. There are now some results in this area.

From the very start, health and sanitation has been a top priority with Local Council. The main health problems in the 1920s seem to have been venereal diseases, goitre, and tuberculosis. (The ladies labeled V.D. "a scourge," "a secret plague," or "that foul canker eating at the heart of the nation.") According to L.C.W.'s 1919 Health Convener, venereal diseases then affected 10% of the population. L.C.W. persuaded the school board to include in its curriculum information on "How to avoid contacting contagious diseases," had warning notices posted in public lavatories and other public places, and were instrumental in the compulsory reporting of V.D. Perhaps the most important result of Local Council's work in this regard was its success in getting legislation making mandatory the treating of babies' eyes at birth to prevent blindness – a tragedy frequently following a birth to V.D. parents.

Goitre was apparently widespread, and little was being done about it when in the early 1920s Calgary Local Council women decided that the public should be "awakened to the fact that it was a serious menace." They became vocal and busy, interviewing doctors, publicizing facts and preventative procedures, holding public meetings, and sending off resolutions to local, provincial, and federal governments. The Alberta government tried to apply the brakes, suggesting that it would be bad publicity for the province if the problem was publicized – even though it was then a national problem. The women had more success locally. Treatment was provided for children in the schools, and the adult population was alerted to the seriousness of the situation to the point where they began to demand action toward eradication.

As for tuberculosis, much progress has been made on a national scale in the diminution of T.B., due largely to National Council of Women's persistent and successful campaign for compulsory testing of herds. Calgary L.C.W. had done its part in demanding that milk delivered in the city come from T.B. tested herds. But the disease was still rampant. As pigs were thought to be the culprit, the women dug up statistics showing that 25% of swine killed were tubercular as a result of being fed milk from tubercular cows. Also, they said, T.B. was taking more young lives than any other disease. On the assumption that an inability to pay for treatment was one reason for the epidemic proportions of the disease, L.C.W., jointly with the Women's Labor League and United Farm Women, called a public meeting to get support for a request that the sanitarium be supported by taxation and free treatment provided for all. They were successful. Presumably believing that prevention is better than cure, the Local Council women urged stricter enforcement of the city bylaw prohibiting spitting on sidewalks and in streetcars. When in 1934 it was rumored that the office of Lieutenant Governor was to be abolished, they came up with the tongue-in-cheek suggestion that the money thus saved could be used to build and maintain a much-needed sanitarium. Mrs. Wm. Carson, a worker and long-time member of Local Council, devoted much of her energies to the improvement of conditions at the sanitarium.

Worrying about the cost of maternity hospitalization, L.C.W. members talked a lot about some kind of pre-payment by installment. Getting nowhere, they eventually came up with something better – free hospitalization. It came in 1944.

In 1924, L.C.W. asked for and was granted the establishment of classes in Home Nursing under the Department of Health. Also, a registry was made available of classified helpers who could be called on by the public when temporary services of a nurse, housekeeper, or other household help was required.

Sanitation being what it was – or was not – in those days, it was a natural subject for investigation by the Local Council women. They took their enquiring noses into all kinds of places and sent delegations to the mayor and health officer to report their findings. They asked for better inspection of eating places and medical inspection for food handlers. Foodstuffs were not protected from public handling, they pointed out, despite the bylaw passed at Local Council's urging a decade earlier, and there should be government supervision of stockyards and cold-storage plants. Dairies must do something about unclean milk bottles. Their intervention in these matters nearly always brought results, although sometimes not immediately.

We are apt to think of drug trafficking in schools as a modern dilemma. It may come as a surprise that it was a serious problem as far back as the 1920s. Appalled by the amount of drug use among school children, L.C.W. sought to have "scientific truths about drugs" taught in the schools. They were not successful but got some satisfaction out of diligently watching to see that what laws there were covering drug trafficking were strictly enforced.

In the "nothing-new-under-the-sun" department is a resolution passed forty-five years ago by Calgary L.C.W. asking the city for a bylaw that would provide punishment for "persons knowingly offering for sale animals or carcasses which they knew to be diseased." As this history is being written, a number of meat distributors in eastern Canada are being taken to court for the same crime.

Letters were sent to churches asking them to consider using individual communion cups. The women must have given up on beauty parlor sanitation, for they sadly suggest that it would be wise to take one's own toilet articles when visiting a beauty parlor. A Beauty Parlor Act was proclaimed later.

The campaign for a pure water supply for Calgary was as old as the Local Council itself. It was stepped up considerably during the twenties, due largely to the tireless dedication of the Health Convener Mrs. C.R. Edwards during her nine years in that office. She saturated herself with information about filtration, talked to the mayor about it, and often suffered ridicule for her forward-looking ideas. She was responsible for arranging a series of lectures on a variety of health subjects by members of the medical fraternity. The lectures were so popular that requests for repeats came from rural towns and even from men's organizations. Most of the worthwhile L.C.W. projects in the field of health and sanitation during this period can be credited to her initiation and hard work.

Two very special and original L.C.W. projects of this time were Confidence Week and Letter Day. Letter Day was visualized and publicized by the women as a day when everyone – children and adults – would write letters to relatives and friends in eastern Canada and the U.S. extolling the virtues and beauty of Calgary and inviting them to visit the Calgary Exhibition, which that year was introducing a new feature – a stampede and barbecue. They must have been successful in transferring their enthusiasm for it was estimated that twenty thousand letters were sent out on that day in June 1922. The women gave pep talks over radio, in clubs, and in schools and encouraged everyone to wear Stetson hats and kerchiefs during Exhibition Week.

Confidence Week was the brainchild of the 1922 executive. Actually it was the forerunner of the Winter Works Campaign. They gave it wide publicity, inviting citizens to undertake constructions or renovations that could be carried out in winter to relieve serious unemployment and keep money in circulation. Local Council minutes report with pride that more than two thousand jobs were created that week, with as many more in the weeks following, as a result of the campaign. Its success is evidenced by the fact that enquiries for details came from other Canadian cities.

Among the brightest stars in L.C.W.'s crown is the establishment of a pre-school health clinic in Calgary, which is still carried on today. The idea was originally presented to Local Council by the Child and Family Welfare Association in 1917, but it took five years of joint lobbying of City Council before the first clinic became a fact.[5] City council evidenced its trust in the judgment of Local Council women by asking them to submit their view of a necessary clinic staff, which was implemented *in toto*.

The Local Council had a Moral Standards committee in the 1920s, whose members kept under close scrutiny dance halls, theatres, and literature of all kinds. Movies and theatre performances were thoroughly monitored. When a Grand Theatre performance included girls in scanty attire, they told the mayor that "those girls must wear more clothes or be cut out of the program." The picture of a nude outside a theatre was removed when they complained. They continuously peppered movie house managers with their criticisms and suggestions, but in spite of that seemed to get a surprising amount of co-operation. By the 1940s they had a nice thing going for them – they persuaded the theatre managers to issue two passes to facilitate their investigations. Talk about putting ammunition into the hands of a potential enemy!

They were for strict censorship in those days and waged a long fight for it, with some success. The committee chairman's report of 1920 noted "an increase of over 200% in juvenile crime in Canada," claiming that much of it was attributable to the moving picture show. She expressed the hope that "soon every picture suggestive of theft, murder and immorality would be banned!"

Magazines also came under the watchful eyes of these moral guardians. What they called "unelevating literature, detrimental to Canadian ideals" entering Canada duty-free from the U.S.A. so incensed them that they pledged themselves not to buy Hearst publications, and sought the support of service clubs in requesting the federal government to ban them.

Because of the perils they saw lurking for unwary young people in unsupervised dance halls, two Local Council members were appointed to check dance halls to make sure that young girls had the consent of their parents to be there. And L.C.W. was influential in having a bylaw enacted regulating cabarets and making it mandatory that a matron be on hand at all times in dance halls.

The slot machines found in many city stores were seen by the ladies as devices for leading young people to perdition, and they had considerable input in a mid-twenties bylaw outlawing them. They were getting somewhere with a declaration enshrined in a 1919 resolution that "the standard of movies, theatre productions and dance halls must be raised."

Ever mindful of the children and young folk, they continually bombarded the city fathers for better enforcement of the curfew bylaw, and they nearly succeeded in having a light installed atop the monument in Central Park "so that no unseemly conduct can be carried on under cover of darkness." They congratulated themselves that the city had budgeted for it, but there is no record of a light ever having shone or even having been installed. Concern for young people sparked a request that the city take over control of all amusements in city parks. The city co-operated.

The school board was never allowed to forget that the eyes of Local Council women were constantly on the moral, mental, physical, and spiritual welfare of the children under its jurisdiction. Some of the problems discussed at that time bear a remarkable resemblance to those of today: overcrowding in schools, low grades because of an overabundant social life, circulation of objectionable literature and drugs among school children (students were expelled for this), and poor reading habits. They took the latter deficiency to the Parent-Teacher Associations, suggesting that "more attention should be paid by mothers to what their children are reading." A Better-English-Week was lightly talked about but came to nothing. That was all in 1923; it could be 1975.

Speaking of better English, Miss Donalda Dickie, the well-known novelist, who was Local Council's Education chairman in 1928, was scathingly critical of the poor English used on bill-boards and in comic strips, advertisements, and elsewhere. "How can you expect a child to attend the teacher's instructions on the use of the adverb" she asked, "when 'Go Slow' stares at him from the school gate." We are still asking the same question – and with greater reason.

Miss Dickie also recommended to the school board that more labs and workshops be provided in high schools for those who, for some reason, would not be going on to university, contending that "there are twice as many hand-minded people as academically-minded people."

A fascinating encounter between Local Council and the school board was L.C.W.'s long battle to have scripture reading introduced into the schools. Having prodded for years without results, the women went into high gear around the mid-twenties. What they wanted was: (1) compulsory reading of scriptures without comment, followed by reading of the Lord's prayer, (2) a copy of the ten commandments to be placed in each classroom, and (3) scripture selections to be memorized. The school board hedged, but the women would not be sidetracked. They eventually got classroom scripture reading and, to break a stalemate about the other issues, the ladies asked "How about stickers to be placed in school readers?" This was finally okayed by the board, with the suggestion that eight thousand be provided. The ladies ordered forty thousand, to make sure that there would be at least a four year's supply.

The history book then being used in Calgary high schools was *Myers History*. It was, the Local Council Women said, "an insidious piece of literature, repudiating God, attributing victory in war to the Americans, and having pro-German sentiments." They demanded that the Minister of Education have it removed from the curriculum. It was removed, but the minister's obfuscation is implicit in his remark that the history had been used in Alberta for twenty-two years.

The scant supply of books in school libraries and their deplorable condition came to the attention of L.C.W. spies in 1921. Learning that the reason was the withdrawal of grants to school libraries a few years earlier, they managed to have the grant reinstated, with the proviso that school boards would provide matching amounts.

Education to Local Council women was not just the 3Rs. Children must acquire the saving habit, they maintained, so they hatched up a savings plan for children to deposit 25¢ a month, and with the co-operation of the Bank of Commerce and approval of the school board, it was introduced into some schools, although it was not universally adopted. Children must develop an appreciation of art, so they offered prizes for school children's art work at the Calgary Exhibition for some years. Children must learn early about brotherhood. So L.C.W. introduced "World Goodwill Day" into Calgary. This called for all grade seven children, in all schools, to write a goodwill message to children of the world. The letter judged as the best was publicized over the air and sent all over the world. To implant a love and knowledge of nature, Local Council women took an active part in the celebration of Arbour Day. Not only did they help in planting trees, but they gave classroom talks on the care of trees and boulevards. Physical training in schools and an annual physical examination for all school children were also matters taken up with the school board by L.C.W. They were influential too in having hot soup and milk provided for children who lunched at school.

Immigrants always brought out the mothering instinct of Council Women, both national and local. The number coming to Canada from Britain and Europe in the 1920s was quite high. Colonization schemes, fostered by a variety of organizations, the railways, and the government's Family Settlement Scheme, also the Soldiers' Settlement Scheme, brought a continual flow – most of them to farms in the West. Calgary Local Council seemed to feel a special responsibility to make the adults feel welcome and to make good citizens of the children. To this end they managed to have a weekly flag drill instituted in schools, "to instill Patriotism," and sent textbooks and other reading material to rural schools, going to the trouble of getting names from the teachers so that none would be overlooked. Magazines and household items went to the parents and a liaison person was appointed "to further mutual intercourse and understanding," which entailed quite a bit of personal visiting. At one point, Local Council adopted three immigrant Dutch families and were able to report later that "they are settled and making good citizens." A novel personal touch was the sending of flower seeds to all those who came as newcomers to the province under the Soldier's Settlement Plan. And they endorsed the idea put forward by the Social Service Council that a resident woman agent be stationed in Calgary to supervise new Canadian girls during their first two years here. They also asked the Government to establish vocational training schools for immigrant boys and girls.

Inspection of boarding houses, remember, was on their very first agenda. But even by the twenties it was still not adequate enough to suit L.C.W. So they formed a Girl's Friendly Protective Society to give advice and help to friendless newcomers. And for girls who were neither friendless nor newcomers, Local Council, in co-operation with the Y.W.C.A., set up social centers to keep the girls off the street.

Daylight saving time is unnecessary, was the opinion of the 1921 Local Council women, and they went on record as opposing it. When another daylight saving plebiscite was held five decades later, another generation of Council women expressed themselves as in favor.

Charging that "the game of politics has been played long enough in this city," the 1922 L.C.W. membership was unanimous in endorsing a resolution that went to the city requesting a full-time city manager. They suggested a plebiscite, but the city officials took refuge in the fact that a new commissioner form of government had recently been instituted, claiming that would take care of things.

Surely Calgary motor traffic could not have been as hectic in the 1920s as it is today, but we find those women telling the mayor that there should be better control. They even suggested that car drivers should be licensed!

Street car steps were too high, they continuously complained, and so were the fares. Lower steps for new streetcar purchases were specified, but a request repeated monotonously for a five cent fare was never granted, although some adjustment of schoolchildren's fare was agreed upon.

Considering the number of pricks and jibes frequently directed at city hall personnel by L.C.W., and city council's tendency to co-operate where possible, it is rather amusing to note the reply of Local Council to a request from the city clerk to supply twenty copies of any documents sent. They said: "As Local Council of Women is composed of ratepayers, and its affiliated societies are not paid – get the copies made at City Hall."

Chapter Three

The 1930s

THE DEPRESSION YEARS must have been a frustrating time for women with the well-developed "mothering" instincts of Local Council members of that era. Dire need surrounded them. Knocking on bureaucratic doors either got no response or the answer "no funds," which, although they wouldn't admit it, was probably a justifiable excuse at that time.

Stopping only long enough to retort "Find some other ways of economizing" (like "a cut in interest on Calgary bonds"), they plunged into work with other groups and individuals in practical ways of bringing comfort, thus keeping up morale where possible. Typical was the club for unemployed girls, ventured into jointly with the Y.W.C.A. Meetings held at the Y provided something for both mind and body. The girls were taught sewing, remodeling clothes, meeting procedures, etiquette; and they held debates. Sports, such as swimming, basketball, and other types of recreation, were also included.

L.C.W. members collected and distributed food and clothing, hampers at Christmas time, and games, magazines, socks, and mufflers to the city-operated camps for unemployed men and women. These camps concerned them greatly. They found conditions intolerable and predicted mental as well as physical deterioration, even revolution, if young people had to continue living in such circumstances for very long.

The women were not too busy to continue their sniffing out of unsanitary conditions round-and-about. They found them in as wide an assortment of places as the women's section of the employment bureau, women's police cell, the C.P.R. station, and Banff campground. The employment bureau was surely a busy place in those days, but, as the Local Council watchdogs persistently reminded the city fathers, there was no excuse for it to be unsanitary. Besides, it had no toilet. The answer they received to their complaint was: "Women are not here long, and we've provided seats. We think this is the limit of special provisions that should be made." It took a year or more, but the bureau was eventually moved to better quarters, which satisfied the women as to cleanliness. But it still had no toilet!

The disgraceful condition of bedding and mattresses in women's police cells was brought to the attention of the appropriate authorities and was corrected. L.C.W. was also successful in having the cells removed from the damp basement to the first floor and having a matron on hand at all times. Without a hope was the request that went with their critical comment on conditions at the C.P.R. depot: that separate waiting rooms be provided for women.

There were some civic and school board economies that Local Council women objected to as indefensible, even in depression times: curtailment of Domestic Science and Manual Training classes in public schools, a proposal to close the commercial and technical high schools, the abolition of music instruction and discontinuance of clinics in schools, and reduction of garbage collection to a bi-weekly schedule. All were false economies, to their way of thinking. They sponsored a mass meeting ("crowded to capacity") out of which emerged several resolutions: one protesting the cuts in education programs ("programs that are even more important than formerly, and in no sense less desirable than many of the so-called academic subjects"), another giving motherly advice to school board and teachers about trying to co-operate, and one directed to the public at large, urging citizens to pay their taxes early to help ease the school board's difficulties. No favoritism or discrimination there. The city council's "action" regarding L.C.W.'s protest about reduction in garbage collection (they simply filed it) galvanized the women into action. They got up a petition and gave it wide circulation. The city commissioner, on the defensive, claimed that it was never intended that the curtailment would be operative in the summer months – the city wouldn't think of jeopardizing the health of citizens for the sake of saving half a million dollars!

Besides pressing for schools to be kept open, L.C.W. also asked for the elimination of examination fees. It does seem a strange time to put pressure on the board for the establishment of a junior high school, but that's what they did in the midst of the Depression. They also chose that time to suggest that French should be added to the school curriculum in the lower grades and to begin a continuing petition for some sort of adult education. But they emphatically protested the reinstatement of cadet training in the schools. No war preparation for them.

One cannot help wondering, too, why L.C.W. would, in the prevailing economic climate, propose that money be spent to improve conditions at the dog pound. Moreover, to wonder why – as the mayor's reply informed them – $1000 had already been requisitioned for that purpose.

Perhaps it wasn't a good time either for them to bring up the subject of equal pay for equal work. But cuts in salaries of nurses and teachers, and the discovery of a significant spread between the pay of male and female teachers, gave them an opportunity to reiterate their oft-repeated stand on such discrimination. They didn't get far with the salary matter, but their efforts toward having the working hours for nurses reduced from twelve to eight were successful. L.C.W. also had a hand in getting separate living quarters provided for nurses at the general hospital.

Relief for the unemployed in 1933 was $3 a week, raised to $3.50 by 1936. "This is not enough to maintain health, let alone provide a minimum standard of living," Local Council women complained, as they joined with the C.C.F. women and other organizations in attempts to have it increased; they sent a spray of letters flying out in all directions to members of all legislative bodies.

In 1933, L.C.W. approached the city and the chamber of commerce, asking them jointly to call a conference of city groups to arrange a "Spend for Employment" campaign and to "search for ways and means of relieving the present distressing situation, instead of cutting wages." They saw unemployment, deteriorating health, and loss of individual dignity as an inescapable chain reaction that must be stopped, not only to relieve the current distress, but to prevent its recurrence in the future, and, to this end, proposed the introduction of unemployment insurance (contributory, for the preservation of dignity). The resolution sent to the federal government in May of 1931 read as follows: "We, the members of Calgary Local Council of Women, do call upon the Government of Canada to take immediate steps to organize and set up a system of contributory unemployment insurance, that shall insure workers and their wives and families against privation and want when unable to secure employment, and no longer leave the victims of industrial organization subject to hasty and inadequate schemes of public relief or private charity."

For the same reason, some sort of health insurance was also needed, they insisted. "People are not seeking the attention they should have because of unemployment and lack of money," they pointed out in their petition to the government. Their concern also made them bold enough to invite doctors to do their share towards relieving the situation by reducing fees proportionate to the general reduction in wages. As we take for granted unemployment insurance and medicare today, we should give credit to the foresight of those pioneer women of the early 1930s.

A shortage of hospital beds was something L.C.W. was frequently bringing to the attention of the city's medical authorities. But city officials were probably unprepared for the ways-and-means suggestion added to Local Council's plea for more hospital accommodation in 1931. It suggested that construction on the proposed 4th St. subway should be delayed and the money used instead to pay for an addition to the general hospital, with modern laboratories and facilities for research. The 4th St. subway was built, of course; but thirty years later, Local Council was still asking for more hospital accommodation.

The plight of deserted wives, made more poignant by the circumstances of the 1930s, had been an ongoing concern of Calgary Local Council women from the beginning of their history. As far back as 1914 they had begun a move for Mothers' Pensions, and constant pressure had been kept up subsequently by Mrs. Maude Riley, Council's Laws Convener, whose pet project it was. In her report to a Local Council meeting in 1919 Mrs. Riley commented: "It is a disgrace that any Christian country should compel a mother to go out and slave over a washtub in order to provide a meager existence for the nation's best asset – its children." A 1936 L.C.W. resolution pointed out that, under the Mother' Allowance Act then in existence, widowed mothers received a pension, but deserted wives and children were on relief. Council's effort was to have deserted wives granted the same status as widows insofar as eligibility for Mothers' Pensions was concerned.

One of the well-known stories of the Depression is that of the "On-to-Ottawa Trekkers" – the group of unemployed who, in 1935, marched from Vancouver to Ottawa to voice their grievances and caused a riot in Regina on the way. They paused in Calgary for a while and thereby got into this history. The big-hearted Local Council women sent a delegation to the mayor asking that food and shelter be provided for the trekkers during their stay in Calgary. It was. But when the trekkers became involved in the Regina fiasco, and Calgary L.C.W. was approached for a donation towards legal fees for the trekkers' defence, they said no – that was against Council policy. But that didn't mean that the women had hardened their hearts. They took up a voluntary collection from members in addition to sending a letter to Prime Minister Bennett asking that the trekkers be given a fair hearing.

A very commendable program entered into jointly by the federal and provincial governments in the mid-1930s was the Dominion-wide Youth Training Plan. One phase of it – Home Service – was set up in Calgary, its purpose to train young girls in all kinds of home activity to prepare them to enter the field of domestic service, as well as to upgrade the profession. It goes without saying that Local Council women became involved immediately in something so dear to their hearts. They played an important part in the renovation and furnishing of the Lougheed House, which had been donated for carrying out the training program. Mrs. Blight, a past president of L.C.W., was chairman of the plan's Calgary advisory board during that time, and was highly praised by the Dominion supervisor for making the Calgary unit the best in the country. Mrs. Margaret Lewis, another indefatigable worker for women workers on the provincial level, and an officer on the Local Council Executive for many years, later became chairman of the board. She was followed by Mrs. Selby Walker.

Calgary Local Council's stature in the community at the time of the Depression is indicated by the invitation received to participate in a number of conferences and committees attempting to find ways of solving Depression-created problems. Such varied groups as the Ministerial Association, the Board of Trade, Labour organizations, and many voluntary groups sought assistance and advice from the Council. In 1931, L.C.W.'s Housing Convener was invited by the city to sit on the newly-formed Town Planning Commission. The news media, too, recognized Council's influence in the community. When the National Council of Women held its Annual Meeting in Calgary in the spring of 1933, the *Herald* welcomed the delegates with a four-inch banner front page headline, and the city granted $100 out of its Depression budget.

How the Calgary Local Council managed to stage a national conference at such a time is a mystery. Both national and local councils had felt the pinch of the Depression. During

1931, Calgary Local Council found itself out of funds and had to bail itself out of its temporary difficulties with voluntary contributions from executive members. And economic conditions forced the National Council to cancel its 1931 Annual Meeting, which had been scheduled for Calgary, as well as the 1937 National Annual, which was to be held in the West that year.

There seems always to have been an active interest on Local Council's part in art and music in the city. Both in the 1920s and 1930s Calgary Council sponsored several exchange exhibits between western and eastern artists. Some came under the umbrella of National Council's exchange program, and it was on National's recommendation that, in 1928, the Calgary Local Council began giving the annual prizes for children's art exhibited at the Calgary Exhibition (first prize $3, second $2, and a special award of $5) . This lasted until 1933 when an annual $25 scholarship for an outstanding student at the Institute of Technology and Art was initiated. This was later raised to $30, then to $50, and in 1950 to $100. Such well-known artists as Matt Lindstrom, Margaret Shelton, and Gerald Tailfeathers were among the winners of these scholarships. A change was made in 1971, and a $50 scholarship is now awarded to a woman wishing to retrain herself for re-entry into business.

In the 1930s there was a close liaison between the Musical Club and L.C.W., each ready to help the other when needed. At one point the Musical Club put on a concert to raise funds for L.C.W. And for several years, the Local Council purchased two Musical Club season tickets to be used by specially selected students.

Local Council's avid support of home-grown talent was not confined to the arts. The members were frequently reminded to buy products made locally or provincially. In 1931 they decided to carry their enthusiasms to the general public by venturing into a "made-in-Calgary-and-Alberta Exhibit." It was such a success that it was made an annual event. It was eventually taken over by a newly formed Southern Alberta Development Board, with the ladies of Local Council serving tea as a money-making project for themselves.

One of the most useful enterprises of the practical-minded L.C.W. members of the thirties was the organization of self-help groups. Under the supervision of Council women, girls and women on small salaries learned how to make their own clothes, preserve fruit and vegetables, and other thrift-oriented activities. These self-help groups became self-perpetuating – the first students eventually becoming the teachers and administrators. This project is typical of how Council works – by initiating then withdrawing to a background supporting role once the project is off the ground.

Toward the end of the thirties, when the pressures of the Depression were easing, Council felt it was not only timely but necessary for women to broaden their horizons. They organized a Women's Forum with the aim of educating women in matters of general interest, through speakers and discussion. As they saw it, "when everyday bread-and-butter needs are diminishing, this is something for the mind." They seemed to have no difficulty in enlisting outstanding speakers and inciting good attendance, and it continued over several years.

L.C.W.'s attitude toward birth control (or family limitation as it was sometimes euphemistically called) in the 1930s was pro. In 1932, after an emotional speaker had noted that contraceptive information was available to the rich but not to the poor, Local Council adopted a resolution requesting the government to "establish clinics in Alberta for the dissemination of scientific information regarding family limitation." As a result, the Council lost one of its affiliates – the Catholic Women.[6]

It was not a subject to be bandied about, however, as the party or parties responsible for circulating advertising material about a book on birth control on the streets during Stampede

Week in 1929 found out. On a complaint laid by Local Council of Women, the street salesmen were arrested and fined.

We complain today about too great a variety of sizes displayed on grocery shelves and insufficient information on labels. It seems that consumers suffered the same problem forty years ago. In April 1936, Local Council asked that sizes be standardized and recommended that weight, grade, and quality be clearly indicated. They pointed out that the great number of sizes of canned fruits and vegetables "is confusing, and leads to misleading advertising."

Alice Grevett was President of the Calgary Local Council during 1933–34 and again in 1938. The 1939 L.C.W. Year Book featured the following 1938 President's address:

'The wise need not be told that man without man's past is meaningless."

Time marches on. Another year has come and gone and now recorded as history.

Since we last met in Annual meeting, many of our faithful members have slipped through the open door of immortality.

We here record our Love and Affection, and re-consecrate ourselves to the tasks they have resigned.

John Carlyle says: There is no merit in just belonging to anything. The merit comes entirely through whatever personal effort we give to make the organization function. An organization is not an Entity; it has no life or meaning in itself. It is simply a line of functioning individuals. When one individual fails to function the whole line is affected. The greatest possible idea that can be put across in relation to any organization is the idea of *personal* responsibility for *corporate* action.

It is of feelings with both sadness and pleasure that we review the activities of the Council since its inception 26 years ago. Many of our fellow-workers have passed on to a higher sphere; others of our members have removed to other scenes of activity, and are lost to our Council at present.

A Pageant is being staged at this Annual Meeting to portray the growth and development of the Council idea, and if we catch the vision we shall see how it has changed with the changing needs of the community. Look back in imagination over the years and see the Council as a part of the Woman's Movement by women for women; see it as an expression of the community's needs, attempting to bring the need for remedial legislation to the attention of the provincial authorities, to serve the women and children of all creeds; see it as a manifestation of democracy in a country whose people have come with differing traditions from all nations and races.[7]

"Since the present comes out of the past," let us take a glimpse at the accomplishments of the past, and the needs of today.

There are at least two reasons for knowing something about the early days of the Council.

First, we can understand it, as it is today, only if we know how it came into being, and get an idea of its purpose, and how necessary it has been to change continually to adapt its forms to the needs of women and children in particular and the community in general.

Second, such understanding gives us an appreciation of our heritage in it. The pioneer women achieved scores of reforms, which are today an accepted part of our social, economic and political life.

Twenty-six years of organized service to the community. We were organized to be of mutual helpfulness and understanding. Founded on the Golden Rule in society and custom. To help build a Christian Order; to try to educate public opinion by our own experiences as to what the needs of that order are, and as to conditions of today which must be changed if we are to give women that fullest kind of life, and now we are reviewing our successes and noting our weaknesses so that we may build better in the future. The conditions of today are a challenge to our womanhood. Well could we exclaim with Barrett-Browning, "Might the women of the world become one confederate sisterhood ever onward." In this world of conflicting opinions and emotions we find dictators using religion and race differences to further their own ends; a world where bombing innocent women and children is defended as a means of gaining objectives; a world that seems bent on destruction in a new World War.

The increasingly tragic plight of our refugees and stateless persons, for whom assistance, the right to work, and possibilities of rehabilitation, should be assured, continue to present a grave problem.

We must urge upon our governments that some temporary means of dealing with this distressing problem, so that pending a final solution, which can only be brought about by concerted effort, the sufferers may a least be protected against further violence. The concerted efforts of certain governments and the helping hand of several national and local committees have given us reason to hope that positive results may be obtained in the near future. We must continue to call public opinion to the urgency of this problem, and to support every effort to alleviate the fate of these unfortunate, unhappy human beings and to come to their aid in the misfortunes that have befallen them.

Unemployment and Relief are real problems in the lives of our people; we are just beginning to face our responsibilities to a generation of youth growing to maturity without much hope of a home or job. The Dominion-Provincial Youth Training is at last a step in the right direction.

The recognition by the government of the need for trained certified domestic help in the home and the care of children should result in legislation for hours and wages and a higher status for the worker.

As we face the days ahead with faith and confidence in our new leadership may we, as members of this organization, dedicate ourselves anew and shoulder our responsibilities with fresh courage and joy. And in closing I would like to repeat the appeal made by the first President of our Council, Mrs. R.R. Jamieson:

"The times are strenuous and it is difficult to always keep up the work with so many conflicting interests; but the work of the Council is so far-reaching in its effect on women and children that the help of every affiliated society, and the help and unqualified loyalty of every woman is asked for."

I would like to take this opportunity to thank my officers, and all those who contributed in any way, to make our Year Book a success.

Chapter Four

The 1940s

STRADDLING THE END of the 1930s and the beginning of the 1940s was World War II, and, of course, war work took precedence over everything else. As in the first World War, Calgary Council women manned government booths, selling war stamps and handling ration cards. Following a directive sent from National Council at the outset of the war, they co-operated with recognized organizations already specializing in war work rather than setting up new projects of their own in order to conserve effort and prevent overlapping.

However, one outstanding contribution to the war effort sponsored and carried through by L.C.W. in 1941 was the exhibit in Calgary of the Princesses dolls. Gifts of the French government to Elizabeth and Margaret, the dolls were being shown across Canada to raise funds for European refugees. It was quite an undertaking, involving considerable publicity work and detailed arrangements. It was pronounced a smashing success. Almost $2000 was raised – a sizable sum in those days.

Another wartime activity that Local Council could call its own was the Soldiers Sailors and Airmen Committee, with Mrs. Millicent McElroy as its chairman. This was the same Mrs. McElroy who chaired a similar committee in the first war and did such a memorable job of welcoming returned men and caring for their families. She repeated that fine performance, providing entertainment for returned men wherever they congregated, visiting their families, even attending funerals and keeping L.C.W. informed of the needs and condition of veterans.[8]

After the war, Local Council added its collective voice to many others in its protest against the importation of Japanese goods and the exportation to Japan of material that could be used for war purposes. And to back up their protest, the women pledged themselves to not purchase enemy-made goods. The soft-hearted, motherly women even went so far as to ask the federal government to relax immigration laws to permit refugees in danger in Europe to escape into Canada and, what's more, to contribute to their upkeep. And with low income people in mind, they asked the National Council to request the federal government to remove all sales taxes imposed during the war.

Perhaps it was an after-effect of the war, but the Local Council chairmen's reports in the early 1940s present a gloomy picture of conditions at the time. They deplore a criminal waste of food, an alarming increase in illegitimacy, venereal disease spreading at a great rate, and nation-wide malnutrition. "Sunday as a day of worship seems to be old-fashioned," one convener lamented. Another said, "Beverage rooms have become incubators of crime." And the convener of the Moral Standards Committee, in her 1945 annual report, bemoaned the fact that "in Alberta last year three times as much was spent on liquor as on welfare, charitable grants, hospitals, asylums and gaols put together."

Food wastage combined with the widespread malnutrition seemed to bother them. They came up with advice and action. To conserve food and be ready for emergencies, they urged the government to establish warehouses where surplus food could be canned, dried, or preserved, and new methods researched. A Food Conservation Board would also be a good idea, they added – with women on it. They joined other organizations in a campaign to salvage surplus food for starving people in other countries. The result of this effort is not recorded; but they probably met with the same lack of success as they did in the 1960s; Local Council members who tried to put the same idea into motion were told that transportation difficulties made it impossible. They supported the city's malnutrition classes and urged the federal Minister of Health to inaugurate an educational program. The poor and the unprotected woman was their main concern. "How can we have a healthy people when the allowance for a mother with one child is only $25.00 a month?" they asked the government when reiterating their earlier plea for an increase in Mothers' Allowances, which, they said, had not even kept up with the escalating cost of living.

Child welfare legislation was receiving considerable attention in the 1940s. Procedures of adoption were a special cause of complaint. Not only L.C.W. but other organizations asked that a survey by outside specialists be made. The government appointed a commission and a new act was passed. L.C.W.'s then Child Welfare chairman (Mrs. Wilma Hansen) pronounced it a good bill but warned that its administration needed watching. Her fears were not groundless. In 1948, the government proposed changes to the act which, without doubt, would have diminished its effectiveness, and Local Council was among the first to challenge the action.

Back in 1919, the Calgary L.C.W. had endorsed – and supported with cash – a plan of the *Herald*'s Sunshine Society to establish a day nursery, and during and after the war had helped in providing care for the children of working mothers.

In 1942, the Local Council appointed a special committee to work with the Council of Social Agencies (with whom they were affiliated) in a comprehensive survey of day nurseries in other cities and other countries, with a view to establishing one or more in Calgary. By the beginning of 1943, with satisfactory results from their research, they were looking for a suitable house and hoping that a nursery would soon be opened, funded partially by a grant from the Dominion government. But that grant was contingent upon the province taking advantage of a 50/50 offer from the federal government, which they seemed loath to do. What must have been a surprising turn of events was when the L.C.W. president returned from that year's National Annual Meeting with the information that the feeling of eastern members was that the cost of day nurseries was something that should not be added to taxes. It was also the opinion of the majority of eastern members that women should return to their homes after the war. Women's Lib. hadn't arrived yet. That opinion was not shared by Local Council women in Calgary. They continued their efforts locally, without a clue as to where the money was to come from. Uncertainty changed to disappointment when, in the spring of 1944, the province turned thumbs down on a day nursery for Calgary. However, by the fall of 1944, the women had managed to get together enough money and cooperation to begin operating a nursery class in the James Short School, in a classroom made available by the school board (with some equipment provided by the school and some purchased cheaply by L.C.W. or scrounged). It operated until the end of the war.

The war had taken women beyond the traditional home-bound limits and given them ideas they had not had before. That at least some were disturbed about this is reflected in the president's address to the 1944 Annual Meeting of Calgary L.C.W. Such things as nursery schools and community kitchens must continue, she said, until the returned men are absorbed into civilian life – but no longer, if home and family life is to be kept intact. On the other hand though, women in business should not be asked to step aside for men of less ability. Then, with prophetic insight, she added: "We are now facing a real crisis in the history of womanhood – a crisis which, unless we meet it sanely, may overturn the whole applecart of existence."

But "mothering" was still paramount in the thoughts and action of Local Council women. For mothers travelling with little children, the Local Council approached both railway companies and the Department of Transport, asking that a special nursery coach be made a part of all trains. "Men have smoking compartments," they snidely commented. They got a sympathetic hearing and a promise that, while a whole coach was not feasible, special arrangements would be made.

They saw a problem with children running on the street when the school board decided in 1944 not to open schools that year until October 1st in order to give older students a longer earning period. However, they did not succeed in getting the board to change its mind, and the government clinched matters by bringing in legislation setting the opening date "for the duration of the War." In that case, said the women, we shall see that there is more rigid enforcement of the curfew law.

One of L.C.W.'s 1946 project was to have the Juvenile Delinquency Act amended, raising the age to 18, so that the young person under 18 would not be imprisoned with hardened criminals. In this they were eventually successful.

At the war's end, Local Council came with an inspired suggestion that would solve two problems in one stroke. Low-cost housing was needed, for sure, and so was employment for returned men. Why not combine the two? Build small compact homes on a wholesale scale, using veterans to construct them. They asked all three levels of government to consider this but got nowhere.

Among the highlights of the 1940s was the culmination of two long-fought campaigns: the appointment of women on the Calgary Police Force and free hospitalization for maternity cases. The history of L.C.W. up to that time was liberally sprinkled with repeated interviews, resolutions, and letters asking for women constables. It is a wonder the city could have held out so long. There had been matrons for jail and court duty. Now there were two women on the police force for the first time, and Local Council women rejoiced.

It is only a comparatively short time since city libraries have been made available to the public on Sundays. Yet Local Council of Women saw the need back in 1945, when they asked for public use of library reading rooms on Sundays, holidays, and Wednesday afternoons. They began a campaign for branch libraries at the same time.

Chapter Five

The 1950s

THERE COMES TO MOST volunteer organizations a periodic low, when activity goes on but growth stops and excitement is lacking. It happened to Calgary Local Council of Women around the end of the 1940s and again in the mid-1950s. No yearbooks were issued in the years 1953 to 1958, and if minutes were kept, they cannot be found. Yet there were some worthwhile things accomplished during the decade, and recognition of the Local Council's viability, even when not fully functioning, is implicit in the fact that that L.C.W. was given permission to hold its meetings in the city hall council chambers – a privilege granted to no other organization before or since.

With the smallest number of affiliated societies in Local Council's history, a new executive, with Mrs. Russell Clark at its head, began picking up the pieces in 1951. The revival was evident in the success of its first undertaking: the establishment in Calgary of a branch of The Council of Christians and Jews. At the banquet held in celebration, all races, colors, and creeds were represented, and the head table was heavy with city dignitaries.[9]

"A memorable day for Local Council," was the way one member described it. So successful and well-received was the project that members immediately voted to make the banquet an annual affair. Today the Brotherhood of Christians and Jews is a valuable part of Calgary life.

Their next project was aimed at having vitamins made available to children of poor families. The best way to accomplish this, they thought, was to have vitamin tablets provided free to all school children. The Medical Officer of Health approved the idea, but retail druggists protested, and the school boards needed convincing. However, a vitamin program was ultimately instituted in Calgary Schools.

The Rehabilitation Society was another crown jewel of this period – spearheaded by Mrs. Ruth Gorman, Council's Laws Convener, who was well-known for her interest in the handicapped. Council women found a meeting place for the newly formed society and helped to organize and encourage them in every way possible until they became the viable and self-supporting organization it is today.

Alberta Clark served as Calgary's Local Council's president from 1951 to 1955. In her February 24, 1955, address to the Annual Meeting, she summarized her "quiet" year's work and feelings on her long service.[10]

It is most fitting that our Local Council Annual Meeting should fall in Brotherhood Week. Our founder, Lady Aberdeen, had the idea of all peoples working amicably together many, many years ago. It was she who chose for Council the motto – the Golden Rule – "Do unto others as you would that they do unto you." The Council is composed of women of every faith and color. Local Council meetings are traditionally opened with a moment of silent prayer, so that each person in her own way, may commune with God. Let us never forget the full significance of this moment of silence.

Local Councils study almost every phase of our complex modern society with two exceptions. These exceptions were set down by Lady Aberdeen – partisan politics and theology. She was a wise woman, for these are the differences which will spark an argument and bitter wrangling at a moment's notice. We do well to follow the advice of our founder – and we do so proudly.

In what way does Council differ from other women's organizations? For it is different. Most clubs are made up of individual members whose interests are similar, or whose husbands are in a certain profession or business. Council, on the other hand, invites organizations as such to become members. Each club appoints a representative to attend meetings. So, though the number of women attending Council may be relatively few in number, they represent a great many individuals of divergent groups. So when a subject of vital interest to the community is discussed; or a brief prepared for presentation, to City Council, for example, each affiliated group is informed and given the opportunity to express their opinion through their representative. This gives Council much more authority than that of a single organization. In the same manner, any affiliated group which has a resolution or brief which they wish to present to a city committee or board, they can present this to the Local Council who will in turn seek support of their other affiliated societies. In this way we help each other.

What have we done this past year? We were off to an auspicious start in '54 with a lovely tea at the Palliser Hotel. Although this affair was essentially an advertising scheme it was a most delightful social function. About one hundred representatives of women's clubs were invited. The table was a symphony in blue – dark and light blue flowers, elaborate candles and a cake to match. Even the walls of the Sun Room blended with the table setting to make a most charming picture. We were proud and happy hostesses!

Our Vice-President, Miss Una MacLean, gave us an address on "Equal Pay for Equal Work." This provoked an interesting discussion.

At the time that City Council discussed the opening of the Glenmore Dam site for recreational purposes, we planned an open meeting, for full discussion of the subject with a panel of experts. However City Council abandoned the plan and our meeting was cancelled. Prior to the Civic Election however,

Local Council sponsored a public meeting for the women of Calgary to hear our three women candidates. The response was most disappointing. Why are our women so apathetic, when our predecessors fought so long and so violently to gain for us the privilege of the vote?

We had, throughout the year, many interesting reports from our convenors and representatives. Mrs. Johnson reported on many welfare meetings attended; Mrs. Battiste on the Safety Council; Mrs. Hutchison for United Nations; and Mrs. H.F. Clarke our representative, and the only woman, on the Unemployment Insurance Commission. Mrs. Clarke gave us a splendid talk at a recent meeting, and brought forth several ideas for future programs.

Our scholarship winner this year was Miss Wanda Goota, of Spruce House, Saskatchewan, and to her we send our congratulations and best wishes. This award is for fifty dollars, and is given to an outstanding student of Art at the Institute of Technology and Art.

A letter in the form of a resolution was sent to the Safety Council. We commended the city's long range plan for improved street lighting but urged a speeding up program, and asked especially for better lighting in three areas – Red Cross Hospital, Coste House, and Grace Hospital.

We co-operated with our National Council by writing our Members of Parliament and soliciting their support for certain revisions in the Succession Duties Act. Suggested revisions were presented by a parliamentary delegation headed by our National President, Mrs. Turner Bone. Both our members, incidentally, indicated their support.

At one of the meetings of the Association for the Handicapped it was our privilege to serve the refreshments – a very rewarding experience.

This has been a quiet year in Local Council. It supports my theory that no President should stay in office too long. I did – and proved my point! However, I wish to thank my executive for the hours of work they put in for Council; for the willing co-operation they gave me at all times. I have enjoyed not only the past year, but all the years I have been your President.

I will miss the wonderful teas, meetings and other delightful occasions when as your President, I have been invited on your behalf. Though I leave the chair, I'm not leaving Local Council and though I say "Good-bye," I'm not going – Thank you for everything. (Glenbow archives, file M5841/30).

Her report on presenting National Council's brief to Prime Minister Diefenbaker and his Cabinet Committee appeared in the 1962 Local Council Yearbook:

> To be a member of the Parliamentary Committee of National Council of Women, and to assist in presenting a brief to the Prime Minister and his cabinet, was indeed an honor and a privilege.
>
> The morning of February 7th we were escorted into the Prime Minister's office. With Mr. Diefenbaker were: Mrs. Fairclough, Messrs. Fulton, Monteith, Dinsdale and Nowlan. We were received with friendly courtesy; and the meeting was most informal and interesting.

Calgary's Local Council president Grace Stonewall also highlighted the event:

> We are basking in the reflected glory of one of our members who was elected this year to the very important post of Vice-President of National Council of Women. We are delighted that Mrs. Russell Clark's years of devoted service to Council has been recognized in this way. It is also a matter of pride to us that Mrs. Clark was invited to speak to the Resolution on Sex Deviates when it was pre-

sented by National Council to the Government in Ottawa recently. (It is worth noting with satisfaction that this was originally a Calgary Council Resolution. Which proves that study on the local level can reach the highest authority of the land through our affiliation with all the organized women of Canada in National Council). (1962 L.C.W. Yearbook, "Message from the President," p. 2–3.)

After the doldrums of the mid-1950s, a revitalized Council bounced back into activity. One of the first projects undertaken by the new executive in 1959 was a survey of conditions for women in prison. The new president, Mrs. Jessie Hutchison, personally undertook an inspection tour of the women's section of Fort Saskatchewan jail and was dismayed with what she found. The membership reacted to her report by asking the provincial government to provide a compulsory vocational program within the jail to prepare the inmates for re-entry into community living. Because the majority of prisoners were there as a result of alcohol abuse, their resolution also suggested that female alcoholic prisoners should be segregated and receive special treatment.

With no action forthcoming, follow-up research was undertaken by Mrs. Grace Johnson in the spring of 1960. Her findings confirmed and added to those of Mrs. Hutchison. The report of a complete lack of any constructive use of time spent in prison prompted L.C.W. to repeat its 1959 request to the provincial government to institute activities that would provide mental and spiritual stimulation, to make counselling available, and to consider a centre for rehabilitation on release. ("The men have Belmont Institute; why not something similar for women?" Council members remarked.) There is considerable improvement in women's prison conditions today, and there is a half-way house in Calgary, too.

Two other related resolutions followed naturally from Mrs. Hutchison's 1959 discovery of the vacuum in the life of women in prison: The first was a commitment to take steps toward the formation of an Elizabeth Fry Society in Calgary; the second to back the John Howard Society in its attempt to have a female social worker on its staff to serve the needs of women prisoners and ex-prisoners. A committee went to work gathering information about the Elizabeth Fry Society, interviewing and holding meetings, but it never quite got off the ground at that time. After lying fallow for a few years, an Elizabeth Fry Society branch was incorporated in Calgary in 1965, with L.C.W. representation on its board and executive. The second resolution brought more immediate results. Within a short time, Miss Marjorie Larson became a staff member of the John Howard Society.

In 1959, noting an increased demand for employment by women in the over-forty age group, L.C.W. agitated for vocational training for older women wishing to return to employment outside of their homes. There is no way of knowing how much influence Local Council had, but programs to this end were eventually set up by the government.

Calgary could have had a downtown mall twenty years ago if the city fathers had listened to suggestions from L.C.W. and Alex Munro, the then Parks Superintendent, who first seeded the idea in the minds of the women. It would have been different from our present mall. The street level would have been a grassed park with parking, rest rooms, and other facilities underground. This project was an outgrowth of L.C.W.'s year-long study of community planning. It still makes sense.

Following in the footsteps of earlier Local Councils, members of the executive and affiliates helped along the city's "Do-it-now" Winter Works Campaign in the fall of 1959 by acting as hostesses and receptionists at the opening ceremonies. For several years L.C.W. members also participated in courthouse ceremonies welcoming new Canadian citizens.

A leap into uncertainty was L.C.W.'s decision to sponsor a travelogue by Mel Halversen at the Jubilee Auditorium on a 60/40 split-profit basis in the hope of enriching the kitty. This was a sizeable undertaking (and it actually contravened Council's no-fundraising policy). It was well organized, and all the hard work would have paid off had a heavy winter storm not struck that November night, reducing both the attendance and the amount of L.C.W.'s share of the profit.

Council women must have found the experience rewarding, for they undertook a similar adventure in 1962. That time, however, they considered it to be a public service, since the film-showing at which they assisted at the auditorium was to promote public interest in the bringing of the 1968 Winter Olympics to Banff. To Council women, the Olympics in Banff was a boost for Calgary; so, although not financially profitable, it was considered a worthwhile venture.

Under the rubric of education, the high point for L.C.W. in the 1950s had to be the presentation of a brief to the Cameron Commission and the subsequent study by the membership of the voluminous report. The purpose of the commission, appointed by the provincial government, was "to enquire into all phases of education in the Province." A panel of speakers knowledgeable in the field of education discussed the report at a public meeting arranged by Local Council.

There were two hearings by the Public Utilities Board in the 1950s on the subject of price increases for milk, and L.C.W. presented its views at both of them. At the 1951 hearing, Local Council took the stand that if a price increase was necessary, luxury dairy items should bear it, not whole milk. They followed this up with research into the nutritive value of skim milk, presenting their findings. Shortly afterwards, 2% milk was introduced to the market, which today's diet-conscious population is appreciating. An L.C.W. representative attended the 1959 hearings, but Council contented itself with endorsing the Consumers' Association brief, with which it was in entire agreement. That brief asked for a price differential between store and home delivery, also a separate Milk Board independent of the Public Utilities Board.

The early 1950s saw considerable cross-country agitation on the subject of margarine, to which Calgary L.C.W. added its collective voice. Council of Women, both nationally and locally, took every opportunity to express the view that margarine is as nutritious as butter and should be readily available to the poor as a substitute, "without the silly, messy business of this do-it-yourself project" (referring to the separate coloring powder). A similar furor about margarine raged about the land back in 1922, when the federal government banned it. At that time also Calgary Local Council joined the chorus of successful protests as well as the skirmishes about color regulations.

Another consumer problem in which Council became very involved in 1959 was trading stamps. Local Council worked closely with the Consumers' Association in an attempt to publicize what they believed to be the fallacies in such gimmicks. (C.A.C. was a new affiliate. In fact, Local Council had recently been instrumental in the formation of the branch in Calgary). The trading stamp war was a hot one, and officers of both L.C.W. and C.A.C. became actively involved. Presentations were made to the provincial government, which was just as much opposed to the proliferating gimmick, and within the year trading stamps were outlawed.[11]

Sometimes hearts ran away with heads. When L.C.W. petitioned the provincial government to consider paying 25% of any unused unemployment insurance contributions of a worker to their widow or widower, they were diplomatically reminded that insurance is not the same as a savings account.

Chapter Six

The 1960s

A STRONG LOCAL COUNCIL flourished in the 1960s, and made its presence felt in the community. There were several major undertakings in that decade, but perhaps in none of them was more strength and tenacity needed than in the C.P.R. debacle of the early 1960s. That was when the C.P.R. attempted to get agreement from the city to run its railway lines along the south bank of the Bow River. L.C.W. was not alone in its opposition to the proposal – the whole citizenry was embroiled. Articulate groups sprang up – some pro, some con, some motivated by the possible effect on their businesses or homes, and some, like L.C.W., purely altruistic. Local Council's involvement must be told for the record.

Preservation of the river bank had always been a continuing and special priority with Calgary L.C.W. So, when the first rumblings were heard about the C.P.R. relocation scheme, threatening desecration of the river bank, Council sprang into action. At a city council meeting, an L.C.W. representative asked for a definite commitment that a green strip the width of a city block be kept between the river and any tracks that might be agreed upon. This was promised, but when L.C.W. was able later to take a look at the actual agreement the city was prepared to sign – *did* sign, in fact, against the advice of the city solicitor – it was apparent that, despite the promise, not only did it not allow for a green strip, but the tracks would be so close to the river in some parts that fill would be necessitated. From a thorough dissection of the agreement by a specially appointed committee with legal advice, the proposal seemed to embody unfavorable results to Calgary citizens in many other aspects as well. If it were to be implemented, the river would be cut off by a seven-foot-high embankment, pierced in a couple of places with a pass-through for access to Prince's Island, topped by fenced-off tracks. It was not even clear that the new tacks would eliminate those cutting through the heart of the city, for which many would have been willing to make concessions.

As the agreement had not been published (even though citizens were to be called upon to validate or reject it by a plebiscite), L.C.W. sponsored an informational public meeting (crowded to capacity) to review the agreement and give interested citizens an opportunity to discover what was truth and what was fiction in the conflicting arguments whirling around them. A representative panel to answer questions was arranged, but C.P.R. refused to send anyone.

Out of this meeting a citizens group was formed to continue enquiring and informing. When an alderman was forced to resign from his employment because his employer was caught up in behind-the-scenes pressures, and evidences of similar pressure surfaced elsewhere, the citizens group decided there was a moral issue at stake and called an open meeting. The three hundred and fifty people present, representing many and varied organizations, went on record that "it is time the truth is brought out," and forwarded a petition to Edmonton asking for an enquiry by the provincial government. As a result of this and similar action by other groups, legal injunctions were imposed and an official enquiry by the government concluded that the contract signed by the city was not advantageous for Calgary. The city and the C.P.R. broke the contract by mutual agreement. Thus, Prince's Island was saved for the people.

A later resolution, initiated by the citizens group and endorsed by Local Council, asked the provincial government to (a) amend the City Act to make it an offence to threaten or take reprisals against municipal officials or employees because of the manner in which they vote or express their opinions concerning public issues, and (b) institute a judicial enquiry to determine the nature and extent of rumored "pressures and undue influences" was withdrawn in the interests of peace.[12]

Prince's Island has since had a facelift and is now a beautiful park enjoyed by young and old. One of its outstanding features is the cupola removed from the old James Short School when the school was demolished. The preservation of that bit of Calgary's history was another L.C.W. undertaking with a happy conclusion. The "save the cupola" project had its beginning in 1960 when rumors of possible demolition of the old school to make way for a bus depot first surfaced. L.C.W. asked the school board to spare the cupola as a bit of Calgary's past, and Mary Dover, a former alderman, offered to put it on the grounds of her lovely estate. When the school's death warrant was actually signed, L.C.W. reactivated its 1960 request and appointed a Historical Committee to follow up. City council members were divided on the merit of spending the money. The situation was at a stalemate when an anonymous "angel" donated $10 000 to restore and move the cupola to a final resting place.[13]

Local Council's choice of location had always been Prince's Island, and that's where it stands today, within sight and sound of the city's upstart high-rises.[14]

For the couple of years the cupola had languished forlornly in the city's storage yard, it was not entirely abandoned. In addition to L.C.W.'s watchful eye, the *Calgary Herald*, to its everlasting credit, kept interest alive with occasional photographs and supportive editorials, while suggestions as to a location for the relic appeared in "Letters to the Editor" columns from time to time.

Local Council of Women's final salute was given when, in April 1974, the National Life Members in Local Council planted a tree nearby during Environment Week, the visiting National President, Mrs. Gordon Armstrong, officiating at the ceremony.

From saving a piece of Calgary's past from destruction, Council women turned their attention to focusing public opinion on what they believed to be a much more serious form of destruction – ravaged environment from strip mining operations. In 1964, mining interests were lobbying the government to allow mining exploration in the National Parks, and L.C.W. had strongly protested such exploration at that time. By 1968, coal mining was proliferating in Alberta's mountain areas. Photographs revealed terrible scars in the landscape, and reports told of destruction of fish and wildlife through silted rivers and environmental disruption. At a regular L.C.W. meeting, at which the deputy minister of Mines and Resources was invited to speak, members were surprised to learn that government regulations applied only to surveyed land (i.e., farming and ranch land), which meant that there were no rehabilitation regulations of any kind on mountain terrain outside of the National Parks where most of the strip mining occurred.

For public motivation and education, L.C.W. sponsored a symposium in December 1968 – its theme: "This Land is Your Land – Beautiful or Scarred." The panel of eight speakers included representatives of the coal industry, a power company, conservation, forestry, a geologist, and the western director of National Parks. Spirited discussion at least aroused public interest and concern, even though the provincial government took no action on the ensuing resolution that asked for protective legislation. The petition was repeated in 1970. At the time of this writing, there is double action: legislation is being considered on the one hand, while on the other hand, mining permits are being issued as usual. It is not yet clear how the two will balance out.

In the area of environmental concerns, L.C.W. also participated in the Bow River Beautification Plan sponsored by Chief Justice McLaurin in 1965. Mr. McLaurin's plan was to sell tickets at $1 each to provide a fund for correcting slippage on the north bank of the river and plant it with beautifying greenery.

Having helped to save the south bank, the women were more than ready to do the same for the north bank, and Mr. McLaurin found many willing saleswomen in Local Council and affiliates to help him raise the money.

Not only pollution of the land but pollution of the air bothered Council women when they saw the slowly growing bank of smog on Calgary's horizon in 1960. With statistics showing Calgary to be almost at the top of a Canadian list of cars per capita, they decided something ought to be done before Calgary became another Los Angeles. Deciding that the elimination of exhaust from buses would be a good place to start, the superintendent of Transportation was approached with the suggestion that after-burners be fitted to buses. (Los Angeles was then making the installation of exhaust purifiers mandatory.) He was not interested, nor was the public concerned. An open meeting called by L.C.W. to discuss pollution was poorly attended.

Around the same time L.C.W. offered another helpful suggestion to the city: the establishment of a fertilizer plant that would use the city's garbage. It seemed a sensible idea, since garbage disposal sites around Calgary were becoming scarce and fertilizer from such a plant was being sold in Calgary. However, despite a pile of factual information collected by the women and presented to the appropriate city officials, the search for landfill sites which would not bring roars of protests from citizens still continued.

Pollution of Calgary's drinking water was on the minds of L.C.W. women when they wrote letters to the city in 1967 deploring the fact that apartment buildings were being allowed around Glenmore Lake – the source of the city's water supply. There was some response, and building was curtailed at that time, but developers still press.

One of the saddest facts coming out of Mrs. Johnson's 1960 investigation of conditions for women in prison was that 70% of women in Alberta jails were Indian, and that 50% of them were there as a result of alcohol-related troubles.[15] Such a need could not be overlooked, and the idea of an Indian Friendship Centre in Calgary was born. It would be a central point where Indian men, women, and children in town for the day from neighboring reserves could meet and have a cup of coffee; mothers could rest themselves and feed their babies and young girls would have a place to go instead of becoming vulnerable to trouble by having to walk the streets.

To discover what support there might be from both the general public and the Indians themselves, L.C.W., in conjunction with the Council of Community Services, held an open forum with a panel of Indians and non-Indians. After a long evening of frank exchange of thought, the meeting went on record that there was indeed a need for such a centre. This gave L.C.W. the go-ahead signal to look into the possibilities of location, administration, and financial support, utilizing Indians and representatives of other city associations that had shown interest in the welfare of Indians. At first, Local Council worked closely with the Council of Community Services. But, when it seemed that the latter organization had in mind a lengthy research program leading to a much more elaborate type of centre than the Local Council had envisioned, the parting of the ways was inevitable.[16]

After intensive work, volunteer help from many quarters, and a few miracles, the Calgary Indian Friendship Centre, with an administrative board composed of both Indians and non-Indians, was opened with pomp and ceremony in October of 1964. While the work and support of many people made that day and the difficult days that followed possible, much credit must go to Mrs. Grace Johnson, chairman of Local Council's steering committee, whose dedication not only had much to do with bringing the project to its successful conclusion, but with keeping it afloat in the shaky early years of its existence. The establishment of a Rest and Information Centre for Indians in

Calgary must be counted as one of Local Council's most important accomplishments in the 1960s – indeed, of its whole life.

Calgary Local Council's interest in and support of the Indian reaches back to the 1940s, when the well-known champion of the Indian Dr. Laurie pleaded their cause at a Council meeting, and L.C.W. there and then endorsed the formation of an Indian Association in Alberta and passed a resolution asking for equal rights for Indians. Mrs. Ruth Gorman, L.C.W.'s Laws Convenor, became solicitor for the Indian Association and personally fought and won many battles for them. Mrs. Gorman's dedication to the betterment of conditions for Indians is probably at the root of L.C.W.'s sustained interest and support.

In 1946, L.C.W. asked the federal government to appoint a royal commission to look into the matter of education for Indians; and, in that same year, endorsed a petition of the Alberta Indian Association that sought to obtain full treaty rights for Indian women who marry outside the ranks of treaty, as well as full treaty rights for children of such marriages under the age of eighteen.

Indignities to Indian bands at the Stampede grounds were brought to the attention of the authorities in 1951. And in 1957, the Calgary Local Council was among those recommending to the federal government that an Indian should be appointed to the Senate. Senator Gladstone represented his people well in the Senate for many years until his death in 1972.

In 1959, L.C.W. asked to have a restrictive clause in the Indian Act removed so that an Indian could vote without fear of forced removal from the reserve. In 1964, the area of concern was the need for industry on reserves. Members felt strongly that with small factories, stores, or garages on the reserve, Indians would more easily get the training to prepare them for entering urban life or even replace non-Indian instructors – besides the added bonus of improving life on the reserve itself. Surprisingly, this met with some opposition in its passage through National Council. But time and experience are proving the merit of the Calgary viewpoint, and such programs are now in successful operation on some reserves.

When Calgary's new police station was opened in 1962, it contained something new in the identification centre whereby witnesses could view the line-up of suspects without being seen, removing the fear of reprisal. The police chief had kept his promise to Council women who had asked for this innovation.

The advantages of dogs on the police force was something else L.C.W. took to the police chief about the same time, only to discover that the police department was already looking into the possibilities. By the summer of 1960, three trained dogs were ready for action.

Three important anniversaries fell in the 1960s. The first was Calgary Local Council's fiftieth birthday in 1962, which was celebrated with a banquet, a three-tiered cake, and a pageant based upon the Council's history. An evening of fun, Mrs. Saul Hayes, the National President, came to join in the festivities.

The other two were the fiftieth anniversary of the granting of the franchise to the women of Alberta (1966), and Canada's Centennial (1967). Calgary Local Council of women marked both with very special functions.

The week of October 16 to 22, 1966, was proclaimed "Women's Franchise Week" by the provincial government. As a send-off, L.C.W. organized a conference on women ("Pots, Pills and Politics" was the title they chose) with Doris McCubbin Anderson, editor of *Chatelaine*, as keynote speaker. While primarily a tribute to the pioneer leaders of the franchise movement, the advertising frankly stated that it was "intended to inspire women to take more interest in world affairs; to realize the importance of their role; and to make them appreciative of their duties as well as their privileges." It was a very successful conference.

As part of the celebration, a search was made for Calgary women then living who had voted for the first time fifty years before. As a result, two hundred and four names were collected and inscribed on a scroll, which is now lodged with the Glenbow archives. To close Franchise Week, the three Alberta Local Councils, under the aegis of the Provincial Council of Women, participated in a banquet held in Red Deer, which was attended by Lt. Governor Grant McEwan and Premier Ernest Manning.

In commemoration of Canada's Centennial, Calgary Local Council arranged a two-day symposium entitled "The Responsibility of Today's Women Toward Their Community, Province and Nation." It was held April 28 and 29, 1967, at the University of Calgary, with the cooperation of the University's Department of Continuing Education. Its suggestive title was "The Hidden Talent." This conference – which could be called a sequel to the one held in Franchise Week – was a very serious affair, focusing in on discrimination against women in business and politics, and attempting to arouse women to do something about it. It succeeded to the point that a steering committee was elected to look into the status of women's civic rights and motivate women to become more active in civic affairs. Named "Action Calgary," and only loosely connected with Local Council, it was quite active for a short time but was unable to overcome complacency enough to reach its goal of "Power in the Community." As a further recognition of Canada's Centennial, L.C.W. presented a specially made visitors book for use in the new Centennial Planetarium.

A very special occasion was the National Council's Annual Meeting held at Banff School of Fine Arts on June 10–13, 1963, with Calgary Council as hostess. The eighty-five miles between Calgary and Banff made the preparatory arrange-ments a bit difficult for the committee in charge, but every-thing went off without a hitch, unless you count the time there was a shortage of buses for a side trip, and the National President found herself riding in the company of the school's garbage on its way to town. "Squaw" dresses, white Stetsons, and western atmosphere were introduced wherever practicable, and the visitors' response to the unusual informality was gratifying.

Emphasis on the child ran through the programs of the 1960s, as evidenced in resolutions on "The Battered Child," "Kindergartens," and "Day Care Centers"; all of which were preceded by much study and attempts to get public involvement. Local Council women learned that, coupled with an increasing number of abused and neglected children, there was a general hesitancy to report incidents of such abuse. The resolution that went to the provincial government in 1965 asked for an amendment to the Child Welfare Act to make mandatory reporting by doctors, hospital personnel, welfare workers, or anyone who has information about abuse, or injury, or need for protection of a child. This was just the beginning of a continued enquiry and lobbying. There was some success by 1973.

Kindergartens within the school system – or early childhood education – was given intensive study and publicity by Local Council's Education Committee over a period of two years. T.V. interviews, a brief to the government, public meetings with knowledgeable educationists participating in panel discussions, culminated in a request to the provincial government to make funds available for kindergarten classes within the school system. Ten years later this is finally happening.

Daycare centers was something L.C.W. had always advocated and supported. It was a hot subject in 1968 following a study financed by the city's Preventive Social Services, aided by the Social Planning Council, which revealed a wide gap between the need and the supply of daycare for an increasing number of working mothers. Subsidization was being urged upon the City, and Province, and L.C.W.'s voice was included there.[17] Local Council was also involved in the formation of two daycare projects at the time. Bowness-Montgomery Centre was organized but seeking funds and help when L.C.W. gave its financial and moral support with a cash donation and representation on its board. Local Council was also one of the six city organizations that joined in planning an ambitious Model Daycare program, which was to include top-notch care, research, and education, besides serving as field experience for city institutions offering training courses in child care. It was a worthwhile idea, but perhaps ahead of its time. It did not get off the ground.

The watchdog instincts of Local Council women were on the alert when, in 1965, the Alberta Legislature was considering a new Human Rights Act. In the draft bill, the word "sex" was omitted from among the conditions and classifications against which discrimination shall not operate. An emergency resolution was hurriedly passed asking that this omission be corrected. It was.

Human Rights – or at least human consideration – is implied in two requests that were granted by the government. Both had to do with the handicapped. One was medical assessment for the province's physically handicapped, followed by appropriate treatment and training to make them self-supporting. The response was quick and satisfying. A pilot project employing a team of medical men was set up in 1961 and later transferred to the new Foothills Hospital. The other – a reiteration of an earlier request – asked for the provision of facilities for mental patients while adjusting to a return to the normal stress of life. Great strides have been made in this direction since then.

As had been said many times, Council of Women is not a fundraising organization; its very make-up precludes that sort of activity. However, a plea that could not be ignored came in 1960. In that year, Canada undertook to staff and maintain a new food technology training centre in Mysore, India, where students from Southeast Asian countries would be taught practical methods for processing, preserving, packing, and storing foods grown in their own countries that was going to waste for lack of knowledge and equipment to preserve it. The federal government initiated a nationwide "Freedom from Hunger" campaign, and National Council of Women, among several other national organizations, was asked to spearhead the fundraising. At the National Council's request, Local Councils across the country rallied to the cause. Led by Calgary L.C.W., Calgary organizations managed to raise monies for this worthwhile cause with such projects as the sale of Maunchadi seeds, distribution of coin cards, an international music and dance concert, and an austerity lunch.

A long-time campaign to get some stiffening into legislation covering sex offenders gathered momentum in 1960 after the gruesome murder of a 9-year-old Calgary girl by a sex deviate. Up until that time there had been many petitions presented to the government with no results. In the 1920s, Local Council women's thoughts leaned only to punishment (castration for molesters of children and whipping for rape). The need for something more positive was recognized in the 1940s when a resolution called for treatment to be coupled with more severe sentencing. The repeated requests of the 1950s were that recidivist sexual offenders be considered habitual criminals and be committed to continuous detention with medical care until there could be assurance that they were no longer a menace to the community. The evolution of the women's thinking is evident in a 1960 resolution which went a practical step further and asked for diagnostic clinics where sexual deviates could be observed and treated after conviction but before sentencing and where voluntary application for treatment would be possible. With such clinics, it was argued, sentences would be based on knowledge of the extent of the offender's future danger to the community and the possibilities of cure or rehabilitation. This resolution followed an in-depth study by Local Council members of the McRuer Report and a very successful panel discussion at one of its meetings. The resolution was presented in person to the then Federal Minister of Justice, Davie Fulton, by a delegation from the National Council of Women (having gone through the regular procedure of being assented to by all Local Councils at the National Annual Meeting), who received assurances that amendments to the Criminal Code were contemplated in the current session of Parliament. However, replying to a letter sent by the Calgary Local Council, Mr. Fulton pointed out that while the federal government could amend the Criminal Code, enforcement was the responsibility of the provincial government. The result was a 1967 petition to the Alberta government asking that "Forensic Clinics be established at or near a seat of learning, such as a university or hospital, so that teaching and research facilities may be part of it."

During 1968, Council's Arts and Letters Committee took a look at facilities in Calgary for the enrichment of cultural life, and found them wanting. Citing the facts that more leisure time was becoming available to people and that growth in numbers and industrial development of a city required a more active cultural life to go along with it, a resolution was adopted by the membership asking for a cultural complex to be established, to be geared to the widest possible use by all citizens, including ethnic groups, and to provide facilities for art exchanges with, and exhibitions from, other countries. It also requested that a cultural board be set up to manage the complex, with representatives from all segments of society.

The resolution was presented to city council in January 1969, and the following October, the Calgary Regional Arts (C.R.A.F.) was created with the task of equitable distribution of all civic grants to the arts. While this was not all that L.C.W. had asked for, it was a gratifying result. C.R.A.F. is currently functioning well, with L.C.W. representation on the board.

A brief rundown on other 1960s activities of Local Council Women:

- Took a stand on capital punishment (retain the death penalty for murder)
- On daylight saving (contrary to their 1933 sisters), the 1960 members were for it[18]

- On autonomy for the University of Calgary – endorsed it by resolution and aided in publicity
- Complained about too much sex on T.V.
- Sent letters to supermarkets, shopping centers, radio, and T.V. stations asking them to refrain from publicizing Christmas until after Thanksgiving Day
- Told newspapers, radio, and T.V. stations that releasing news of accidents without names is a scare tactic that serves no useful purpose
- Passed a resolution requesting the government to see that flammable synthetic materials bear a warning label (most of them do now)
- Asked the provincial government why the amendment to the Credit Loan Agreement Act had been assented to but not proclaimed (The answer was that a suitable formula could not be found – L.C.W. sent them one!)
- Were joint sponsors of a Short Course in Money Management and Related Subjects
- Assembled periodically a list of names of women willing to serve on juries at the request of the city sheriff (At last – women on juries. National Council had been asking for this in 1923.)
- Collected books for the Lady Aberdeen Memorial Library in Waterloo – a library of books by, for, and about women, inaugurated by National Council of Women; also collected Canadiana for the library of the new University of Calgary
- Sent a representative to sit on the Charitable Appeals Board at the request of the city

Two events designed to create closer liaison between the executive and affiliate members were initiated in the early 1960s and proved to be worthwhile.

The Presidents Coffee Party, now held annually in the fall, was initiated in 1962, with executive members as collective hostess and presidents and representatives of the affiliated societies as guest. The opportunity for unstructured exchange of information – even complaints – proved to be a good introduction to new members and a new season.

It was in that same year that workshops were introduced as a means of arriving at ideas for future programs and discussing ways for implementation. These workshops have continued, although not on a regular basis.

Chapter Seven

1970–1975

Dr. Ruth Gorman's April 22, 1970, Critique of the Local Council

Delivered at the Highlander Motor Hotel during the Annual Meeting.

FELLOW MEMBERS of Local Council and guests. I was delighted to find my speech was titled a critique. Because to be a critic is one of the easier jobs of this world! Almost any fool can be after wise or criticize other's actions – the tough job is to be the activists. However, it's a rough form of natural justice that this is my lot now because after 25 years of being your convenor of laws and resolutions and over fifteen of those being the chairman of the nominations committee who gathered together your governing body, I usually got the brunt of the criticism. Now it's my turn and it's much more fun and easier, I can assure you, to merely make a speech from the other side of the fence from the real creators and doers.

I carefully reviewed your year's activities. Your executive were more than loyal in their hours they gave. On reviewing their minutes I found they were still assisting in several activities that were originally created for this city by L.C.W. For instance, in connection with the rehabilitation of the disabled, they were protesting the need for disabled children to attend schools. A representative attended the Indian Friendship Centre, another project that was supported and almost created through L.C.W.'s efforts. They also had a resolution supporting Indian rights. Brotherhood Week, again a project they actually initiated. They continued the fight to prevent a destruction of a natural park in Southern Ontario and the Inglewood Park and also reminded City Council of the promise they had literally wrenched out of City Council in a three year battle re: green strips on the riverbank, and passed a resolution re: strip mining. They continued the work they have always done in schools by preparing a good brief on religious education in schools, one that followed up some of the most successful experiments, already begun in other parts, of incorporating it into the entire curriculum rather than by a rote formality. Their committees met with the city planning department and, although they were not actively to participate, they did get the word across and passed a resolution re housing costs. The old cupola, part of our heritage, was saved from destruction and although I have been accepted on their committee, that job has not yet been completed any further than some consultation and a dinner invitation. But the cupola has been saved and they will have to do consulting with us, or go back on their word.

In the field of criticism of the media they are still active. I, myself, got launched into becoming part of the media and doing the most difficult job I have yet tackled, of trying to keep alive a western publication, as a result of a local council meeting some years ago. This year your president attended a series sponsored by a local paper, labeled "the media friend or foe" and I can tell you eight years ago I don't think, without our criticism, the word foe would have even been in the title. They also listened to a review on the controversial Canadian Radio and Television Media.

One of their most creative actions was the culmination, after several years of study in actual board participation and limited fund participation, in the privately financed first Day Care Centre, largely financially supported by the Junior League. A day centre that may eventually persuade government of the great need and public support and will be a tremendous aid to future women and children.

They also became concerned in a study the Junior League had undertaken, re Calgary's need for a museum and art gallery, although they did not approve of the firms employed plans for placing it on Prince's island and thereby using up the only space L.C.W. have been fighting, for over six years, to preserve as an exciting downtown park. However, placing it on the banks of the Bow facing Princes Island Park would be ideal, provided Calgary City Council do not ruin that area and our green strip with the expensive Bow Trail traffic throughway that will run right through our downtown area, destroying our river beauty area and our revenue property.

Executive and councils and National Council have fortunately faced the need for more women representation on the numerous non-political boards that now semi govern many of our very important city activities. It was unfortunate some of our ablest women who were recommended were not included, and I refer to the Hospital Board appointment.[19] However, Betty Garbutt was appointed to the Educational Committee. Grace Stonewall and Mrs. Wilma Hansen serve on the University of Calgary Senate and Grace on the City of Calgary Library Board. I also serve on the Provincial board on Penology, and there are a few others. The Local Council of Women were complemented and asked to submit a list of suitable women and one was collected, but I have a criticism, or I suppose a warning, I feel I must give Local Council of Women about this matter. To get a few women, who are the minority on these boards is not enough. It is a fine effort but in turn it will now be vital to the women of Calgary if they are then not kept informed of these boards' actual efforts to protect women and children. So, I would suggest you plan, next year, to devote one meeting to requesting brief reports of what has or has not been achieved by the women on these Board positions.

I did note however, your executive was plagued by too much actual social planning re: teas, coffee parties, etc, and although these proved exceptionally popular, one of my criticisms or suggestions would be that a larger social committee should be appointed to take this burden off your executives' shoulders and allow them to concentrate on the quantities of problems in today's overburdened cities.

Now we come to what was achieved at our general meetings. The get acquainted coffee parties and teas that included actual reports from affiliated societies were happy and useful, but I would recommend in future at these, a printed summary of Council's expected topics of study and possible resolutions be distributed by L.C.W. to the affiliate presidents, and also, that a short notice of each meeting be properly aired in all media, well before each meeting, with the possible resolutions that would be considered. If this was done it would double their efficiency and involvement of the whole community.

I have another real criticism to make of your general meetings. I note that Local Council of Women is being more and more used by affiliate clubs and non-affiliate clubs as a source of promotion of their own club's projects, some of which are social, others for a financial campaign, some only to find volunteer help. This is not Council's function – we are the protestors, the leaders, in reform, not merely to be used to promote either individuals or any other club's projects. Resolutions from those clubs are all important, but these other matters, although important, are not our function. At present, a large part of the meeting's time is now, of necessity, being taken up with reading and reporting these. I realize they are of interest to our women and often of importance, but if there is one thing that plagues modern woman it is her actual shortage of time that she has for her own club activities. In a busy large city like this we will soon be swamped by such notices and requests. I would like to recommend, in future, that we initiate a notice board and all these matters and notices be posted on it at each meeting so any one concerned may read it. That would include thank-you letters, etc. It would still allow us to serve as a clearing house for matters of concern and interest to women but leave us much more time to get down to the "nitty-gritty" matters that are presently plaguing our civilization. The financial report and the president's report of the meeting and teas attended could also be posted there and this information, if kept in a book throughout the year, would still be available to any member or any executive or the press.

Now, as to the planned general meetings of matters of concern to the general public. I would like to suggest that, although panels do bring information to our women today, it is often only information by persons that have previously, or could be, as well aired in the press or on TV or radio, and too often speech is limited to only their own special topics or job. I would like you to give serious consideration to holding several "Town Hall Meetings." It could be a debate or a short speech by a person, or even a Local Council chairman who has a matter the executive have okayed by pre arranged plans as one we should consider at such a meeting. More time could be given to actual participation by the audience and our affiliated clubs. Let's not be just "talked at." Let's consider and participate more.

I note that the meeting on youth problems, where Mrs. Stonewall specifically invited outsiders, university and teen groups to attend, was well attended and this brings me to another criticism I must make of Local Council of Women.

We have tended to limit ourselves to an approved group of women's clubs. At the moment women's clubs are having difficulties in attracting new members and younger members. This is not because they are poorer clubs. The demise of the Women's Liberal Club is a sad example. The majority of today's women are divided into three classes. The young married woman who, without sitters, finds participation in one club almost impossible, never mind participation in the club's affiliate Local Council of Women. The second is the career girl who, if married, has no time and if not, is so tired the club must then excite her or help her solve her problems. And lastly, the older woman who just may be, but is not always, dangerously out of touch with the violent swift-changing problems of our day. Yet the tragedy lies in the fact women probably today have the most problems. We desperately need a Local Council of Women.

For that reason I would like to recommend that next year you attempt two, or more, "Town Hall Meetings" – open to the public and well advertised in advance. Let us offer this, so our concern be shared by all.

I have fortunately been chosen the honorary advisor for National Council for several years. All over the country we are concerned over what the role of the Local Council of Women is. I think the report made by Mrs. Waite was valid in many aspects.[20] National Council is too far away – we need more local autonomy and also we need to, somehow speed up our resolutions. You had some fine ones this year. But the fact we have to send a resolution through only one representative back to another society or club to be presented to their group for ratification often means it is three months before we can even speak with authority about it in this fast moving world. It is too late! If it is a national resolution, too often it takes over a year.

I would like to recommend your executive, at their first meeting after this annual one, review National's resolutions and our own ones that are not yet implemented; and send such a list to all affiliates also requesting any they are considering presenting. I also recommend that the first general meeting be a resolutions one. The executive should attempt to list the resolutions in order of their need and mail those out to all affiliates and then design, as Mrs. Neve did, this year's meetings to discuss these.[21] Affiliates should be informed that these are open discussion meetings with a factual speaker or whatever committee or affiliate is concerned. At the end of that meeting some recommendations should be passed for the resolution committee to consider and the executive to choose and vote on, and continue to take action on.

These are really suggestions, not criticisms. You must judge their true value and I will in no way be hurt.

There is a tendency today to criticize such clubs as this one. I think if the press and the public carefully reviewed our past performance they would find Local Council of Women in the past thirty years have brought hundreds of needed reforms and new thought to this city. We, who are often labeled as "the little housewives" or "the do-gooders" were the real protestors, the real activists before that word became common usage. For example, today everyone's excited about environmental destruction and air pollution. It was over six years ago we had the city transport official in here demanding he get smog controls on his buses and at that time we were just pooh-poohed by officials. For years we have concerned ourselves with peace and support of the U.N.; for years we have dealt with racial differences and drug problems.

This fore thinking by women in the Local Council of Women is desperately needed today. Let us cut our sail's to today's wind. We can do it. Your executive worked hard, but some new simpler changes in procedure are needed to meet these changing times.

It is wonderful to be back briefly with you ladies who I have worked with for so long. Women who have always been overly kind to me with the honors and teas you have given for me. My personal criticisms[22] and suggestions may seem a small repayment. You have done so well in the past and the world needs you so desperately in the future. Do carry on with increased efforts. (Glenbow Archives, C.L.C.W. fonds, M5841/260).

Barbara Langridge in her President's message in the 1970–71 L.C.W. Hand Book, referred to the need to "search for a better way" of functioning. In the same handbook, Citizenship Chairman Barbara Scott documented the bleak state of affairs as follows:

Your chairman constituted the sole member of L.C.W.'s Citizenship Committee. This is an unfortunate situation, faced by other committees as well. If a variety of points of view is to be brought to bear on an area of L.C.W. concern, such as citizenship, then it is clear that regular and standardized procedures for involving affiliates and individual members in committee work will have to be found.

During the past year, your citizenship chairman was responsible for an L.C.W. general meeting, on citizenship participation in local government.

Your citizenship chairman also participated in several community consultations on the Citizenship Act, preparatory to a planned consultation with the Minister Responsible for Citizenship, Robert Stanbury.

Additionally, your citizenship chairman took part in a review of L.C.W.'s constitution and bylaws, with a view towards strengthening the use of proper organizational procedures and enhancing L.C.W.'s opportunities to voice effectively its affiliates' positions on matters of community import.

The Publicity Report submitted by Chairman Frances Roessingh read, in part:

> The media have shown no interest in extending advance coverage beyond a simple notice, listing chairman and speakers, and the subject under discussion. This is disappointing in view of the successful efforts of our own program chairman to attract well-known and competent speakers to our meeting.
>
> Reporting on the meetings reflected the attendance of our own members. The evening meetings were poorly attended, and the papers did not send reporters. No reports on those meetings were carried in the press. At afternoon meetings, reporters were usually present and press coverage was very satisfactory.

It is desirable that an effort be made to conduct a stronger and more direct publicity campaign amongst the members of our affiliates to get a better attendance at the very worth while meetings.

The early years of the 1970s were a time of flux in the world of women. Until some time in the 1960s, the word "feminist" was associated with the turn-of-the-century suffragettes. But Betty Friedan changed all that when she issued her clarion call for the liberation of women in her Feminine Mystique published in 1962, and a new feminist movement was born. For the next few years, sporadic demonstrations by shouting women waving the feminist flag made headlines, but the action was mainly south of the border. "Women's Lib," as it came to be called, did not surface in Canada until the 1970s, certainly not in Calgary.

It was in this climate that the report of the federal government's Status of Women Commission's Report was released in 1972. It stressed the need for drastic changes in legislation concerning women, and made specific recommendations for action. When there was no sign that implementation of those recommendations was being considered, it is understandable that the newly roused women would not take the delay lying down. The Women's Liberation movement really got underway in Canada then.

It was against this backdrop that Calgary Local Council functioned in the five years of the 1970s that are included in this history. It was inevitable that the new restiveness among women would be reflected in an organization like the Local Council – composed of women of all ages, religions, and political and social stripes – particularly when that organization's founding objective was the preservation of family life, which sometimes seemed threatened by the freedoms demanded by the Feminists.

However, many of the Status of Women Commission's recommendations echoed changes which the Council of Women had striven for since its inception, and it goes without saying that the Council welcomed the Commission's findings and prepared itself to take action whenever possible. In 1972, the National Council appointed a Status of Women Committee to keep *au courant* of the situation, and advised its locals to do likewise. Calgary L.C.W. appointed its own Status of Women Committee to liaise with other involved groups.[23] It became one of the busiest committees during this period. L.C.W's. influence had much to do with the establishment of a new flourishing Status of Women Action Committee in Calgary, and support of that wide activity continues.

To acknowledge that the cries of women had been heard, the federal government proclaimed 1975 International Women's Year. The Hon. Marc Lalonde, Minister of Health and Welfare, was appointed to initiate or fund suitable activities, conferences, literature, etc. As the year came to a close, Calgary Local Council, jointly with the Calgary branch of National Jewish Women, Hadassah Wiso, and the Junior League, arranged a very successful public meeting as a "wrap-up" to I.W.Y., and Mr. Lalonde accepted an invitation to speak to that October 29th meeting. He promised the large and representative audience present continued government action beyond 1975.

It was nothing new that L.C.W. should jump in with both feet where women's rights were being trampled on. In 1970 a resolution went to the Alberta government pointing out that its new Human Rights Act contained no provision to prohibit discrimination in employment on the basis of sex or marital status. The omission was rectified.

Another clear case of discrimination, brought to the attention of L.C.W. by a retired lady school teacher, was taken up with the appropriate government department and brought to a successful conclusion. The pension for female teachers had been 13% less than for males, based on the chauvinistic logic that women were likely to live longer than men.

But not all of Council's time and effort was given to women's rights. A strong Nutrition Committee made an in-depth study of the nutritional habits of Canadians. Appalled by the findings, Local Council held educational meetings and sent letters to the Provincial Minister of Education and the Minister of Social Development, seeking an education program on nutrition in schools and counseling for welfare recipients. A Calgary resolution asking that a yearly survey on nutrition be included in Statistics Canada reports and for more action on programs for nutritionally vulnerable groups, was eventually presented to the Prime Minister and some of his cabinet members by the National Council of Women executive, after being adopted by the National body at its Annual Meeting.

Constant threats to Calgary's natural land areas and heritage buildings kept the Conservation Committee and the reactivated Special Historical Committee on their toes for most of the early 1970s.

Rundle Lodge, an old sandstone building, Calgary's first hospital, and currently being used to house senior citizens, was slated for demolition. L.C.W. presented briefs at provincial government hearings and allied itself with a city-wide group of Calgarians. They banded together in an effort to save the historical landmark. Countless hours of intensive work and pleading failed to move city and provincial officials to change their minds.[24] The building came down – most of it, that is. A couple of partial walls in a grassed plot were left to stand as a monument to those men and women – mostly women – who played a part in building the Calgary of today.

A city with a fast-growing population, a housing shortage, and thousands of acres of park or open land on its perimeter, is sure to tempt developers and lead to confrontation with citizens concerned with preserving open spaces and irreplaceable flora and fauna. Calgary has Nose Hill's thousands of acres of natural growth area to the north and the long strip of park land bordering Fish Creek to the south – both prime targets. Many public hearings, meetings of city council and private groups, and discussions all over the place aired the subject. Calgary Local Council of Women let its voice be heard at all of them.

At this writing, Fish Creek has been declared a provincial park by the Alberta government. As for Nose Hill, when the smoke cleared there was an agreement for a 4600 acre park. But the smoke is descending again as some of the administrators are having second thoughts and attempting to reduce the acreage to 2800.[25]

It was Calgary Local Council's determined and continued policy to preserve the beauty of the riverbanks that led them to object in 1975 to a proposal for a private multi-million-dollar athletic arena to be built adjacent to the Bow River close to downtown. Letters to city council were followed by the personal appearance of L.C.W.'s president at a city council meeting called to hear the pros and cons. Some aldermen admitted privately that L.C.W.'s input had had some influence on the vote, which refused permission for the arena to be built on that site. The city found an alternative location for it.

Local Council members keep a close watch to see that the city's promise of a green belt paralleling the Bow River through the city would be kept. It was with smug satisfaction that the city's Bow River Impact Study was received in 1974. One of its recommendations was that no new buildings be erected within two hundred feet of the riverbank – one of the requests in L.C.W.'s submission.

In 1970, L.C.W. asked for a green belt around the whole city, adding the suggestion that, in the meantime, there would be a temporary moratorium on the fragmentation of property lying in the path of future city growth pending completion of the city's growth plans. Perhaps that was too much to ask.

That same year, L.C.W. came to the aid of city cyclists by suggesting to the city that bicycle lanes should be provided on city streets. It is good to note that the city has gone even further, and bicycle paths are appearing cross-town and along the river bank.

By this time the old James Short School had been demolished, and Greyhound was planning to build a bus depot on the site. When Greyhound decided to build its depot elsewhere, Local Council, ever watchful for the provision of open spaces for people downtown, approached the city to reserve the site for a mini-park.

Along with many other groups, Local Council had tried to keep for posterity the gracious old sandstone courthouse. But when the new courthouse was built, the lovely old one came down. At least a mini-park was placed on the site.

Viewed with dismay at this time was the cultural health of the city. In the late 1960s, L.C.W. had been partly responsible for the creation of a civic Cultural Board. Now they asked for civic policy that would promote "a rich, aesthetic environment in the city." In a thoughtful 1970 resolution presented to city officials, they set out some details. Such policy should include (1) civic recognition for excellence in design of new and improved older buildings; (2) tax or other incentives for developers who included green belts or works of art in their designs; (3) civic recognition and encouragement for donations to the arts; (4) yearly civic grants, on a matching basis, to all fund drives for cultural purposes. To shame the mayor, alderman, and board of commissioners into taking action, a list was attached to the resolution documenting the contributions made to the arts by most of Canada's larger cities. Calgary was at the very bottom.

During this period, Calgary Local Council had representation on the Calgary Regional Arts Foundation, C.O.G.S., and on a steering committee jointly with the University Women and I.O.D.E., under the guidance of the University of Calgary's Department of Continuing Education and working with a $2550 federal grant to bring in recommendations on the need and effectiveness of volunteer organizations.

An important 1972 event was the appointment of L.C.W.'s Conservation Chairman as L.C.W. representative on the provincial government's Environmental Conservation Authority.[26]

In 1973, Calgary natives looked north and saw two C.B.C. owned T.V. stations in Edmonton and none in Calgary. Calgary was the largest city in Canada without such a facility. L.C.W. joined in the growing demand for a Calgary station, and it was not long before this justifiable complaint brought results.

The plight of the battered child is today receiving publicity and remedial, if not preventive, action. It was back in 1965 that L.C.W. made a project of the problem and began to seek such action. Between then and 1972, some study and several reiterated requests to government were made, but little progress seemed possible while persons with knowledge of child abuse were afraid to report suspected cases. In preparation for a 1972 resolution, L.C.W. called a meeting where a panel of doctors and social workers discussed the difficulties as they then existed, and the resolution that went forward asked again that reporting of known injury or suspected abuse be made mandatory – all persons reporting to be indemnified. In March 1973, a bill was introduced in the Alberta Legislature by a Calgary M.L.A. who had been in communication with the Calgary Local Council of Women. It covered all the points in the L.C.W. resolution.

More attention is being given these days to the provision in public buildings of facilities to make things easier for the physically handicapped, but no one seemed to have of thought of the difficulties encountered by deaf persons wishing to use a public telephone. In 1973, Calgary L.C.W. took the problem to the provincial government's Minister of Telephones. Persistent prodding resulted in special amplifiers being installed on some airport telephones by the spring of 1974, and the hope is that the program will be broadened. Encouraged by that success, Local Council next asked that such equipment be provided in the homes of the hearing handicapped, with the cost – at least for senior citizens – to be covered by medicare. That hasn't come yet, but it likely will.

The provincial government was next asked to consider and amend regulations that unfairly restricted the amount of income a handicapped person is allowed to earn to be eligible for support. That was in March of 1974, and nothing has come of it yet.

Throughout its history, Calgary Local Council never failed to keep tabs on education, locally and provincially, and has therefore always been ready with input into any investigation on that subject, and has initiated its own share of research and investigations. In the 1960s, the Local Council had presented a brief to the province's Cameron Commission on Education. In 1972, Dr. Worth was inviting submissions in accordance with his mandate from the provincial government to look into all phases of education in the province. In October of that year, Calgary L.C.W. presented its researched conclusions in a brief.

It seems fitting that in International Women's Year, Calgary Local Council had the opportunity of coming to the support of a woman whose rights were in jeopardy because of discriminatory laws. In a case that became a *cause célèbre*, rancher's wife Irene Murdoch sued her husband for a financial settlement in recognition of her contribution to the family farm during their years of marriage. The judge ruled that no matter how much a wife adds to the family property in time, money, or work, she is not entitled to a share of the assets in the event of divorce. To Local Council members, and many others, this was blatant discrimination. Women everywhere were up in arms. L.C.W.'s practical approach was to initiate a public fund, the money to be used for legal fees in an evitable appeal. Donations came from everywhere, and are still coming in at the time of this writing. (P.S.: In October of 1976 the appeal was won, and Alex

Murdoch was ordered to pay $65 000.) It should be the last of such court battles. The cobwebs are now being dusted off the ancient tomes of marital laws that have lain so long in the care of male custodians.[34]

Part Two

Original Source
Documents and
Other Notes

Addendum A

A Matter of Record:
Secretary Reports

The 1920s

1924–25 Corresponding Secretary's Report – Mrs. W.E. Hall

THE CALGARY LOCAL COUNCIL OF WOMEN has just terminated a most successful and strenuous year. Such is the conclusion one must reach after carefully or even casually perusing the official records of this composite body of representative club women.

The Local Council at present consists of 46 paid up affiliated societies – one of the largest in the history of the organization. Four new societies were welcomed into the Council this year, namely, the Military Chapter, I.O.D.E., the Cliff Bungalow Parent Teacher's Association, St. Andrew's Presbyterian Ladies' Aid, and Scarboro Avenue Methodist Ladies' Aid.

During the year there were held three General (including the annual), eight Executive, three Special or Urgent meetings and three sub-Executive conferences. In addition to these, there were two public meetings under the auspices of the Local Council, the first – in June – to hear Miss Knight, on "The Save the Children Fund" of Greece; the second on January 27th to hear Dr. G.D. Stanley on "Prevention of Goitre, Scarlet Fever and Diptheria."

During the year letters of sympathy were sent to Mrs. Carson at the time of her sad bereavement, to Mrs. Riley and

Miss Markle, when suffering from severe accidents, and to Mrs. Kerby when Dr. Kerby was ill. Flowers were sent to Mrs. Riley, at Ottawa, and others to Mrs. MacWilliams and Mrs. Riley's sons when they were ill in the hospital. There were also gifts of flowers to Mrs. Carson and to Dr. Kerby.

Letters of appreciation were voted to Captain J.T. Shaw, M.P., because of his efforts to remedy the Divorce Law of Western Canada; to Wm. Irvine, M.P. for his support of Captain Shaw, and to J.C. Buckley, M.L.A., for the inaugurating of the Scripture Memorizing Contests for Sunday Schools.

The law firm of Short, Ross & Selwood was commended and thanked for their assistance in the O'Leary case.

The *Calgary Herald* was also commended for its stand against the useless slaughter of trees at Christmas time.

Votes of thanks were accorded Mrs. Glass in appreciation of her splendid work in getting out the Yearbook; to the different convenors and all others who secured advertisements for the same.

Assistance was given the Red Cross by securing taggers for their Annual Tag Day. The Humane Society was furnished with information which proved useful in furthering the work of that organization.

A delegate – our convenor of education, Mrs. French – was appointed to the Educational Committee which is endeavoring to secure a Junior College for Calgary. Mrs. Geddes was appointed our delegate to the Social Service Council, with power to choose two other delegates.

The funds of the Council were greatly augmented by the publishing of a Year Book, under the able direction of Mrs. H.G.H. Glass, past president. This book contained a fund of interesting information and was an innovation in this Council. It is hoped that this Year Book will become an annual publication.

A donation of $10 was made to the International Council's Pavilion at the British Exposition at Wembly.

The Committee of Household Economics, which has been in abeyance of years, was re-established at the December meeting on account of the disbanding of the Associated Consumers. Mrs. Ainsley Young was appointed convenor of this committee.

The only speakers during the year were Sir James Outram and Major Walker, who addressed the Council in June on "The Conservation of Our National Parks."

In March, during the Spring Opening, a very successful Tea was held at Parkers' under the convenorship of Mrs. Akitt and Mrs. Birnie.

In May, at Knox Church, the Local Council entertained the delegates attending the Annual Convention of the Women's Institute.

It was with great regret that the Council lost three officers this past year, Mrs. P.D. McLaren, corresponding secretary, who left Calgary to reside in Vancouver; Mrs. B.L. Stavert and Mrs. Reginald Smith, first and fourth vice-presidents, who resigned in December.

The news of the death of Mrs. W.J. Budd, a highly esteemed and beloved former convener, came as a great shock to her many friends in the Council.

Three delegates from the Calgary Council attended the National Convention in Toronto in October – Mrs. W.A. Geddes, our President, who carried the Council's vote; also Mrs. B.L. Stavert and Miss Markle. Mrs. Geddes presented a most interesting and comprehensive report of the proceedings at the November general meeting, stating that although much splendid work had been covered, a great deal of valuable information had to be withheld on account of haste in the business of the convention.

Many splendid reports were submitted by the different conveners during the year out of which arose a number of important resolutions. Your secretary, however, does not intend to report at any length on these, as they will be fully dealt with by the conveners in their annual reports, to be given later. I shall merely give a brief summary of all resolutions presented during the year. They follow in no sequence whatever, merely in order of their presentation to the Council.

RESOLVED –

- That we strongly protest against the destruction of entire trees for decoration purposes.
- That we send only $50 Council aid to the National until that body sees its way clear to pool delegates' railway expenses as other organizations do, the expense of sending our delegate being so great.
- That the Dominion Government be petitioned, through the National Council, to take preventative and curative measures for the goiter malady.
- That we advocate the formation of habit forming centres, in larger cities, for lower grade defectives, outside of institutional care.
- That we request the Federal Government to lift the ban on Dr. Spookes' books.
- That we petition the Lieutenant-Governor-in-Council to appoint women on censor boards of theatres, same to have right to enter any theatre at any time.
- That we petition the Mayor and City Council to legislate prohibiting the employment of white girls in Chinese restaurants.
- That we protest against dances being held in public halls on Sundays.
- That we petition the City Council to enforce rules regarding the sterilization of all toilet accessories used in beauty parlors.
- That we disapprove of the hamlet settlement scheme of Mr. D. Alger Bailey.
- That we request the Parks Department to have proper lighting in Central Park.
- That we heartily endorse the Berean Shield Scripture Memorizing Competition.

- That we request the Public School Board to institute the practice of saluting the flag.
- That we suggest to the Parent Teachers' Association the holding of reading contests in schools during the winter months.
- That we follow the ruling of the National Council re. the five-year term for officers.

(Source: 1924–25 L.C.W. Year Book, p. 25, 27, 29)

1929 Secretary's Report – Mrs. A. Blight

Madame President, Officers and Members of the Local Council of Women:

I beg to submit the following report of our year's work, ending December 31, 1929.

The Calgary Local Council of Women has just terminated a very active and successful year. It is now composed of 45 affiliated societies. There have been seven general meetings, one executive and two sub-executive meetings. At the February meeting the Council endorsed the action of the Child Welfare Association in asking the Government for a censor committee for vaudeville shows.

We also co-operated with the Child Welfare Council in asking that trained experts only be engaged by the City in all work pertaining to Child Welfare.

Mrs. H.J. Collins was asked to represent the Local Council at the Conference in Vancouver from April 8th to the 13th. The Council approved of the establishing of banks among the school children and a committee was appointed to interview Dr. Scott to ascertain if such a system could be established. Owing to crowded conditions in schools this cannot be managed at present.

A petition to Provincial Government and City Council asking that the liquor vendor store at the corner of 1st St. West and 10th Avenue be widened and a door be opened on the Avenue to avoid accidents on special days when this corner was congested with people.

Council assisted the Women's Labour League in sponsoring a tag day for the relief of destitute British miners. A resolution was passed asking the Government through the Provincial Committee to refuse clearance to vessels carrying cargos of liquor consigned to U.S.A. ports.

It was moved and carried we petition the National Council to urge upon the Dominion Government to take steps to co-operate with the League of Nations in revising the Calendar, so that a year composed of thirteen months, each with twenty-eight days be set. A questionnaire was sent to all affiliated societies for their opinion on the new thirteen months calendar.

Under the auspices of the Local Council it was agreed to send pictures for the Art Exhibit to be held in Medicine Hat in March.

The Council assisted in serving tea during Child Welfare Week, April 1st, our President acting as chairman on the Wednesday of Child Welfare Week.

The Annual Empire Tea was held on May 22nd and proved a great success, Mrs. Guy Johnson, convener.

Our President was appointed the Council's delegate to the Annual National Convention which was held in Saskatoon in June.

At the April meeting Mrs. W. Carson, Convener of the League of Nations Committee, gave a very interesting address on the growth of the peace movement throughout the world.

At the May meeting of Council, Mrs. Margaret Lewis, gave a helpful talk on her work as Provincial Factory Inspector.

Mrs. H.J. Collins also gave an interesting report of the Educational Conference in Vancouver.

On Memorial Day the Local Council was asked to convene the flowers for decorating the graves of those who fell in the Great War. Mrs. H.J. Akitt was in charge, assisted by a number of affiliated societies.

In June, the Council entertained at a tea for Mrs. J.A. Wilson, President of the National Council, Mrs. O.C. Edwards, Convener of Laws, National Council, and Miss Lola Francis, Assistant Corresponding Secretary, National Council. All members of affiliated societies were invited.

Mrs. Akitt, our President, entertained the Executive of the Local Council to tea at her home on September 14th.

In October, a committee composed of Mrs. Grevett, Mrs. Hartshorn, Mrs. Blight, Mrs. Freeman and Mrs. MacWilliams were appointed to attend the session of the Minimum Wage Board, held in Calgary.

Mrs. E.G. Hartshorn was appointed to take charge of subscriptions to the World Wide Magazine.

Through the efforts of Mrs. Harold Riley and the Educational Committee, 40 000 stickers of the Ten Commandments have been purchased and are being placed in the school readers. This amount of stickers will last four years.

At September's meeting, Mrs. H.J. Akitt, President, gave a very full and concise report of the National Convention held in Saskatoon. Congratulations were at this time extended to her for the honor conferred by the convention, when she was elected as vice-president of the National Council.

At the September meeting, Mrs. Elizabeth Harper, a member of the Women's Section of the Society for Overseas Settlement of British Women, who had been visiting British Women settlers through the Dominion was present to express her personal gratitude to the Local Council as well as the other Women's organizations for the kindness shown to the women settlers in Canada.

At the October meeting it was reported by our President that the Calgary Council had collected seven hundred ($700) dollars of their six thousand (6000) dollars allotment for the foundation fund. At this meeting it was decided to ask the Minister of Education to make Good-Will Day, May 18, a regular annual day, with the idea of developing an international attitude of mind in the people of the Province.

At the November meeting it was moved and seconded to request the Minister of Education to ask the Dominion Government to supply copies of the World Peace Pact to be hung in the schools of the Province.

Congratulations were sent to the five women of Alberta: Mrs. Judge Murphy, Hon. Mrs. Parlby, Mrs. Nellie McClung, Mrs. E. McKinney and Mrs. O.C. Edwards, whose appeal to the Privy Council resulted in allowing women the right to sit in the Senate. (Source: 1930 L.C.W. Yearbook, p. 27–29)

The 1930s

1933 Report of the Corresponding Secretary – Mrs. A. Blight

The Calgary Local Council now composed of 27 paid up affiliated societies, held eight general and four sub-executive meetings during the year.

The Council sincerely regrets to report the death of Mrs. G. Newhall, a past convenor of Home Economics on the Local Council, and also a past National officer; the resignations through ill health of Miss Marion Hutt, convenor of Natural Resources; of Mrs. A. MacWilliams, convenor of Citizenship, and Mrs. G.R. Fox, convener of Cinema and Printed Matter, who left the city to reside in Regina.

On January 26, 1932, the 20th annual meeting of the Calgary L.C. of Women was held in the Tapestry Room of the Hudson's Bay Co.

In the evening the annual banquet was held in the Elizabethan Room of the Hudson's Bay Co. L.W. Brockington, K.C., was the speaker of the evening, describing women's spheres of greatest influence as the realm of Home, of Education and Social Reform.

Early in the year a letter of appreciation was sent from the Local Council to Prime Minister Bennett on the appointment of Miss Kydd, National Council president, as a member of the Canadian Delegation to the Disarmament Conference at Geneva.

Good Will Day was observed as usual during May. Mrs. Carson, convenor of the League of Nations Committee, taking charge of the messages which were compiled from letters written by the school children of our city. Many were broadcast and others sent to countries all over the world.

The year book of the Local Council was printed again this year with Mrs. H.J. Akitt, convenor, assisted by Mrs. Victor Wright, Mrs. G. Johnson and Mrs. R.L. Freeman.

Under the convenorship of Mrs. F.G. Grevett, tea was served by the ladies of the Council at the Alberta Manufacturers' Exhibition held one week, January 20–26.

Affiliated societies assisted in making violets for the Public Welfare Tag Day.

The Empire Tea was held in the ball-room of the Palliser Hotel on April 23, with Mrs. E. Hirst, convener, all affiliated societies helping to make this function a great success.

In April the Calgary L.C. of Women affiliated with the Calgary Council of Social Agencies.

Mr. Grigori Garbovitsky, one of the group of prominent citizens being responsible for the formation of the Calgary Senior Symphony Orchestra, was an interesting speaker at the April meeting.

Mrs. Harold Riley, convenor of Laws, represented the Local Council at the third Canadian Conference on Social Work held in Winnipeg, June 7, 8 and 9, 1932.

Early in the year, a letter was received from the National Council of Women regretting the postponement of the annual meeting (which was to have been held in Calgary) owing to economic conditions but a statutory executive meeting would be held some time during the summer.

Under the joint auspices of the L.C. of Women and the Daughters of the Empire a tea and reception was held in the sun room of the Palliser Hotel September 16 in honor of Her Excellency, the Countess of Bessborough. Members of the executive of the two organizations were presented to Her Excellency.

On November 19 the Calgary L.C. of Women had the honor of entertaining Miss Winnifred Kydd, the National president, who was making a coast-to-coast trip in the interests of Council work throughout the Dominion. This entertainment took the form of a tea in the Alhambra Room of the T. Eaton Co., with Mrs. H.J. Akitt and Mrs. E. Hirst joint conveners.

Again in the evening of November 19 a mass meeting, convened by Mrs. F.G. Grevett, was held in the First Baptist Church under the auspices of the Local Council of Women, and the League of Nations Society. On this occasion Miss Kydd addressed a large audience on the Disarmament Conference at Geneva.

The Local Council assisted in serving tea during Child Welfare Week in April, the executive also entertained the provincial executive to tea in the Y.W.C.A. rooms at the provincial executive meeting held November 18. Miss Kydd, National president, was a visitor at this meeting. Mrs. Harold Riley, our new provincial president, entertained Miss Kydd and members of the provincial executive to dinner that evening at the Tea Kettle Inn.

During the year several resolutions have been dealt with by the Local Council. In October the Council went on record as opposed to the curtailment of service in the Domestic Science and Manual Training departments in the public schools of the city. A protest was made by the Local Council to the proposal to close Commercial and Technical High Schools of the city.

Resolution from Mrs. H. J. Akitt, convener of Education, resulted in securing eight tickets for 25 cents for student up to 18 years of age.

Resolution that the City Council proclaim November 11 as a holiday in accordance with the Federal ruling was forwarded to City Council.

A letter recommending the appointment of a vigilance committee of men and women was sent to the City Council also asking that a report on morality cases be made. The City Council was also asked to take action in removing the women's section of the Labor Bureau to more suitable quarters.

Stricter enforcement of the law prohibiting newsboys on the streets after 9 p.m. was urged by the L.C. at the September meeting.

A recommendation was also sent to the Calgary School Board that they continue the school clinic, believing this service to be of untold benefit to our citizens, also suggesting that other ways and means of economy be found other than by eliminating most desirable and valuable services.

There have been several other recommendations brought into the Council, which are not given in this report, as they will no doubt be given in the various reports of the Council's convenors.

Mrs. G. Johnson, president, has represented the Calgary Local Council at several social functions during the past year, among which was a banquet given by the Business Women on international night, a luncheon to Mrs. Kydd by the Women's Canadian Club and luncheon by the League of Nations Society.

Numerous letters have been received and answered during the past year, also many letters of thanks and appreciation to the merchants of Calgary and others who have helped the Council in various ways. (Source: 1933 [Souvenir] L.C.W. Year Book, p. 33–35)

1935 Report of the Corresponding Secretary – M.A. Hall

In summarizing the work of the Local Council of Women for the twenty-second year of its existence, one realizes that it has been carried on with well sustained interest and varied activity, the officers and conveners showing the same noteworthy zeal and ability that have characterized the executives of the past.

Educative and legislative as is the nature of its work, the Council deals chiefly with resolutions, petitions, appeals and requests, with, of necessity, follow-up work to implement, in many cases, the resultant reforms.

Resolutions and petitions fall into three classes: those directed to the National Council or Government of Canada for Federal action, those to the Provincial Legislature, and others to municipal authorities or boards. These various resolutions will not be dealt with in this report, merely mentioned, as no doubt they will all be outlined in the annual reports of the several convenors originating them.

During the past year five important resolutions were sent to the Federal Government: re Government control of exports of nickel, the establishment of a Central Bank, elevation of moving picture themes, the lowering of age for old age pension recipients, and desertion a just cause for divorce. In addition to these, the Minister of Justice was petitioned for clemency in the case of Mrs. Dranchuk, sentenced to death in an Alberta court. This petition was endorsed by affiliated societies and no doubt helped to secure the commuting of the sentence.[27]

To the Provincial Legislature have been directed three resolutions: re using funds for upkeep of Government House for sanitarium if available, re the careful choice of the new Deputy Minister of Education, and a request for information re settlers in the Back-to-the-Land Scheme.

The City Council was petitioned in regard to: garbage collection, reduction in car fares, women supervisors in playgrounds, protection of children in congested areas, training or recreation for youth in leisure time, interns in hospitals, women on hospital board, and restoration of cuts in relief.

The City Council went on record as favoring the establishment of a Community Chest in Calgary, the candidature of women in civic offices, and on the directorate of the new Bank of Canada.

The second annual scholarship was awarded for merit to a student in the Provincial Institute of Art, Myrtle Jackson of Gadsby. Jack Robb, last year's winner, kindly loaned a number of his sketches and drawings for a showing at the May meeting of the Council, when his mother expressed her thanks to the members.

The text book fund of the Home and School Federation was helped by individual donations, as well as several needy families appealing for clothing and school books.

Funds were raised by the securing of advertisements for the Year Book – an outstanding success this year – by a luncheon at the Hudson's Bay Company's Store, convened by Mrs. Stuart Brown; a tea at the home of Mrs. Maurice Groberman, convened by Mrs. A. Blight, and by the fees of the Societies. The Council will greatly miss the excellent services of Mrs. F.A. Sage, who is retiring after six years as treasurer.

Thirty-two paid-up affiliated societies comprised the Local Council in 1934, but of these two have disbanded, the Central W.C.T.U. and the Unemployed Women's Association. Two societies have withdrawn, while four societies, Women's Section, Canadian Labor Party, Women's Section, Douglas System of Social Credit, Association of Graduate Nurses, and the Local Branch, Canadian Authors' Association, have been welcomed into the Council.

During the Council year from February 1934 to January 1935, there have been held eight general monthly meetings, six sub-executive and 6 executives, four of the latter being special emergent meetings to consider: Nominations for National Council, taking any action in the Brownlee-Macmillan case,[28] petitioning for Mrs. Dina Dranchuk of St. Paul, Alberta, and a protest against cut in relief food quotas.

Through the kindness of a number of speakers the Council has heard several cultural and educative addresses at its general meetings given by Mrs. Amelia Turner, Mr. I. Gislason, Miss C. Maberly, Mrs. A.T. Spankie, Miss Pansy Pue and Miss Ruby Campbell.

On Decoration and Remembrance Days, wreaths were placed on the Cenotaph by Mrs. Grevett in the name of the Local Council.

A chart for registering attendance of delegates, designed and executed by Jack Robb, was presented to the Council. The winner of the pennant, presented by the President, was the Women's Institute with 100% attendance.

The Council was represented twice at the Legislature in Edmonton, by Mrs. Grevett in January and by Mrs. Grevett and Mrs. Freeman in September; at the Child Welfare Council by the President; at the Social Agencies by Mrs. Grevett and Mrs. Victor Wright; at the Women's Peace Council by Mrs. Wm. Carson; at the League Against Fascism and War by Mrs. D.W. Hunt; and the National Council of Education by the President, Mrs. Grevett.

Tea was served to the delegates at the annual meeting of the Provincial Council in October, when the Council was represented by Mrs. Grevett, Mrs. Freeman and Miss Helen Steeves.

A reception at the home of the Corresponding Secretary was held by the Executive in honor of Mrs. Grevett, on her return from Ottawa in October where she had been elected a National Vice-President. As delegate of the Local Council, the President submitted a comprehensive report at the annual meeting of the National Council.

A congratulatory cable to Miss Winnifred Kydd, in London; a telegram to Mrs. Grevett in Ottawa, and 72 letters were sent out by the Corresponding Secretary during the year, as well as 38 petitions re: Mrs. Dranchuk, nomination blanks to 30 societies, and final agenda, totaling 56 copies, to all societies, officers and convenors. (Source: 1935 L.C.W. Year Book p. 15–17)

The 1940s

1941 Corresponding Secretary's Report – Mary Goldie

The Calgary Local Council is made up of twenty-five affiliated societies and three individual members. During the year 1940 eight general meetings, eight executive and three sub-executive meetings were held. The banner, award for highest attendance, was won once again by the Calgary Branch of the Women's Institute.

In pursuance of its duties and policies, the following petitions, recommendations, and resolutions were presented to various departments of the Legislature.

February: A recommendation was forwarded to the Street Railway Department urging the necessity of a five-cent fare. Some consideration for rates to Keith Sanitarium was again solicited. Both unsuccessful.

March and April: The Local Council of Women supported and endorsed the following:

To the City Council – Immediate increase of 25% on the relief quota.

To the Provincial Government – That the Provincial Government should establish a basis rate of relief 25% higher than the current rate.

A letter was sent to Premier Aberhart asking that Alberta co-operate with the Dominion Government in Unemployment Insurance.

May: A Committee was appointed to present a plea for raising the allowance to unemployables by 50¢ to 75¢ a week. The Committee reported success – a 50¢ per week increase was allowed.

The Local Council of Women also endorsed a resolution from the Unemployed Women's Association condemning the action of the City Council which cut men off relief whether they could or could not obtain work.

A resolution that pensions age of old age pensioners be reduced from 70 to 60 years was forwarded to ten sources of possible action.

October: We protested the name chosen for the North Hill Cemetery.

A resolution was forwarded to the Federal Government urging an embargo be placed on export of metals, chemicals and machinery that could be used in the manufacture of armaments. Such embargo to go into effect at once against our enemy, Germany, her allies Japan and Italy, and any other state which gives aid to Germany.

November: The President, Mrs. E. Hirst, and Mrs. Fred White attended a meeting held by the Board of Industrial Relations to discuss Protective Legislation for Female Employees, particularly those employed in restaurants. We endorsed resolution to limit hours of labor for women.

The Council is pledged to assist the Council of Social Agencies and the Public Safety Council.

December: A letter from the Department of Defence, in answer to our demand that metals, chemicals, etc., be not exported to Japan brought the following information: "The only metals being shipped to Japan are those that had been contracted for before war was declared."

Motion that we go on record as doing our utmost to prohibit importation of enemy-made goods by pledging ourselves not to purchase such goods.

We are asking the City Council to give those on relief an extra allowance for clothing.

This concludes the summary of our endeavors in the field of Public and Social Service.

To do its part in the promoting of Education, the Calgary Branch of the Local Council of Women has for some years sponsored the development of "Art" in this city. This year's winner of our Annual Art Scholarship is Margaret Shelton. Samples of her work are on display, and I may add that she is considered to be an outstanding artist, for whom a very successful future is predicted.

Our social activities were very happy and successful.

Mrs. H.J. Akitt kindly loaned her home for the Annual Council Tea. Mrs. C.T. Jackson and Mrs. Fred White convened this tea. The sum of $50.95 was realized.

A bridge party was held in the Auditorium of the Gas Company, with Mrs. Rothwell convening. This also was a very enjoyable event.

Under the auspices of the Council, Mrs. A.E. Pearson, Convener of Citizenship, arranged an interesting programme for International Day. Mr. Calhoun was the speaker.

Other speakers heard during the year were: Mr. John Burns, Chairman of the Provincial War Savings Committee and Honorary President of the Alberta Division of the Red Cross, who spoke on "The Need for War Savings"; Lieut. Roger D. deWinton, Officer Commanding the Calgary Division of the Royal Canadian Naval Volunteer Reserve, who spoke on "Naval Activities"; Mr. D.W. Clapperton, on "Anglo-Saxon Co-operation"; and Mrs. G.W. Duncan, who reviewed most ably Dr. James Roberts' book "From Subjection to Citizenship."

One thousand copies of the Year Book were issued under the convenorship of the President Mrs. Hirst, and distributed through the Province as well as in the city.

The President, Mrs. E. Hirst, has represented the Local Council as a member of:

- The Local Committee of the National Council of Education.

- The Advisory Board of the Dominion-Provincial Girls' Training School for Domestics.
- The Alberta Council of Child and Family Welfare.
- The Council of Social Agencies.
- The Alberta Section of the Western Canada Food Distribution Council.

The President assisted in arrangements for services, etc., for Decoration Day. She made a wreath, which was placed on the Cross of Sacrifice in the name of this Council. Accompanied by Mrs. McElroy, Convenor Soldiers' and Sailors' Committee, she was present also at the Cenotaph on Remembrance Day, again placing a wreath in tribute to the men who gave their lives in the Great War.

Mrs. Hirst, as President of this Council, assisted on Public Welfare Tag Day. She is at present actively engaged upon both Platform and Reception Committees for the visit of Mrs. Dories Neilson, who, as you know, is the only woman member of the Federal House. The visit of the "Royal Dolls" is also being arranged for by Mrs. Hirst, in collaboration with the Hudson's Bay Company. Money raised by this means is to be devoted to the fund for Refugee and Evacuee work that is not sponsored by the Government.

The Local Council was represented at the following social affairs by the President:

- Annual Banquet of Business and Professional Women's Club.
- Jewish Council Luncheon.
- Alberta Council Child and Family Welfare Banquet.
- Old Folks' Home Tea.
- Luncheon sponsored by the National Council of Education for the Poet, Alfred Noyes
- Y.W.C.A. "Burning of Mortgage Ceremony."
- Langevin Junior High Home and School Association Tea.

- Women's Institute Tea.
- Several Graduation events at the Training School.
- Ramsay Home and School Association Tea.
- Garden Party, held at the home of Mrs. Fred White, in behalf of the Women's Section, Dominion Labor Party and C.C.F. Clubs.
- Y.W.C.A. Christmas Tree for Self-Help Group.
- American Women's Bazaar and Tea, and others.

(Source: L.C.W. 1941 Year Book, p. 15–17)

1944 Report of the Recording Secretary – Edith Patterson

The Local Council of Women, Calgary, is at present composed of nineteen affiliated organizations and three individual members. It has held eight general and five executive meetings during the past year.

As usual, in conformity with its reason for existence, it has used its influence upon many matters affecting the welfare of the community.

CHILD WELFARE

Child adoption, Placement of Provincial Wards. Having reason to believe that many children are placed in unsuitable homes, we sent a questionnaire to the Department of Health, asking for information re the procedure of adoption: (a) Are homes carefully inspected and recommended before children are placed in them? (b) By whom are the recommendations made? (c) How often and over what period are homes inspected and supervised after child placement? We followed this with a resolution asking that a survey be made throughout the province, by outside specialists, and upon learning that a commission was to be set up, recommended the names of Dr. John Davidson and Miss Charlotte Whitton.

In June a committee was appointed by order-in-council to enquire into, (a) the best method of dealing with neglected or delinquent children, (b) the best method of administering the Child Welfare Act, of the Juvenile Court Act, and to make recommendations for amendments of said Acts.

The Council of Social Agencies, to which we are affiliated, prepared an extensive brief to submit to the above committees, and that report we endorsed.

Following this a Home Investigating Committee was appointed with the responsibility of determining what homes are suitable for child placement, and to follow up children in homes after adoption.

Upon enquiry we were told that the committee appointed was composed of persons well qualified for that type of work.

Juvenile Delinquency. Realizing that the causes of juvenile delinquency are not well understood, Miss Annie Campbell, at our request, prepared a paper for the Council on the subject. The causes of delinquency are found to be many and complicated; such as poor physical condition, various kinds of handicap, nutritional needs, poor housing (a very common reason), lack of suitable activities and recreation, home disturbances, increased during the war, etc. We objected to the former police headquarters being utilized for a detention home for delinquents, as we believed that it was not suitably located (on a lane), nor had the potentialities for what was required. The building, now altered, will also be used for other children, not classed as delinquents, until their cases are dealt with.

We wrote to the City Council asking for enforcement of Curfew By-law. The letter was referred to the Chief of Police for a report to the Legislative Committee.

Playgrounds. One of the preventives, and a remedy for delinquency, being supervised recreation and play, we heartily endorsed a resolution of the Alberta Council of Child and

Family Welfare, requesting the City Council to make provision for the appointment of a Playgrounds Supervisor and for the further training of supervisors. A committee of our members visited a number of city playgrounds, and following that, we sent a letter to the City Council urging that there should be some housecleaning, and improvements made on some of the play-centers. This letter was favorably received by the Parks and Playgrounds Committee of the City Council and referred to the Parks Superintendent with instructions to remedy faulty conditions.

Day Nurseries. The committee appointed by the Council to act with a committee from the Council of Social Agencies. Research work was continued concerning local needs and Day Nursery organization and progress in other cities. The chairman of the committee, Miss E. Patterson, visited several Day Nurseries in Toronto. A sub-committee composed of Mr. Wodell, chairman of the Council of Social Agencies; Dr. Hill, superintendent of the City Health Department, and the former chairman, endeavored to keep the matter before the City Council, locate a suitable house, and explore avenues of revenue. Later a larger committee was set up under the chairmanship of Mrs. W. Hobson, and a brief, setting forth information as to local needs, etc., has been presented to the Mayor.

A resolution from this Council went to the Provincial Government asking that the government accept the Federal-Provincial arrangement of Day Nurseries on the fifty-fifty basis.

HEALTH

We renewed our membership in the Canadian Society for Control of Cancer; protested against fees being asked for treatment in Isolation Hospital; Commended Dr. Cross, Minister of Health, for granting free hospitalization in maternity cases; made enquiries concerning the presence of fluoride in drinking water as a preventive of tooth decay; and requested a chemical analysis of city water.

STREET RAILWAY FARES

We continued to press for lower fares, and for cheaper fares, at least, during light traffic hours. We presented a statement to the City Council showing that the 5% taxation on revenue, with the surplus transferred from Street Railway to General Revenue, effects a saving of 1½ mills, but might be used to reduce fares. We expressed our approval of the re-establishment of the depreciation fund.

REFUGEES

We forwarded a resolution to the National Council of Women, asking that they urge the Dominion Government to relax the immigration laws to the extent of permitting refugees now in danger of their lives in Europe to enter Canada; also that the Government do all in its power to assist such refugees to escape, and further, that the Government be asked to contribute toward the upkeep of such refugees as have escaped to neutral countries and are now without means of escape.

The Local Council endorsed the petition similar to Clause I of above which was circulated by the National Council for Relief of Refugees and sent copies to affiliated organizations. About half of these were returned with signatures to the secretary. The quota set for Calgary was 10000 signatures. Up to date less than half of that number have been received by the committee in charge.

WARTIME PRICES AND CONTROL

The Local Council of Women have co-operated as individuals and as a body with the Boards, believing that rationing, price control, salvage, etc., are in the best interests of the community, and have from time to time made various suggestions. We requested our National Council to ask that prices be not advanced on tea and coffee at restaurants and public eating places; that quantities of flannelette be increased; that more varieties in widths and lengths of children's shoes be produced; that more textiles and that better quality in rubber rings for home canning be released.

AFFILIATIONS, ETC.

We renewed our corporate membership with the League of Nations; our affiliation with the Council of Social Agencies, appointing Mrs. Ervin Hirst as our representative; with the Community Council of the Alberta Adult Educational Association; awarded our annual Art Scholarship of $30 to Miss Emma Driega, a student at the School of Technology and Art.

The Council and this department of our work lost a loyal worker in the death of Mrs. Mary Butler, who at the time was Assistant Corresponding Secretary. Her energy, original ideas, and her support of humanitarian projects was always inspiring.

Mrs. F.S. Ditto, our President, represented us at the Wartime Conference of the National Council of Women, commemorating the 50th anniversary and held in Toronto last June. (Source: 1944 L.C.W. Year Book, p. 11–13)

The 1950s

1959 Secretary's Report – Joan Hollingworth

The Calgary Branch of the Council of Women is coming alive again due to the sincere efforts of our president and some few willing workers which she filled with her own enthusiasm. The increase from seven reports given at the Annual Meeting in 1958, to twenty-six in 1959 is concrete proof of this effort.

Following are the highlights of what the Council of Women of Calgary has accomplished during the ten months previous to the Annual Meeting in February, 1959:

- a study of the education system of Alberta, a brief presented to the Cameron Commission on Education for Alberta.
- a study of the problems of the working woman. A Resolution asking vocational training for the older worker presented to Provincial Council.
- a representative appointed to the Local Branch of the National Unemployment Commission. Active participation in the Winter Employment Campaign.
- research and study of women's prisons in Canada, special emphasis on Alberta institutions. Personal inspection tour of penal institutions taken by the president. Resolution passed re Rehabilitation of Women Prisoners. Research committee set up and still active.
- study of community planning. Resolution re down town park and toilet facilities accepted by Town Planning Committee of Calgary.
- study of Legal Rights of Women. Resolution sent to National re Estates Tax Act.
- study of the native Indian, under Friends of Indians Society, resulted in resolution re the revision of the Indian Act. Further study of adult education for Indians under way.
- backed the sale of Christmas Card and the Hallowe'en Shell-out for UNICEF.
- presented a resolution asking for coloured margarine for Alberta.
- awarded a scholarship to an art student in the Provincial School of Technology and Art.

Programs for monthly meetings, held on the fourth Wednesday of each month, in the Council Chambers of the City Hall, featured special speakers and panels of experts on the subjects under discussion and study.

Special honors awarded to Calgary Council women were as follows:

- Mrs. Russell Clark, Past President, elected President of the Provincial Council of Women of Alberta.
- Mrs. A.R. Hutchison, President, invited to represent the women of Calgary at the opening of the Provincial Legislature.
- Mrs. Frank Fish, Vice-president, appointed to the National Library Board.
- Mrs. Ruth Gorman, Laws Convener, elected Woman of the Year by Local Council of Women.
- Mrs. Addison Wilson, Corresponding Secretary, first Canadian elected to the executive of the International Toastmistress' Clubs.
- Alderman Isabella Stevens, elected Woman of the Year, by the Calgary Junior Chamber of Commerce.
- Mrs. Ralph Johnson, Education chairman, elected to Calgary School Board.
- Mrs. Evelyn Leew elected to Calgary School Board.

Special congratulations to Mrs. N.I. Zemans, first Western woman to be elected President of the National Council of Jewish Women of Canada, and to Miss Una Maclean elected president of the Alberta Liberal Women's Association. (Source: 1959 L.C.W. Year Book, p. 21, 23)

The 1960s

1963 –64 Recording Secretary Report – Mrs. George Lee

At the end of our 1963–4 year Calgary Local Council of Women has 33 Federated Societies affiliated with it. Looking back to the 1960 year book we find that our affiliates at that time numbered 23. This is an indication of the numerical growth in the last four years.

During 1963–4 minutes have been recorded for ten executive meetings and eight general meetings.

The March meeting was a panel discussion titled "Highways or By-Ways," and dealt with a new approach to vocational training through an academic-vocational school to be opened in the fall. Members of School Boards and School Principals were panel members.

The easy access to obscene literature was exposed at our April meeting, a factor often contributing to juvenile delinquency. Two members of a newly-formed group "Citizens for Good Communications" pointed out that this group is seeking, not censorship, but enforcement of the laws as they now stand in the Criminal Code.

In October we held our second annual Workshop, when the membership breaks into groups to look at the past, and future possibilities of our committee work.

Our study of juvenile problems was continued in November, when a panel studied the question "Does Early Marriage Create a Problem Today?" The three panel members, all from Calgary Social Agencies, were in agreement that certain clauses in the Marriage Act of Alberta, indicate a need for revision.

Civic Affairs occupied our attention on several subjects. The proposed CPR Relocation plan brought about a Resolution intended to preserve a strip of park land bordering the south bank of the Bow River. This issue has been kept alive by a "watch-dog committee" appointed in November.

Representatives from Calgary Local Council were appointed to the following civic-minded committees: The Town Planning Committee, and the Citizens' University Committee. Also, through the efforts of our affiliate, the Faculty Women's Club of the University of Alberta, Calgary, supported by Council, a woman representative was finally placed on the Hospital Board.

With the convention of National Council being held in Banff in June, Calgary Council, as hostess, became involved in convention arrangements.

Our closing meeting in May featured the playing of a tape on the life and work of Lady Aberdeen, founder of the National Council of Women in Canada. At this meeting, Mrs. Russell Clark was presented with a National Life membership. Our third National Life Membership was awarded to Mrs. Oscar Stonewall at the Annual Meeting in February. At the February meeting also three local Life Memberships were presented to Mrs. Clarence Irving, Mrs. T.W. Kelter, and Mrs. Chris Crum, bringing the total of Local Life Memberships to 19.

Perhaps the foundations laid this year towards establishing a Rest and Information Centre in Calgary for Indian people will have more far-reaching results than any other phase of the year's activities. In March, a steering committee was formed, under the chairmanship of Mrs. Harry Johnson, with three sub committees to deal with finance, location and administration. Mrs. Johnson brought reports throughout the year of meetings with Indian people in the city and on the Morley and Sarcee Reserves. A count of Indian people (upon which a Federal grant would be based) is being undertaken by a newly-formed Indian Services Committee, composed of Indians and non-Indians, with Mrs. Johnson as Chairman and Mrs. G. Service of the University Women's Club as secretary.

In January we focused on Mental Health, with a play-reading and a talk by a social worker on the problems of rehabilitation for discharged mental patients. The Calgary Home

Economics Association, one of our newer Affiliates, followed this up with a Resolution requesting that the Council undertake a study of rehabilitation services for patients discharged from mental hospitals in the Calgary area.

Increased attendance at meetings, despite sudden changes of meeting place and other minor set-backs, indicates that Calgary Local Council of Women continues to progress along the lines of interest and active participation of our Affiliates, in all phases of our work. (Source: 1964–65 L.C.W. Hand Book, p. 33–34)

1968–69 Report of the Recording Secretary – Mrs. K.L. Vine

There were eight meetings of the Executive Committee and six General Meetings during the year February 1967 to January 1968. All Executive meetings were held in the Herald Board Room, and all regular General Meetings, with the exception of one evening meeting and the Annual Meeting, were held in City Hall Council Chambers.

At our Annual Meeting, held in the Highlander Motor Hotel, February 22, 1966, we presented to the new Planetarium a specially-made Visitors' Book, as a Calgary L.C.W. Centennial project. At this meeting Local Life Memberships were presented to Mrs. J.R. King, Mrs. Frank Fish, Mrs. A.C. Luft, and Mrs. A.D. Winspear. Luncheon speakers were Mr. James Gray, who spoke on "The Welfare State"; and Mr. Milton Wright, who gave the history of the Calgary Allied Arts Council, of which he is Director. Mr. Gray autographed copies of his recently published book "The Winter Years."

Our March meeting program was a discussion on the need and value of a forensic clinic, by a panel consisting of Mr. L.F. Werry, a businessman; Dr. Irial Gogan, Executive Director of the Holy Cross Hospital, and Dr. Etzcorn, psychiatrist.

The speaker at our April meeting was Mrs. Ruth Walker, a Nutritionist, who discussed some aspects of nutrition, and reviewed the work done by a committee studying the need of a School of Home Economics at the University of Calgary.

April was also the month of a successful symposium arranged by Calgary L.C.W. under the joint chairmanship of Mrs. J.M. Johnson and Mrs. A.D. Winspear, and held at the University. A reception on the evening of April 28th was followed by a full day of lively discussion on "The Responsibility of Today's Women Towards Their Community, Province and Nation," under the title "The Hidden Talent." A feature on this Symposium was to have been the presentation of a membership in National Council of Women to Mrs. Mary Dover, O.B.E. as representing Calgary Women who had, through the years, accepted "the responsibility of today's women towards their community." Due to the storm which prevented her attendance at the symposium, the presentation was made at a special Tea and Reception held at City Hall later in the month.

In April too, presidents and representatives of our federated societies met with executive members at the Indian Friendship Centre to bring together their thoughts on the National Resolutions coming to vote at the National Annual Meeting in June, and to instruct our delegate to that Meeting.

Arranged by our Education Committee, the May meeting was held in the evening, in the hope of drawing a wider audience to participate in a discussion of current educational needs, and what can be done about the "Drop-out." The panel consisted of a public school teacher, the president of the local branch of the Alberta Teachers' Association, an administrator at Foothills General Hospital, and the Assistant to the President of Mount Royal Junior College.

Our September meeting took the form of a Workshop. In September also we held our Annual tea. The Centennial theme was used, and all hostesses and waitresses wore period costumes, which fitted in nicely with the large rooms and beautiful surroundings of Scenic Acres where the Tea was held.

In October we heard of the work of the Food and Agricultural Organization (Unicef) in Africa. Mr. A.W. Beatty, who had just returned after several years with this project, showed his interesting slides.

No meetings were held in November or December. (Source: 1968–69 L.C.W. Hand Book, p. 14)

The 1970s

1970–71 Report of the Recording Secretary – Mrs. Pat Waite

Since taking office two years ago 19 Executive Meetings have been recorded, along with 10 General Meetings and one Annual Meeting. Two President's Coffee Parties and two Award Teas have also been held. Executive Meetings, with one or two exceptions, were held in the Board Room of the Calgary Herald.

The practice of sending minutes of Executive Meetings, innovated last year, has been discontinued, and has been replaced by "Focus," a newsletter. The Executive minutes are now sent to the Executive Committee members monthly.

The compiling of a calendar of events for L.C.W. was continued, and 154 copies sent out.

An Awards Tea started the season with an innovation. Instead of selling baked goods, funds were raised by the sale of herbs. This was most suitable, considering the event was again staged at the Conservatory of the Calgary Zoo, the first week of October.

October 28 was the first General meeting, and the subject Citizen Participation in Calgary. It was chaired by Citizenship Chairman, Barbara Scott, and held in the evening at the Calgary Power Building.

The November meeting, November 25th, held in the afternoon, was chaired by Kay Swinton of the Welfare Committee, and titled "Can We Do More to Protect the Battered Child?" Her panel consisted of Dr. Gerald Holma, Head of the Department of Paediatrics, University of Calgary School of Medicine; Miss Nora Clark, supervisor Social Development Department, City of Calgary, and Dr. John Reid. All gave an interesting informative picture regarding the illness, present legal restraints, and suggestions as to further action which could be taken by this group in combating this illness and protecting the child.

January 27th was a meeting with the subject of the United Nations and its present and future role. Mrs. Pat Waite chaired the panel of Professor Anthony Parel, Dean of Political Science; Mr. Don Peacock of the Albertan; and Mr. Peter Kent, of the Calgary Herald. Unfortunately Mr. Art Smith could not attend a most spirited debate on the United Nations and Canada's role in the international sphere. Members of the Calgary United Nations Association were invited to this meeting.

February 24th, again at the Calgary Power Building, in the evening, saw a classical debate on the legislation following the War Measures Act and its invocation due to F.L.Q. activities. Mr. Mel Shannon, local lawyer, and Mr. Max Wolfe, lawyer and president of the Calgary Civil Rights Association tangled "horns of logic." The meeting was chaired by Mrs. Mary Ellen Johnson.

The March 31 meeting, in City Hall Chambers, will be chaired by Mrs. Joni Chorny, Education Chairman, who will host Mrs. I.C. Martini, Calgary School Board; Dr. W.R. Castell, Director of the Calgary Public Library; Alderman Roy Farran; and Mrs. M.A. Vaness, supervisor for the Library Service Centre of the Calgary School Board. They will be challenged by the subject, "School Libraries and Public Use – Feasible, Practical, or Possible?"

No meeting was held in December.

The Annual Meeting was held on April 22, 1970 at the Highlander Motor Hotel. Dr. Ruth Gorman gave "A Critique of L.C.W" based on the year's work 1969–1970 and some suggestions as to how the community role could be strengthened. Luncheon guest speaker was the Venerable Archdeacon Cecil Swanson, who spoke on "Reflections of the Early Days of the Yukon." He was introduced by Pat Waite and thanked by Cynthia Aikenhead. A refreshing and delightful afternoon. (Source: 1970–71 L.C.W. Hand Book, p. 14–15)

1971–72 Report of the Recording Secretary - Margaret Ziebart

The Annual meeting was held Wednesday, April 28th, at the Summit Hotel. Luncheon speaker was Lola Lange, Commissioner on the Royal Commission of the Status of Women.

Following the luncheon a discussion on the four man items of Women's Liberation: day care, abortion, equal opportunity, equal pay, was held.

Speakers were:

- Lola Lange, Commissioner, Giving the status of women's viewpoint
- Mr. D. Norris, business man, giving a man's viewpoint.
- Dr. Charlotte Ziebarth, psychologist of U.A.C., giving the women's liberation viewpoint.

At the May General Meeting Mr. Art New, from the Eco Centre, discussed community cable T.V. and its challenge to volunteer groups, individuals and all segments of society.

September General Meeting held at City Council Chambers, in the afternoon. The program was the many achievements of Local Council of Women, chaired by Grace Johnson.

The October meeting was held in the afternoon at City Council Chambers, October 27th. Ann Van Heteren spoke on the Seminar held on October 1, 2, and 3. It was interesting and informative.

Coffee party held December 1st, at 10:00 a.m. at the home of Mrs. Jean Leslie. It was delightful and well attended.

February meeting held in the afternoon at City Council Chambers. Program "The Role of Women in Politics." On the panel were:

- Social Credit: Mrs. Ethel Wilson, Edmonton
- Progressive Conservative: Mrs. Lillian Knupp, High River
- Liberal Women: Jean Reid, Calgary
- N.D.P.: Helen Freeman, Calgary
- Moderator: Mrs. Jean Leslie

March meeting held in City Council Chambers in the afternoon. Program: Sgt. K. Johnson, from the Calgary Police Force, Home and Personal Safety. (Source: L.C.W 1912–1972 Diamond Jubilee Year Report, p. 13)

Addendum B

Worthy Causes: Standing Committee Convenor Reports

The 1920s

Citizenship Committee – Magistrate Alice J. Jamieson, Convenor

ONE OF THE GREAT NEEDS of Canada today is the awakening of the submerged half of women members of society who do not trouble to think about matters pertaining to civil affairs or else nurse an impenetrable ignorance and apathy that keeps them from the polls, or cherish a sense of superiority in ignoring merely secular activities. The average woman has yet to learn it is not only her privilege but bounden duty to exercise the franchise so dearly won for her. Calgary in this respect is much better than many cities, her womenfolk showing an intelligent comprehension of the issues at stake, but there is room for improvement and every adult person should be urged to get out and cast her vote in municipal, provincial and federal elections.

The Boy Scouts, Girl Guides, Trail Rangers, C.G.I.T. and other movements which have as their object the making of good citizens, are growing and advancing each year. In many cases community clubs specialize in work of this kind, one club in the city backing the Boy Scouts, while others get behind movements of like nature. It might be a good idea if the Local

Council would make an endeavor to aid and encourage the Girl Guides; there is a great need for such help and surely it would be worth while.

An appeal has been made that the word "newcomer" be used instead of alien or foreigner. This might have a tendency to make an immigrant, a future citizen of our country, more at home.

Much progress has been made throughout Canada in the last few years in the study of civics. The I.O.D.E. have made it a part of their educational programme. Many organizations in Calgary have formed civic clubs which are proving a source of interest to all members.

That the question of good citizenship is arousing nation-wide interest was shown at the recent International Council meeting held in Washington, when a special time was set aside to discuss such methods of training children for world citizenship as would lead to a realization of their international obligations. This, in my opinion, should apply to families already in Canada and to those who intend to make Canada their future home. It is well to remember always "The child of today is the citizen of tomorrow." (Source: 1924–25 L.C.W. Year Book p. 33)

Public Health - Mrs. C.R. Edwards, Convenor

In presenting the report of my Health Committee for 1925, I do so, not with the keen satisfaction of having accomplished all that we would like to. During the year resolutions were submitted by the Health Committee and passed by the L.C. of W., and sent by the Secretary to their various departments, namely:

1. A letter to the Mayor and Commissioners congratulating them on their success in securing the scrubbing of the gas, thus adding greatly to the safety and comfort of the consumer.

2. That the L.C. of W. recommend that the City Health Department keep on hand a sufficient supply of antitoxin for cases of scarlet fever, and that in cases where patients were unable to pay physicians, can secure same free of charge, if necessary.

3. That the city Health Department be requested to take steps to control the smoke nuisance, and that all factories and vulcanizing stations be compelled to use appliances as will eliminate the same.

4. That a letter be written the heads of the various religious denominations asking them to consider in the interests of Public Health and Sanitation, the use of "Individual Communion Cup." One reply was received to this.

The first three resolutions were sent by the Secretary, Mrs. Hall, to the Mayor's Office. To date no reply or acknowledgement has been received from any department relative thereto.

I may as well be frank and state plainly the Health Committee of L.C. of W. has not had the hearty co-operation from our M.H.O., Dr. Gow, that we have had from his predecessor.

We have tried to be fair and reasonable in all requests. As a committee our work has been constructive, not destructive, and "co-operation" our watchword in all matters concerning the welfare of our city.

A few weeks ago complaint was made that the Health Committee were lax in the fulfilling of their duties, namely, that cooked foodstuffs were not protected from handling by the public. Candies, bread, cakes, meats, were all exposed to contamination almost anywhere you have a mind to look, spitting in street cars and on sidewalks was a common occurrence. Rotten fruit with a good layer over the top to mislead the public, was being sold at the markets. Ladies, I have phoned the department governing these things until I am almost ashamed to do so any more. Might I suggest that you constitute yourself a vigilance committee, and assist your convener by calling up these various departments, requesting enforcement of the bylaw governing these things. I wonder how many of the citizens of Calgary would be willing to have the bylaws governing these things removed from the books?

The epidemic of scarlet fever and diphtheria has been reduced to almost a minimum. This is, I believe, attributed to the use of toxins as a preventative.

We have at the present time an epidemic of German measles, and which is considered of a mild type. There is need of precaution for fear bad results may follow. Personally I have known where robust children have suffered delicate health for years following a supposed mild attack of German measles.

Your convener spent an afternoon at the Gyro's clinic, and was very interested in the work carried on there, particularly in the lesson on the remodeling of old woolen garments into garments for the new baby. Nor can I pass on without comment on the splendid report that appeared recently in the press upon the work the Victorian Order of Nurses are doing in our city. Only a few of the things Calgary has to her credit are the diphtheria prevention measures employed by our physicians to eliminate this disease. A splendid lecture was given by Dr. Stanley on this subject, under the auspices of the Health Committee.

In the standardization of hospitals of United States and Canada, Alberta ranks high. The General and Holy Cross meeting the requirements.

The hospitals have 100 beds or more. 14 000 000 pass through the United States and Canadian hospitals annually.

It is worthy of note that Calgary has the lowest death rate from the disease of cancer in the Dominion, covering the period from 1915 to 1925.

Calgary also has the distinction of being the home of the "Prize Baby" for the British Empire, having won the prize at the Wembly Exhibition. Mr. and Mrs. Angus MacDonald are the proud parents of baby John Duncan Claude MacDonald.

In health activities throughout the world great strides are being made. Time permits only a few of the results in scientific research being touched upon.

The endeavor to isolate the Cancer germ, the discovery of Insulin as a cure for Diabetes, the success of compounding Insulin in crystal form instead of liquid, thus making the shipping of Insulin, which is an expensive article, more safe and more likely to reach its destination in good condition.

It is also noteworthy that three of Britain's great men have joined forces in an endeavor to bring about the golden age of health. These men are the Earl of Oxford and Asquith, the Earl of Balfour, and Mr. Ramsay Macdonald; who together with other prominent physicians and hygienists have formed a society called "The New Health Society."

There is one other matter your convener would like to bring to your attention, namely, the interest being taken at the present time in the problem of the care of sub-normal children. Your convener would like to see the time come when the State, together with the parent will unite in giving the unfortunate child the best remedial scientific care available, thus providing the possibility of the child becoming of some benefit to itself, the State and society, and when it will no longer be looked upon as a menace. For the care and protection of such children, even in the planning of such care, we as women must necessarily play an important part. (Source: 1925–26 L.C.W. Year Book, p. 72–74)

Soldiers' Pensions – Mrs. George. (Millicent) McElroy, Convenor.

The National Council has decided that the necessity which called into being a "Soldiers' Pension Committee" in the program of the Council of Women, no longer exists, the interests of the returned men being now taken care of by the establishing of pension and appeal boards, and the appointment of secretaries whose sole business and duty is to investigate and bring to notice all such claims, also the organizing and amalgamation of service clubs, such as the Canadian Legion, Amputation Association, etc., as well as the Government Department of the S.C.R. The Council feels that the object for which the soldiers' pensions committee was appointed has been attained, and, as such, will no longer function. Our women, however, will continue their aid, support and co-operation in any cause to promote the interests of the "Service Man" and his dependents.

We have endeavoured to assist in every way possible all such efforts during the year – visiting the sick, the bereaved, and the hospitals. Your Convener was honored by a request from the Daughters of the Empire, to present and assist at the unveiling of the South African Memorial in the Central Park, which, having been completed, was formerly handed over to Mayor Webster for the city; also at the Armistice Day Service, in the Memorial Hall, as on former occasions, and on the Memorial Day committee. We are informed that Dr. F.W. Gershaw, Liberal member for Medicine Hat, has announced that he has been successful in interesting the secretary of state in the proposal to create the anniversary date of the Armistice a national holiday, so the date will no longer be confused with Thanksgiving Day.

We should like to put on record our appreciation of the very generous help given in the arranging of entertainment programs at both the Col. Belcher and Keith Hospitals. The C. P. R. Male Voice and the Scottish Choirs gave splendid service, also the owners of cars, who, in most adverse weather, were responsible for their transportation, also the Hayden Quartet, and many others who have rendered most cheerful assistance in the Sunday night song service, and the Rev. Capt. McCall, whose ready co-operation and bright messages have been a source of help and encouragement to many still "shut in" and whose lives are a daily sacrifice, because of service for us which can never be repaid, and should claim our unflagging and lasting gratitude and solicitous care. It is of interest to learn, and cause of great gratification, and a source of comfort, that the original wooden crosses in the war cemeteries of France, which marked the last resting place of so many of our boys, are being re-placed by slabs of stone, quarried and carved in England. In front of each is about 18 inches of soil, wherein is growing old-fashioned garden flowers – Roses, Pinks, Canterbury Bells, Sweet Williams, and in front of them, three feet of grass, carefully mown. The wood crosses bore the desolate inscription, "An unknown soldier"; on the stone slabs, the far better and much more suitable inscription – "Known Unto God." (Source: 1926 L.C.W. Year Book, p. 64)

Equal Moral Standards – Mrs. M.A. Harvey, Convenor

To give a report of the work of this committee is a very difficult matter. It might almost be termed a "vigilant committee" as its chief function is to watch and be on the lookout for any phase relative to this part of the Local Council's work. That Calgary is awake to the importance of safeguarding and protecting the morals of women and children is evidenced by the fact that they have two women magistrates in the city.

The National Council stands for equal moral standards, and not long ago were gratified when their petition asking that divorce be granted on the same grounds to women as men, was granted.

While the Council takes this stand on equal moral standards, it is opposed to bringing the standards of women to that of men. From time immortal certain things have been considered as men's rights, and while women have this same right in regard to moral standing, it is not expedient or wise that they should follow these lines. We must remember "God's greatest gift is a womanly woman," and she is not wielding her greatest influence if she does not set an example for all that is best in the Home and elsewhere. In regards to this point, it is interesting to note that certain hotels in the province have barred women from their beer parlors.

Divorce is still on the increase, and parental control has relaxed. In this advanced scientific age in which we are living, it is well to remember two great truths given by our Lord and Master, "Whom God has joined together let no man put asunder," and "Honor thy father and mother that thy days may be long in the land." There is great promise in these last words and a great blessing to those who practice both. (Source: 1926 L.C.W. Year Book, p. 65)

Films and Printed Matter – Mrs. A.V. Pankhurst, Convenor

The motion picture is now a factor in our lives, and must be recognized as such. As local council members we should demand only the best. One cannot always judge a picture from the title, which may be misleading. We may find ourselves patronizing something of which we heartily disapprove. We may register complaint at the office, but how many of us do? It has occurred to me that if on the programs there were left a blank space for this purpose we could register our opinion and pass the slip in at the office upon leaving. It would be a guide to the theatre managers as to the opinion of the public. We know that the majority of our people desire good, clean, amusing and educational pictures.

We do not want such films as "Twinkletoes," the scene of which was laid in the limehouse district of London, when there are so many beautiful scenes and historical settings in the old land for pictures of an elevating nature.

We do not want such pictures as the "Unknown Soldier" shown during Armistice Week, rather do we want shown something of the work of the League of Nations, or pictures of prosperity and happiness among peoples, during Peace.

The highest ideals of Life should be constantly kept before our children through the movies. What better way to impress upon the child the home training of righteousness, truth and clean living than through the pictures. We all know that many of our juvenile crimes are traceable to something seen on the screen.

There should be some way by which pictures could be advertised or described so that parents would know the type of picture to be shown before allowing children of an impressionable age to attend.

The thought has occurred to me that the National Committee might prepare a list of films which have been approved by them as right and desirable for children to see. These lists to be had by all societies wishing them. Our local managers could be asked to present these Saturday mornings or during holidays. Church societies and parent-teacher associations should make it a policy to discourage attendance during the week. Was there ever a time when children needed more guiding and guarding than now?

Closely allied with the films are the cheap books and magazines which are flooding our markets. On the list of indecent magazines and books which come into Canada there is one from Germany, two from France, and one from England and about sixty-two from the States. Eleven of these are books, in reference to which Mrs. Wilson, National Convener, is urging that lending libraries be licensed, as many of these books are to be found on their shelves. Let us heartily support our National Convener in this important matter.

Again, may I refer to our appreciation of the prompt action of Mayor Webster last fall in confiscating all copies of a magazine which had a nude woman as a cover picture. Let us all be alert in liker manner and report what we consider improper.

It is very easy to condemn, so let us bring forth some constructive ideas, such as making easily available lists of good books and magazines which have been arranged by experts. We can encourage the supplying of school classroom libraries of the very best reading matter available for the different grades. The local children's librarian could supply lists, and I am sure in the interest of good reading would supervise all libraries if requested. While we realize there are no improper books in our schools, sometimes there are those of an indifferent type which could easily be replaced with something good. The very best procurable is none too good for our young Canadians. As loyal and patriotic citizens of our country we should heartily support our Canadian Authors Week, encourage our stores to have displays of the works of Canadian Authors. At our club meetings that month have a local writer give an address. Buy our local authors' books to send away as Christmas gifts, or send a year's subscription to a Canadian Magazine to a distant friend.

The Magazine Publishers' Association of Canada is doing a great deal to keep our popular literature free from taint, and to keep out the objectionable publications from other countries. Let us give them our hearty support.

Your committee is making an investigation of the local book stalls to ascertain if there are many of these objectionable magazines offered here for sale and will report at a later date.

During the year I have been requested to attend only one picture, which I did, and only one complaint, which I investigated and reported upon. I shall be pleased to do what I can if anything is brought to my notice. (Source: 1926 L.C.W. Year Book p. 66–67)

The 1930s

Employment of Women – Mrs. J. Drummond, Convenor

Instead of employment for women I am afraid this report will have more to say about the absence of employment, as this aspect of the situation has been very forcibly presented to us during the past year.

Many factors have contributed to this distressing situation which is almost world-wide in its scope and to try and find a solution for which economic experts are busy in every civilized country.

While unable to get the exact statistics for 1930, the provincial report not being completed, the following figures from our local bureau gives a very fair estimate of the general conditions throughout our province.

In conversation with the official at the employment bureau for women, I found that the peak of unemployment was during the months of October, November and during the early part of December. Christmas activities provided a short respite, but the situation now shows little signs of improvement in the near future.

While during 1929 and years previous to that, a young woman seeking work as a domestic help had a choice of positions, the situation is now entirely reversed, which also applies to stenographers, clerical and other workers. So far very few applications are coming in for help in rural homes, due I suppose to the distressing economic conditions of the farmers.

In response to numerous complaints about the Government Employment Bureau for Women, a committee of investigation was appointed by the Council, who, finding great room for improvement, waited upon Mr. Smitten, Labour Commissioner, and Mayor Davison, with the recommendation that better accommodation be provided. While they gave us a very sympathetic hearing it was not productive of much success, but it resulted in a resolution being brought in, which was passed by the Council, petitioning the Government to provide a separate employment bureau, which we hope may in the near future bring about this much needed reform.

To relieve the situation and in response to the solicitations of a number of our women, accommodation was provided at the City Hall where all unemployed women were asked to register, which was taken advantage of by a large number.

To be unemployed under any circumstances is an unmitigated evil, but to be without a job in the winter time and away from home, was the terrible experience of many young women in our fair city during the last few months.

To cope with this serious situation a number of Calgary's prominent women citizens formed themselves into a committee to assist these girls in their need, and have been the means of finding homes for many of them. Where, in return for board and lodgings, and in some instances the addition of a small wage, they have undertaken to assist with the domestic duties in the home, being also provided with the opportunity of keeping a look-out for a position in the sphere for which they are most fitted.

Through the activities of these ladies, assisted by the Women's Auxiliary to the Locomotive Engineers, and other donations, a Christmas dinner was provided for a number of these homeless girls who otherwise would have very little chance of having any share in the general Christmas festivities.

Abnormal situations require abnormal remedies, and while we, as members of the Local Council of Women, appreciate very highly the efforts that have been put forth on behalf of these homeless girls, we trust that these and other merely palliative measures for the present situation, will not result in lowering the minimum wage standard which the Council fought so hard to obtain. This we must strenuously guard against and strongly recommend that employers of labor reduce the number of working hours, rather than lower wages, which even at the present standard simply insures a bare living.

In this connection I am glad to report that since July 1st, 1930, the minimum wage act has been extended to cover all of the province, so that now girls working in the country have the same protection in this respect as if they were in the cities.

From a study of the experiences of 14 000 women engaged in 20 different types of work it was found that 43% of the women were engaged in clerical work, 19% in teaching, 10% in sales and publicity work, 6% in health work, 4% in finance, the remaining number being scattered through 15 other kinds of work. Regarding their earnings, the following conclusions were drawn from this study:

- That the chances of high earnings were twice as great for women working in commercial and manufacturing organizations as for those employed in educational institutions, and a much larger proportion of women in sales and publicity work have high earnings, than in either clerical work or teaching.
- Earnings increase with experience for the first twenty years, remain fairly constant for the next ten years, and then decline.
- Earnings increase with age up to 50 years, very little between 50 and 60, and decline thereafter.

This study also showed that the qualities entering into the question of success were proved by an analysis of eight cases of persons who had lost their jobs. In none of these instances were the girls dismissed because they could not do the specific task assigned to them, their failure being mainly due to the lack of such social qualities, as good manners, acceptable standards of personal conduct, and the ability to co-operate. (Source: 1931 L.C.W. Year Book, p. 47, 49, 51)

Immigration Committee – Mrs. Walter S. Woods, Convenor

The work accomplished by the Calgary branch of the Local Council of Women during the past year has been of two characters – studying the various immigration schemes now in existence for bringing immigrants to our country and helping those immigrants who are already here to become interested in their newly chosen home.

In the opinion of your convenor we should not, because of our domestic labor situation, do anything to encourage the movement of newcomers to our country at the present time.

Looking to the future our greatest need during this present lull is a close and intensive study, by those who will be responsible for the next movement of immigrants, of such vital questions as:

- From what countries should our future immigration be encouraged or admitted?
- In what number can we assimilate them?
- What requirements should we stipulate as to assets and health?

The present lull in immigration is an excellent opportunity to discuss and determine our immigration policy for the future so that we are prepared with intelligent suggestions when conditions warrant a resumption of immigration.

The population of Alberta is forty per cent foreign and while in many instances the members of our Council and our affiliated societies have helped these foreign immigrants in their problems, our main effort has been with the new arrivals from Britain.

Our second Canadian Club, organizing the Ukrainian women into an active Canadian Club, is doing splendid work.

After the arrival of immigrants by family or individual, a definite attempt has been made by your convener or by members of our affiliated societies to establish a contact between the new arrival and the facilities that already exist for his or her help and guidance, such as placing them in touch with:

- The Women's Hostel or similar facilities.
- The Church of their denomination.
- The Y.M.C.A., Y.W.C.A. and the Boy Scouts Troop.
- The Women's Institute.
- The Canadian Club.
- The I.O.D.E., and
- The Land Settlement Branch of the Immigration Department for advice on land settlement.

This latter organization has, in the past, been glad to furnish wrappings and postage for any donations which our societies cared to make to the newly arrived British families.

At Christmas the I.O.D.E., the Kiwanis Club, the Boy Scouts and various individuals send boxes of gifts to newly arrived immigrants and to those farm families who have been unfortunate.

During the past few years thousands of Canadian magazines have been sent to the people on the land.

One of our members, in seeing the enormous amount of flower seeds going to waste in our city parks each year, conceived the idea of getting permission from Mr. Reader, our City Parks Superintendent, to gather these seeds. Not only did Mr. Reader consent to this plan but he donated two thousand large clumps of perennial roots to be sent to immigrants.

Two thousand and seven hundred packets of seeds were gathered in the parks.

Mr. Grisdale, of the Olds Experimental Farm, donated an enormous amount of shrubbery and berry plants as well as bushels of splendid vegetable seeds. Other Experimental Farms made generous donations, and Lady Cecil sent over forty pounds of choice English flower seeds from the London Horticultural Society.

As a result every immigrant family that has arrived in the south half of Alberta under the three thousand family settlement scheme has been given enough vegetable seeds for a good garden the first year in the country, enough annual flower seeds to make a cheerful flower bed and sufficient perennial roots or perennial seeds to establish a permanent flower garden

Our member who has looked after this work for the past four years, has left our district, but we hope to carry on the work in a smaller degree, as by this widespread distribution of seeds we have been able to determine just who will cultivate flowers and those who take no interest. We hope to establish contact with those who are interested in gardens and as individual members we can gather two or three packets of seeds from our own gardens and make some lonely woman happy by sending her a cheery letter and a few seeds for her garden.

This has been an unusually hard year and it has been necessary to give more donations of clothing and food than we usually consider advisable. It is unfortunate that some people, if they find willing givers, cease to rely upon their own initiative.

Your convener suggests that a letter of encouragement be given each woman upon arrival inviting her to keep in touch with the Local Council of Women who will always be interested in her welfare, not with a view to giving and making donations which, except in extreme cases, should be strongly discouraged, but with a view to extending a welcome, a friendly interest, and most of all, the feeling that in our great Dominion we are always anxious to welcome and help establish the people of our own race, so they will have the same loyalty and the same love for Canada that we, ourselves, possess. (Source: 1931 L.C.W. Yearbook, p. 52–53)

The 1940s

1943 Child Welfare – Mrs. Jean McDonald, Convenor

Madame President and Members:

May I submit to your organization our report on activities during the past year. We have brought to the attention of the Government the urgent need for Police Matrons being placed permanently so young girls should have proper protection.

We also supported the suggestion to open a day nursery for the use of working Mothers. It will give peace of mind to a woman if she can go to work knowing her little ones are safe and comfortable.

Taking the case of the unmarried Mother, we suggest that proper care be given her, and that children born to these young women, during the War period should not be considered illegitimate, thereby throwing a slur on the child itself who is not responsible for its birth. Children born in Britain during the last War were considered legitimate.

In studying maternal deaths, we feel much unnecessary suffering could be eliminated, were expectant Mothers given special pre-natal care. A bonus could be given and investigations made by the medical authorities. Three questions occur to me which have a definite bearing on the well being of the expectant mother.

1. Are they properly housed?
2. Are they able to get plentiful supplies of health giving foods?
3. There is too much fear and worry to the family of limited means when an increase is expected to the family circle.

Statistics show eleven (11) maternal deaths were reported for a rate of 4.2 per thousand live births, as against seven (7) deaths, a rate of 3.1 a year ago.

This new record of births set a much higher figure than in 1941. Two hundred and ninety seven (297) more babies were born during 1942. The net birth rate being 28.8 as against 25.9 a year ago.

The death rate was eighty two (82) per thousand as compared with 38.5 per thousand for 1941.

Our attention has been brought to the fact that canned milk cannot be bought except for babies. We consider a child should drink milk daily in order to build a healthy body. Owing to the fact that milk spoils quickly unless kept in a Frigidaire or ice box, it is not always possible to keep a supply of sweet milk on hand. Therefore it is often necessary to use canned milk, so let us not be over enthusiastic in denying the children this much needed food item. Or else in the days to come we will be facing an enemy in the shape of malnutrition which we will not be able to cope with.

We would suggest more care be taken when placing young children in foster homes and feel that a strict follow up system be established to continue till the child becomes of age. We are constantly faced with problems on child welfare, but these can be taken care of by an active and intelligent committee. We must give of our best to the cause of our young people for The Child is the Nations best asset. (Source: 1943 L.C.W. Year Book, p. 33–34)

Economics and Taxation – Maud Butler, Convenor

Events of the past year have been both interesting and instructive. The experiments of the Wartime Prices and Trade Board have been carefully watched by the women of Calgary. While wishing to co-operate with the government and prevent rises in the price of commodities, yet the women feel helpless to do much about it. The little blue books[29] called for too much duplication of effort on the part of the women and were not as helpful as they were supposed to be.

Many felt that a posting in the stores of the prices of goods which were sold during the basic period would eliminate much uncertainty and misunderstanding. This request was forwarded to the W.P.T.B.

Liaison officers were appointed for most affiliated societies.

Believing the prices of cakes and pastries had risen since the basic period and that some items had deteriorated in quality and size, the Calgary Local Council of Women asked the Wartime Prices and Trade Board here to check up on the matter. In response to this request eight bakeries were reported investigated, the bakeries claiming there had been no increase in their prices since the basic period, no deterioration in quality, nor change in size or weight.

Calgary Local Council of Women are definitely opposed to any waste in food, either at home or elsewhere. Last summer they set up a committee to co-operate with the Selective

Service Bureau here. The aim was to encourage boys and girls or other suitable persons to go to British Columbia and help save the abundant crop of berries and other fruit. About one hundred and fifty boys and girls were sent from Calgary for the berry crop, and later fifty more went for the apple picking. Inexperience, hurried planning, and extremely unfavorable weather prevented the plan from being a complete success. But much fruit was saved, and the experience gained should be valuable later.

A community kitchen, to conserve fruits and vegetables, was operated during the summer by the Self-Help Group, and many jars of fruit were added to the food supply of those who attended. It was a lesson in co-operation and thrift. The women were given the opportunity to come and can more cheaply and easily than they could do the same at home, and many availed themselves of this help. This home supply lessened the demand for canned goods in the stores.

In Alberta quite a number of people who were hoarding tea and sugar were prosecuted and fines imposed. Few cases were noted of the publishing of fines imposed on business houses for infractions of the regulations of the Wartime Prices and Trade Board.

The Local Council of Women favor the appointment of more women on any boards set up to deal with problems with which they are familiar, and especially on those which affect the home.

While not exactly so serious as it was before the war, a measure of unemployment is still with us. In the past we have spent time and treasure in trying to alleviate the ills caused by it. More and more we are becoming convinced that relief and charity solve nothing. As a good doctor tries to remove the cause of sickness, so must we remove the cause of our economic ills. Much talk goes on re post-war reconstruction, economic security, the Beveridge Plan and kindred subjects.

We are realizing that our energy and resources should be used for the benefit of all. Those who have charge of post-war planning or reconstruction must not be afraid of change. The old cruel, unscientific order of uncertainty, want, privation, and misery, must never be allowed to return.

Women, especially, should develop greater interest in all constructive measures to bring about a better Canada. (Source: 1943 L.C.W. Year Book, p. 35–36)

The 1950s

Trades and Labor Committee – Mrs. A.A. Frawley, Convenor

At the monthly meetings of the Calgary Local Employment Advisory Committee, attended by myself, the changing employment picture is thoroughly reviewed and discussed. Ways and means of improving local conditions, such as the Winter Employment Campaign, are dealt with by this committee.

Mr. E.J. Wilson, local manager of the Unemployment Insurance Commission, reported at the last meeting that, while there are various comments on the reported increase of unemployed persons throughout the Dominion, the Calgary area is doing better than hold its own. Total number of unemployed registered shows an overall decrease of 535 as compared with last year. While we continue to have a steady increase in our working force, the number of unemployed is noticeably less, and there is no doubt that the Winter Employment Campaign has been a major factor towards a better employment level during the winter season.

A recent survey shows that approximately 65% of the women registered were in the 20 to 40 age group, many of whom are married with young families and difficult to place. Others have been disassociated from their occupations for varying periods of time and require re-training before they can re-enter the employment field.

Two resolutions, relating to vocational training, have been passed by the Local Employment Advisory Committee and forwarded to Regional Employment Advisory Committee for ratification. Though these resolutions are a duplication of those submitted by the National Council of Women, the committee felt such duplication would facilitate passage of same on the federal scene.

Recently your chairman had the honor of appearing on CKXL's Public Opinionaire panel, the topic being Equal Pay for Equal Work. It was agreed that, although this is sound in principle, and is now on the statute books of both provincial and federal governments, it is difficult to enforce. We must do more than give this legislation lip service. We must make it work. One quarter of the labor force in Canada is composed of women. Adequate representation on various labor boards throughout the country would do much to ensure that working women would receive more consideration in this regard.

Dominion Bureau of vital statistics recently disclosed that last year the number of women workers on farms had increased considerably. This might well be the direct result of automation. In future years we may expect automation of open still other new fields of human endeavour to women from all walks of life. We must be ready and willing to accept the challenge. (Source: 1959 L.C.W. Year Book, p. 27)

The 1960s

Economics – Mrs. K.F. MacLennan, Convenor

During the past year, the trading stamp war flared up again in Calgary and in Edmonton: the protagonists – a national grocery chain, backed by a stamp-promoting company, and the Alberta Government. The chain, spurred on by a Supreme

Court judgment handed down about a year ago in favor of a stamp issued in Manitoba, decided to move in on Alberta and test the validity of the provincial law on stamps and premiums by keeping its stores open and issuing the stamps after the Government had revoked store licenses on the stamp issue. In the resulting court case, the District Court Judge upheld the provincial legistlation banning "giveaways." The stores were fined and have now discontinued their stamp distribution.

However, an appeal is being made against the Judge's decision, which means that the issue is not dead.

Local Council of Women has repeatedly expressed its oppositionto the use of trading stamps and other such gimmicks, and the present situation suggests that we must continue a program of watchfulness and education in this matter

While Local Council took no action in connection with the controversy about store closing hours which raged during the closing months of 1961, we kept in close touch with its progress. in fact, some of our executive members undertook a private survey of opinion among friends and acquaintances. City Council eventually decided on a "hands-off" policy, which leaves the situation much as it was – most stores remaining open only one or two nights a week. According to the L.C.W. private poll, this is an acceptable pattern. Almost all of those questioned felt that one – perhaps two – open nights in the week was a good thing so that families could shop together but that more than two was quite unnecessary and uneconomical.

A Federal Government 1961 regulation should be mentioned because it was initiated by one of our affiliates and because it is of interest to all women. That is the Canada Standard Sizing legislation. After about ten years of research by a committee composed of Government, manufacturers, retailers, and Consumers Association representatives, and the measuring of thousands of children, the new sizing will put an end to the uncertainties and variations in clothes sizes for children from pre-school to high-school age. The framework is ready for proceeding with garments for women, but the go-ahead signal awaits a review of the reception given children's CS garments. The new regulation is not mandatory. It is therefore the responsibility of consumers, through their retailers, to make sure that manufacturers adopt the new sizing. (Source: 1962 L.C.W. Year Book, p. 33–34)

Social Welfare – Mrs. Oscar (Grace) Stonewall, Convenor

With Mrs. Anthony Santapinto as co-chairman, our committee covered the following aspects of welfare which deeply concern us.

John Howard Society. Mrs. Santapinto attended all meetings and was active on the service committee of the John Howard Society. She toured Spy Hill Jail and Bowden Institute, and brought interesting and enlightening reports back to Council. She is also serving as volunteer driver, taking relatives to visit inmates of the jail. She has not only kept us well informed, but has made an excellent contribution in our name to the Society. She now represents the Society on the Advisory Board of the Indian Friendship Centre.

Hospital Board. Local Council of Women were instrumental in the appointment of Mrs. Russell Clark, a Welfare Committee Member, to the Board of the Rockyview General Hospital.

Elizabeth Fry Society. Three of our committee members – Mrs. McCullough, Mrs. Clark and Mrs. Santapinto, attended preliminary meetings on the formation of an Elizabeth Fry Society in Calgary, and reported to them the findings of a study made by Local Council a few years ago. Mrs. McCullough has been appointed to represent Local Council of Women on the Board of the newly-incorporated Elizabeth Fry Society, of which she is Treasurer.

Neglected Girls. Your Welfare Committee is gathering information on facilities and needs in Calgary for neglected girls. This project was first suggested by the North Hill United Church Women and the Y.W.C.A.; and during our discussions concern has been also expressed in this area by University Women, Catholic Women's League, United Church Women and the Salvation Army.

On behalf of the committee Mrs. Winspear and I interviewed Police Chief McIvor regarding the battered child and other matters.

The Welfare Committee arranged an informational meeting when Mr. Don Maeers, Executive Secretary of the John Howard Society, Calgary, spoke on the re-entry of women into the community after serving time in prison.

Council's resolution requesting a change in legislation covering the battered child, was prepared and presented jointly by the Welfare and Laws Committees. Accepted by our affiliated societies, it was forwarded to the Provincial Council of Women, who have passed it and presented it to the Provincial Government.

Your Welfare Committee recommends that our federated societies continue to press for the establishment of diagnostic and forensic clinics for sex deviates by re-iterating our long-standing resolution on this subject. (Source: 1966–67 L.C.W. Hand Book, p. 29)

Education – Mrs. H.C. (Jean) Mekitiak, Convenor

This committee was in charge of Council's first General Meeting of the year, which was devoted to education in keeping with the observance of Education Week throughout Canada. Three speakers were invited: Mrs. D.A. Hansen, Vice-Chairman of the School Board at that time, and Chairman of the University Committee, who spoke on the University; Mr. E.G. Callbeck, Director of the Elementary School Program

Commission, who spoke on education in a changing world; and Dr. H.S. Armstrong, President of U.A.C. who spoke on university autonomy.

Our main project for the year was the study of kindergartens. Mr. Callbeck's Elementary Commission had invited briefs on the elementary program, and we decided to submit our recommendations regarding kindergartens. Mrs. J.M. Johnson, co-chairman of this committee, prepared a 20-page brief outlining the advantages of early childhood education and requesting that kindergarten training be incorporated into the school system. The brief was presented in June. Along with this, our plan was to stir up as much public interest as we could. We arranged two TV programs. For the first, Mrs. H.K. Roessingh and Mrs. J.M. Johnson were interviewed on the subject. On the second program, a 10-minute film of the Happy Hours Kindergarten was shown, and Mrs. Barbara Castle, Co-ordinator of Kindergartens, was interviewed.

Considerable work went into arranging for a public meeting to be held in the fall. In addition to committee members, we called upon Mrs. Merron Chorny, Mrs. Oscar Stonewall and Mrs. H.G. McCullough for help, and Mrs. W.H. Ross guided us in our publicity campaign.

The meeting took the form of a panel discussion, the following being participants:

- Mrs. D.A. Hansen, acting as Moderator.
- Dr. Allan Brown, from the Administration Dept., U.A.C.;
- Dr. John Fair, a practicing Child Psychiatrist;
- Dr. Ethel King, from the Education and Curriculum branch, U.A.C.;
- Dr. Don Mills, Department Head of Sociology, U.A.C.;
- Mrs. J.B. Castle, Co-ordinator of Kindergartens;
- Mrs. J.M. Johnson, Local Council of Women.

The meeting received good publicity coverage by both newspapers and radio.

Our resolution requesting that the Provincial Government make available public funds to the school board which establishes and operates pre-school or kindergarten classes within the school system was adopted by Local Council, and passed for action to the Provincial Council of Women. And on December 13th a delegation headed by the late Mrs. Ralph Johnson and consisting of Mrs. J.M. Johnson, Mrs. Winspear and representatives from Edmonton and Red Deer Local Councils, met with the Minister of Education. I would like to pay tribute to the inspiration which Mrs. Ralph Johnson gave us, and the efficiency with which she carried out this project. (Source: 1966–67 L.C.W. Hand Book, p. 31)

The 1970s

Radio, Television and Films Report – Mrs. Cynthia Aikenhead, Chairman

My committee and I have been, and are, dealing with problems arising from television, radio, and films. We are also studying, in depth, the implications and operational dynamics of television and its cousin, Computerized Data, e.g. what effects their further exploitation will have on all of us.

Letters were sent to the following institutions and daily newspapers' Mailbag Columns: Canadian Parliamentary Committee On Broadcasting, House of Commons, Ottawa (these people are *elected* public servants); Canadian Radio & Television Commission, 100 Metcalfe Street, Ottawa (*appointed* public servants); Canadian Broadcasting Corporation – Television and Radio divisions; Calgary Herald and Albertan; Toronto Telegram and Star; Ottawa Citizen and Journal. The problems "hitting" us in southern Alberta were: to keep SESAME STREET children's superb, award-winning five-mornings-a-week, free-of-commercials, program (11 a.m. till noon) on CBC-TV network; to get a CBC FM radio station located in Calgary to serve southern Albertans with CBC's Radio's *cultural* programs (CBC's new format will cut places like southern Alberta out of this essential listening opportunity – with their "cultural" programs being taken off AM and put onto its FM radio operations – and with their being only CBC-FM radio stations located in Ottawa, Toronto, Montreal, Winnipeg and Vancouver – only five in the whole of Canada!). We were, and are, concerned about Canada's present tendency to put programming-nationalism ahead of programming-excellence. Excellence knows no geographical, political boundaries. And, too, because it is rare, it makes no sense to barricade ourselves against it, and, instead, go after "domestic" mediocrity because it can safely be labelled: "Made in Canada."

I attended a splendid meeting held by our affiliate, The National Council of Jewish Women on February 9th at the home of Mrs. Morris Carnat, the subject of which was TV Education programs in general and saving *Sesame Street* program in particular. Many organizations were represented, including the Public and Catholic school boards. Mrs. Gertrude Lang of the CRTC was there – and witnessed the enthusiasm held by so many people for keeping *Sesame Street* on the CBC-TV network. What's left is to convince Pierre Juneau who heads the CRTC. There is *still* a "tough nut to crack," and requires our continued pressure.

CA/TV is being expanded and the people (you and I) should study this from all angles for their (our) own protection. It matters who runs it; it matters whether or not there are sufficient controls; and it matters how cable television is licensed.

Films. The tremendous popularity of the sensitive and romantic films such as Erich Segal's *Love Story* and David Lean's *Ryan's Daughter* indicates that the days of "movie crude-nudes" are numbered. This is very good news. Regarding

Canada Film-making: things are looking up and there is a breakthrough for the greater distribution to movie-houses of Canadian-made features.

Books about the Media. In closing, may I recommend Nicholas Johnson's informative book called *How to Talk Back to your Television Set* and *McLuhan: Hot & Cool* edited by Gerald E. Stearn . . . the last chapter of which should be, I believe, "required reading" for students. (Source: 1970–71 L.C.W. Hand Book, p. 22–23)

Report of the Special Historical Committee – Grace Stonewall Chairman, Lillian MacLennan Secretary

This committee was originally set up as a special committee to do what it could to have the cupola of James Short School preserved for posterity when that school was being demolished. With this mission accomplished, the committee was retained to keep a watchful eye on other threatened Calgary landmarks. The broader frame of reference required a more comprehensive title, and this year the committee has been operating as Council's "Historical Committee."

With our heritage of sandstone buildings falling to the bulldozer with increasing frequency, we are pleased to be able to give our support to a strong citizen's committee which, for a couple of years, has been waging a battle to save Rundle Lodge – the small sandstone building *which was Calgary's first General Hospital, built in 1894.* Actually this was a natural activity for Council of Women. It was the persistence of a handful of women that brought the hospital into existence in the first place. Appalled by the number of unattended deaths in Calgary, and spurred on by the bequest of one Hundred Dollars and the personal effects (his all) from a Chinese who had died without medical help, they worked hard for financial and physical support until the hospital became a reality.

Rundle Lodge has been our main concern during this past year. We have written letters to the papers on the subject. We have been in correspondence with the Mayor, and we attended a meeting of City Council in January where the fate of the building was to be decided. At this meeting, where speakers for and against preservation were heard, Mrs. Mary Winspear spoke for our committee. As a result of the debate, demolition was delayed to allow for a provincial government study of costs. Without waiting for the result of that study, the Rundle Lodge Preservation Committee (the committee referred to above) is proving its determination by organizing a fund-raising campaign to be kicked off with a $25-per-person dinner dance in June with Rich Little as headliner. As Local Council of Women is not a fund-raising organization, our contribution to this is in providing some needed phoners and publicity. At two public hearings before provincial enquiries, held in Calgary on May 29th and June 28th, Dr. Ruth Gorman made memorable presentations on behalf of our Council. It is our hope that, before our next Annual Meeting rolls around, success will have crowned the hard work and dedication of the Calgarians who see no sense in wanton destruction of our past history.

One other area about which we have had some correspondence, and which will probably need more definite action this year, is the site of old Fort Calgary at the junction of the Bow and Elbow rivers. This is Calgary's birthplace, and we feel, with Alderman John Ayer, that it should be preserved, perhaps as a parkland, with suitable monuments regarding its historical background; and that steps must be taken to acquire land that is not now owned by the City before the rumored apartment developers move in.

We have hopes that the public and the City Fathers will see in these projects a worthwhile way of commemorating Calgary's 100th anniversary which falls in 1975.[30] (Source: L.C.W. 1912–1972 Diamond Jubilee Year Report, p. 17)

Land Preservation and Conservation Committee Report – Chairman Margaret Buckmaster.

The Land Preservation and Conservation committee has been extremely busy this year. We prepared a brief on "Nose Hill," with the recommendation that: "We propose that approximately 3500 acres, bounded on the West by the Sarcee Trail right-of-way, on the South by John Laurie Blvd., on the East by the existing development adjacent to the escarpments of Nose Hill, and on the North by the highlands and escarpments of Nose Hill to and beyond 80th Avenue N.W., be zoned as Natural Parkland in perpetuity."

We became members of the Nose Hill Council, which was appointed by Calgary City Council in July, 1972, to return in one year with a sector plan for North Hill. Although, their policy is not totally consistent with our brief, we have supported their proposal for a 2612 acre Natural Park on Nose Hill.

We joined the Fish Creek Park Association in September, 1972 and were successful in obtaining a 2800 acre park along Fish Creek in February, 1973. We are still working with the Park Association, now working with the Provincial Government in determining the Park's policy.

We continued to support the Local Council of Women's water-course policy in urging City Council to set aside for present and future generations, river-bank parkland on all rivers within the city limits.

We are concerned about the mini-parks, particularly relating to the City Centre. We are anticipating studying a priority site study of mini parks recently completed by the City Planning Department.

A letter was sent to members of City Council, on February 18, 1973, regarding the implementation of Flood Control Measures on the Bow River questioning the validity of a 1968 engineering study. Our concerns were primarily that all research possible be completed before the removal of trees. Our committee also supported the formation of a tri-level Government representation committee to study the long range needs for Planning of large parks in the urban and rural areas of the Calgary region in an area of approximately 75 miles radius of Calgary.

We also had a booth at the Alberta Teacher's Association City Convention to display our work for Local Council of Women in this area.

The Environment Conservation Authority accepted our application to become a member of their Public Advisory Committee in October, 1972 for a period of three years. I, Margaret Buckmaster, have represented Local Council of Women and work actively on the Non-Renewable Resources Study group. There are four other study groups, Pollution, Environment, Renewable Resources, and Education, all of which work continually and present their recommendations to the Provincial Government.

We have been involved in this past year with other interested groups and community associations working on "Park Involvement" and feel it has been extremely beneficial to all concerned.

Lastly, I would like to express my "thanks" to my committee, Grace Stonewall, Mary Winspear, Frances Roessingh, and Marj Norris, who have attended over thirty different meetings, and spent hours helping to prepare briefs and letters. Without their dedication this report would not have been possible. (Source: 1973 Report, Glenbow Archives, L.C.W Fonds, M5841/48)

Addendum C

A Vigilance Committee:
Attitudes, Platitudes, and Beatitudes

THE FORMATION OF the Calgary Local Council's Equal Moral Standards Committee had nothing to do with what was going on in Calgary. Rather it had to do with something that was going on in Medicine Hat. Moreover the committee formed after, not during, the May 28, 1920 executive meeting, as follows:

> An informal discussion followed the Executive meeting, led by Mrs. Edwards. Mrs. Edwards referred to an article in "The Albertan" stating the pupils of the Medicine Hat High school, had a very low percentage of marks, owing to too great an interest in social affairs. It was not desirable that same conditions prevail here. A great deal of discussion followed, all agreeing the lack of discipline on part of the parents was to blame for girls being out at all hours of the night. Parents resent any interference though, and it is a difficult question to deal with. It was finally moved by Mrs. Edwards, Seconded by Mrs. Ross – "that Mrs. R.R. Jamieson be appointed chairman, with power to call her own committee to assist her, and that we stand back of her in any work she may undertake in preventing and combating the moral and social evils amongst us." (Source: Minutes of the 1920 L.C.W. Executive meeting, Glenbow Archives, L.C.W. fonds M5841/24)

The President, Lilie C. Woodhall, and Recording Secretary, Emily L. Akitt affixed their signatures.

Mrs. Jamieson was re-elected to the convenorship in 1921 and at the January 22, 1922 Annual Meeting, her brief report was summarized in the minutes:

> Mrs. Jamieson, Convenor of Equal Moral Standards, reported on Uniform Marriage Law. Age of Delinquency raised from 16 to 18 years, all the provinces excepting Alberta and British Columbia have age raised to 18, both these provinces are asking for it. Equal Divorce Law was also mentioned. Mrs. Jamieson's final report was adopted.

1924–25 Report by Mrs. J.S. Jarrett, Convenor

Every society whose purpose is for the betterment of health and home in a city helps the morals of our young people.

The work of the Social Service and Child Welfare Board and also the Health Clinic, and lectures delivered by fluent speakers of both sexes, are ably assisting the parents to a better understanding of their children.

The practice of teachers and parents exchanging views and opinions on child welfare and training, is to be highly commended and will tend to have very beneficial results. The formation of the Parent Teachers' Association in Calgary was a step in the right direction, as it materially assists the teachers in the training of the children. Church organizations also are giving very valuable assistance in the training of our young people.

From accounts appearing in the public press we note with pleasure that visitors are very favorably impressed with the courtesy and cleanliness of our school children. The habit of courtesy was brought very strongly to my attention last summer when going to a picnic at St. George's Island. On alighting from a street car a boy whose age would be about 14 years, volunteered to carry my rather heavy parcel. Telling him I did not happen to have small change, he replied that he was a Scout and did not expect money for doing a kind act. With such material we may expect to have splendid types of men and women in this country of ours.

The abolishment of the slot machines and other gambling devices will help to elevate the morals of the younger generation and both the federal and provincial parliaments are to be congratulated for their actions along those lines.

We should also show our appreciation for the good work done by the Calgary City Council in giving more illumination for our various parks and recreation grounds.

Another project we should endeavor to see to a successful conclusion is the proposed amendment to the Liquor Act prohibiting women and girls from being served beer in the beer parlors. It is not a very edifying spectacle to see our native women and girls in their twenties patronizing these places.

Summing up, we should all endeavor to make our country a better place to live in for ourselves and future generations and try to give our children the best assistance, both physically, mentally and morally, that will fit them for the battle of life in this great country – Canada. (Source: 1924–25 L.C.W. Year Book, p. 41)

1925–26 Report by Mrs. M.A. Harvey, Convenor

As convener of equal moral standard for the Local Council of Women of the city of Calgary, I have studied the work from many different sources and have given it my deepest consideration, and though it may seem old fashioned to say that the social unit is the family, it is nevertheless true as all history proves. Many forces today seem to be working against the ancient position of the family. We are told on all sides that the family as a unit is fast disappearing; it is composed of individuals whose motto is "each for himself."

Divorce is on the increase and parental control has relaxed. One would think to hold a family intact for the span of their years was an exploit that should have a headline in the newspaper. Is it not all the more important to make sure to take care of an institution which means so much to society? A family saved from dissolution is an asset to the whole community – all social welfare workers instinctively know this, and seek to keep the home intact if at all possible. I would like to see women, particularly mothers, as they have a greater responsibility guiding the youth, to try not to allow yourselves to become over excited at some unfortunate case that may happen in the city, by pressing your way to public places, giving the public officials any amount of trouble who are trying their utmost to perform their duties. As a judge of the Juvenile Court of the City of Calgary, I am very much pleased to say that the morals of the children have greatly improved during the past two years, and I think are on an equal moral standard with any children of the Dominion of Canada. I sincerely hope that next year with the wise counsel of their parents and teachers they will lead in moral standard. (Source: 1925–26 L.C.W. Year Book, p. 43)

1927–28 Report by Millicent McElroy, Convener

This committee on equal moral standards has been spoken of as a "Vigilance and Look-out Committee," a sort of "watch-tower" from which to make observations of conditions, and possibly from time to time sound the note of warning as necessity arises, seek solution of social problems that confront the progress of right living. Now, there may be a wide difference of opinion as to whether the general moral standard of to-day is improving or otherwise, for (although we are startled and pained at times at some shocking revelation of conduct and crime), we must bear in mind this fact, that where a few years ago it would have taken many days, possibly weeks, or even months, for news to travel, in these days of rapid communication, something transpires on one side of the world, and immediately, just a few seconds, wireless has broadcast it to every side and all around, and the action is being discussed by thousands who otherwise might never have heard of it. There can, however, be no difference of opinion as to the great desirability for improvement in many directions. It is said women are the guardians of the morals of the nation, and here is our great opportunity to regard with deep sincerity this sacred trust, and endeavor to prove ourselves worthy.

Can there go forth from this Council a call strong and clear to the members of every affiliated society that WE take a definite, unmistakable position with regard to any tendency to habits and conduct that degrade and impair our Womanhood and endanger the standards of our morals.

There must be NO lowering of the standard. Should we not discourage and discountenance many forms of so-called recreation, pleasures and amusements, some innocent enough and harmless as may be of themselves, but the associations are not such as really do lend themselves to the recreation of either physical, mental, or moral powers, but tend rather to defeat the very purpose for which recreation should be designed.

Our attention has been called to the fascinating, but foolish craze for gambling that is absorbing a large percentage of our people. Here we ask consideration of many games of chance and forms of gambling that obtain. May we relate an incident we heard of? Quite a young man, a mere youth, took from his pocket a handful of notes and money, answering his mother's question: "Wherever did you get all that money?" said, "Oh! I was in great luck last night, a bunch of us were playing and I won the whole pool." Again replying to his mother's horrified exclamation that "Her son, she was an active church member, should play for money like a common gambler," said "Why mother, you taught me to play cards yourself right here at home, and don't you remember how delighted you were later, when I won the prize at the whist drive you gave? What difference? You pay money for the prizes; we just take the money. I don't see the difference to make any fuss about." WE must seek back of the effect and find the causes, which, in the majority of cases have their beginnings in the neglect of cultivating the endeavor to live up to the highest ideals of life. The pernicious cigarette habit, which is (according to the evidence of highest medical authorities) poisoning the blood stream, drugging the heart and demoralizing the nerves of those women and girls – the mothers of our next generation, who indulge the habit. The twin evil of the cigarette, the wine-drinking, and cocktail habit, often accompanied by the rude joke, and vulgar loose language, all, as a rule, acquired thoughtlessly, with no real evil intent, but it is well known, "more evil is wrought for want of thought, than want of heart." These small innocent-looking beginnings lead to tragic heart-breaking results, which constitute a large part of our social problems, hence as consistent women of the watch-tower we must sound the warning note against *all questionable* forms of pleasure and habit, investigate and satisfy ourselves whether or not certain things lead to a higher conception of life, its duties and responsibilities, conducive to clean, pure habits of thought and conduct, conforming to the highest moral standard for all. (Source: 1927–28 L.C.W. Year Book, pp. 49–51)

1928–29 Report by Mrs. G. McElroy, Convenor

In the Year Book, our National Convenor suggests the pertinent question "Why an equal moral standard?" When we speak of a double standard, with regard to sex relations, there is really no such thing; in every illicit act, both a man and a woman are concerned, and consequently the amount of such immorality is exactly the same. The fact has been that only a small number of women, comparatively, have been the partners of a large number of men. A very high standard of moral conduct has been expected of women, whereas the lapses of men, provided there was no open scandal, has been regarded with little concern. This is the double standard, and the double standard is the direct cause of the professional prostitute. It is impossible for all women to be virtuous until all men are virtuous. It is all important then, that men should be educated to accept a single high standard of conduct in sex matters, and that society should look for, and expect from them the same clean living and freedom from "sowing of wild oats," that it expects of women. Only so can an equal high moral standard become a reality. Any measure of consent to a double standard means the lowering of the woman's standard, to meet conditions, and so there is a gradual coming down to a lower standard which can only be fraught with disastrous results for all. We all deplore the tendency of many girls to-day to act like men – smoking, drinking, swearing, etc. Many of them, no doubt, do so merely desiring to be considered good sports. Having chosen then an equal high ideal for men and women alike, we must not hesitate to challenge the double or equal low wherever we meet it. The first and most important step is the education of public opinion until the single high standard has been as widely accepted as the double standard was heretofore. To this end, the combined efforts of all are required, college professors, teachers, social workers, leaders of young people's groups, and parents. Children growing up in the homes and schools where a high moral and spiritual standard is maintained, equipped with knowledge rightly imparted, develop qualities that make for right living, purposeful outlook on life, noble thinking, and sound character, "'tis education forms the mind," "as the twig is bent, the tree's inclined," prevention is better than cure, pre-formation rather than re-formation of character is most to be desired.

During the year a branch of the Canadian Social Hygiene Council (of which His Excellency Viscount Willingdon and

Her Excellency Vicountess are patron and patroness) was formed in the city, with Dr. Singleton as president. Lectures have been given on Community Health, and a series of moving pictures of films illustrating the various phases of disease and prevention were shown. This council will be of considerable service in helping our several organizations to bring this much needed education to their own communities, the need of which has long been felt, but an acceptable method of presentation to the general public was a difficult problem. We are glad to report the interest and co-operation of local doctors and others who are heartily supporting this movement, which is reducing the problem to a gratifying solution. More recently a secretary for southern Alberta has been appointed, whose headquarters will be in Calgary and whose services will be available. (Patron, His Honor Lieutenant-Governor, Wm. Egbert).

We have refrained from quoting figures as to crimes and convictions, or making comparisons with regard to same, male and female, adult or – alas, that it should be – juvenile delin-quents, or the alarming and increasing number of interdicts of men and, sad to say, women, too. The unmarried mother, the neglected child, the work of the social service home, the work at the provincial clinic for venereal treatment, these are all ques-tions calling for our serious thought, inasmuch as "no man liveth unto himself" and the well-being of the community less-er or larger can be of no higher type than the moral health of the individuals who comprise the community, and so we must Educate, by the spoken word, the printed page, picture screen, every means possible, and let us keep steadily before us a high and equal moral standard for both sexes, based on knowledge, self control, and a deepening sense of personal responsibility, and determine, so far as we are concerned, we will not be "found wanting," but each in her own sphere, endeavor to pro-mote and encourage every effort towards this most to be desired attainment, as the late Francis Willard so aptly expressed it, "A White Life for Two." (Source: 1928–29 L.C.W. Year Book, pp. 61, 63, 65)

1930 Report by Mrs. G. McElroy, Convenor

We have received from the National Convenor of this department (Moral Standards), a questionnaire full of interest and helpful suggestion, all of which we hope to submit for your consideration at a later date. One or two of the questions, however, and the information in respect of same may interest you at this time. Almost the first question deals with the League of Nations, and asks, "Are you interested" Do you follow the Humanitarian Activities of the League, etc. and of course we are glad to report that we are kept all the time interested and up to date by a most enthusiastic and active convener of Peace Department, Mrs. Carson.

Section 2 of our question paper opens up with an arresting and most emphatic statement that "Delinquency does not occur among members of Boy Scout, Girl Guides, Sunday School and good group organizations. Are such helpful agencies available? What opportunity does your community afford? What preventive, protective agencies, etc.?

Now it is very gratifying to find that Calgary is indeed equipped along these lines, having several agencies all very actively engaged working for the cultivation and development of the highest and best, both physically, mentally and spiritually. Supervised play centres, two or three vacation schools (for study, games and handicraft) being successfully conducted. We have 14 troops of boy scouts and cubs with an enrollment of about 600. We have a fine company of 50 boys, between the ages of 12 and 18, members of the Navy Boys' League. There are 10 companies of girl guides, 1 ranger company and seven brownie packs with a little over 500 enrolled. Then there are 20 Tuxis groups, 35 groups of trail rangers, 65 groups of C.G.I.T. girls (our splendid Canadian girls in training). The Salvation

Army have large groups of life saving scouts, a boys' band, girl guides and sunbeams. Gym and swimming classes at the Y.M. and Y.W.C.A. A special juvenile 'Y' in the Riverside district with organized classes from little tots of tender years and up. We have most efficient Sunday schools, in most cases, if not all, officered by careful and conscientious teachers.

Most churches have young peoples' societies or Christian Endeavor or Debating Clubs, all these excellent agencies at work in our city. Ample machinery with which to work, ample material with which to work. Do we? Can we realize our share of the tremendous responsibility that by precept, practice and example we encourage and urge our young people to ever seek to attain to the highest ideals of life and character. "A good name is better than riches." 'The Book' teaches and, necessary as money may be as a means of exchange, we must help our youth not to mistake the "Glitter" for the real gold. "He who steals my money steals trash – but he who takes away my good name takes all." An honored name, a life of service, are riches beyond compare, and continue to yield dividends and interest throughout the years of time, and everlasting reward through the Eternities to come.

According to police court records the total number of convictions reported last year for Calgary were 6390 – 5979 males, 411 women. There were 246 Juvenile Court cases recorded in our City during the past year – 238 boys and 8 girls, of this total 227 were under the Delinquent Act, and 19 cases were neglect. There were 75 children up for theft, 11 for breaking and entering, 13 for discharging firearms in city limits, 68 under bicycle by-laws, 1 for smoking cigarettes and 5 for setting prairie fires. Age of delinquents ranged from 4 at 8 years old to 8 at 16.

Dr. Rivers, for some years warden at Lethbridge jail, made a statement recently to the effect that 90 per cent of criminals in Western Canada were 20 years old and under. His conclusions were that "The blame lay generally with parents in that they fail to give the right training in discipline, respect for law and order, and to inculcate ideals of the best, in a day of many attractions outside the home. Children do not have the companionship which makes the home society desirable and the very thought and memory of parents, a "Guiding Star."

Dr. Lindquist, Professor of Sociology at the University of Minnesota, speaking to a St. Paul audience some time ago, said: "Society has consoled itself by saying, Morons and other mentally sub-normal persons make up the criminal class, this is not so, declared the Professor. Not defective mentally but a yearning for thrills makes criminals of our youth. Disintegration of the home and a lack of religious faith are important contributing factors." These are opinions given by experts and demand our serious consideration.

The standard of ideals, principles and character of the home, constitute the standard of morality in the community, inasmuch as it is only in proportion as these are absorbed and assimilated, and become character, reflected in the conduct of our children, that the larger family of communities and nations attain to the ideal, hence the highest must be our objective.

Whatsoever things are true, whatsoever things are honest, whatsoever things are just, whatsoever things are pure, whatsoever things are lovely, whatsoever things are of good report, if there be any virtue and if there be any praise, think on these things.

We have to regretfully acknowledge that with all our splendidly equipped churches, service clubs, organizations and agencies whose qualifications for existence are service, and the good of the community, sin still produces a woeful harvest of corruption, and evil and untold sorrows in a more or less degree to those immediately concerned, and indirectly at large. Do the young people in the circles or groups in which we move, see in our conduct the Christian graces exemplified, because after all, it is not so much what we say or teach, but what we do, and the manner in which we live, that makes its impression on those by whom we are surrounded. You are familiar with the old Truism.

"Actions speak louder than words," and this Association of Women's Organizations must advocate and stand unflinching and unwavering for the highest standard of right living for both sexes, equality of righteousness, equality of responsibility, for the home, for the community and the country. (Source: 1930 L.C.W. Year Book, pp. 48–50)

1931 Report by Mrs. G. McElroy, Convenor

The National Committee is to be commended for the action taken regarding the title of this department, known so many years as "Equal Moral Standards," having for its immediate purpose and object the teaching and stressing of the absolute necessity and importance of an equal standard of purity of life and morals, for both the sexes, in the highest interest of the home, community and national life of our peoples. That the effort was worthwhile and attended with much success is fully established by the very fact that the change in title to that of "Moral Standards" indicating as it does, we are now arriving at the place where, generally speaking, responsibility is on equal basis, and the vision of the possibilities of the work are considerably enlarged.

The cause of Purity like that of Temperance is not merely a moral movement, but also fundamentally and necessarily a spiritual one. "Know ye not that your body is a temple of the Holy Spirit. . . . Know ye not that ye are the temple of God? . . . If any man defile the temple of God, him shall God destroy." Here is the perfect ideal of life and the motive for its realization.

Dr. Mercer defines conduct as "action in pursuit of ends." Moral action may be "self-indulgent" or "self-restrained"; it may also be purely instinctive or the result of habit. Probably there are few things that tend more towards the evolution of a permanent and well-ordered human society than the practice of good morals.

The Christian revelation of what human life, physical and spiritual, is intended to be, has wrapped up in it an incentive to live and work for the realization of the ideal revealed, both for ourselves and others. Temples for the indwelling of the Holy Spirit of God that he may work in us, through us, by us to will and to do of "His good pleasure."

The wages of sin is death but the gift of God is eternal life, and He depends on us – whom he had chosen to be co-workers together with Him in the working out of His Divine Plan for the redemption and eternal security of mankind, whom He created in His own image and likeness, to the end, we should glorify Him. All our work is so small and futile of itself but miracles are worked when we realize it is God that worketh in us, to will, and to do.

Some alarm was felt when it became known a large increase in crime had obtained during the year over the preceding year, and at a specially called meeting of the City Council, to consider the report dealing with juvenile delinquency there was a large attendance of women representing between thirty and forty different organizations in the city, headed by Mrs. Harold W. Riley, Secretary of the Council on Child and Family Welfare, demonstrating the lively interest our women are taking in these matters. It was brought out in the evidence taken that a large percentage of the increase was of minor misdemeanor, still there was ample evidence , and it was emphatically stated, and seemed to be the consensus of opinion that lack of parental authority, discipline, proper home life and training, was the root cause in almost every case, and yet there are those who are not interested and who deem these things no concern of theirs for the sole reason they are not immediately concerned parties in the matter, ignoring the "Golden Rule" and failing to recognize the fact that we are all more or less affected – helped or hurt, to lesser or larger degree by the life and conduct of each other. Solon, "the wise man of Athens," was asked how crime could be abolished by any State. "It will be abolished," said he, "when those who are not hurt feel the same indignation as those who are."

The greatest corrective interest could be exerted in the home, but as one of our Canadian woman magistrates remarked: "Parents cannot bring up children in their leisure time; it is a full time job"; and discussing this matter, a well known inspector of police said; "If there were more home training, there would be less need of police." But parents are not alone responsible, we as citizens are responsible for many stumbling-blocks in the pathway of our youth that we should see removed. The great increase in drinking throughout Canada – Alberta and Calgary not excepted – and the all to prevalent use of narcotics require our earnest efforts directed towards the education of our youth in the effects of these things on the human system and our continued efforts towards stirring up our provincial government to provide the necessary instruction along these lines. May we here record our appreciation of two recent lecturers brought to our city by the provincial government. W.D. Bayley, B.A., of Winnipeg, whose illuminative, highly educative and at the same time most interesting lectures, were listened to with the closest attention and very keen enjoyment by hundreds of high school and business students, and teachers alike. Dr. Margaret Owen, of our own provincial health staff, who spoke on "Sex Hygiene" to a large gathering of representative women whose sympathetic and eager interest in the subject was very evident. We are moving in the right direction and must work for further developments in these matters.

The question of Women Police was again introduced and briefly discussed at a recent meeting of the Local Council. All women will agree upon the principle, that where the law touches a woman or child, the hand of the law aught to be that of a woman. Lately there has been in several countries a great movement amongst well known organizations for women police. The need is keenly felt where they have not been introduced, and where they are, they have been acknowledged a great success.

The White Ribboners Union in England and Wales have had for some time police matrons and probation officers in many courts, but these are now being gradually taken over by the authorities. Scotland has organized women police as probation officers. It is reported that Dublin (Ireland) L.C.W. went on record at their last convention as unanimously in favor of women police. The first three women police commissaries have completed their training in Frankfort-on-Main, Germany, and have been appointed in Cologne, and Breslau.

Many other places have some form of women police guardian. Canada is falling into line, several of our cities recognizing this as one of the needs of the day, have already appointed women to this office. Our neighbor, British Columbia, has now in Vancouver its own women's police bureau and complement of officers.

"Still achieving – still pursuing, learn to labor – and to wait."

A little more patience, a little more effort, and we shall be singing with Longfellow's "Blacksmith" not only "something attempted," but "something DONE." (Source: 1931 L.C.W. Year Book, pp. 77–79)

1933 Report by Mrs. M.A. Harvey, Convenor (Judge of the Juvenile Court, Calgary)

As convener of Social Service for the Local Women's Council, I have studied the work from many different angles, and have given it deep consideration. I have also discussed the subject with many learned workers engaged in moral work, and we think the morals are somewhat better in regard to dress, due to the efforts the women have put forth in this direction.

We must begin with the home. We are told from all sides that the family as a unit is fast disappearing. It is composed of individuals whose motive is each for himself. Divorce is on the increase and parental control has relaxed. Is it not all the more important to make sure of an institution which means so much to society. A family saved from dissolution is an asset to the whole nation. All social welfare workers instinctively know this, and seek to keep the home intact, if at all possible.

I would like to see the mothers, who have a greater responsibility in guiding youth, assist the teachers in their work with the children, for the church and school are next to the home. Some children are liable to play truant, which is a source of other evils, and parents should visit the teachers and ascertain how their children are behaving in school and what progress they are making in their studies. If this were done it would lead to a betterment in the moral standard among children, for one pupil rarely plays truant alone.

For some time past all countries are looking into the welfare of children, especially since the world is suffering such a depression during these times. All over, societies are helping to clothe needy children so that they may be able to attend school.

Fathers and mothers must fulfill their duties to their church, which is doing so much to help the morals of youths, and it must be stressed that children gain more from example than from precept. Life in the home must be a joint undertaking, for there is only one way to make children feel that there are things to be done, and the assistance parents can give is invaluable

I think every boy and girl should have some responsibility from the age of ten years. Something such as a small garden, or something else they will take an interest in. They should be taught that unless they plant something in the earth they shall get no return. Parents will be well repaid for any extra time spent in inducing responsibility.

Very few boys or girls appear in court who have a proper home, where their parents take a right interest in their welfare. I would ask you to study this matter for yourselves. I found it to help many boys and girls in changing their ways and returning to a better path. I shall endeavor this year to get some men to give the delinquent boys a chance in assisting themselves. (Source: 1933 L.C.W. Year Book, p. 31)

1942 Report by Mrs. M.L. Sibbald, Convenor

This work is more important today than ever before. When all lives seem so full of a nervous strain never, perhaps, felt before.

Our cities and towns are full of uniformed men, away from home, looking for diversion, for an "abundant life" while it is to be had.

When beverage alcohol is put to the fore as a means of supplying that "abundant life."

When there is an alarming increase in illegitimacy.

Venereal disease is spreading at a tremendous rate.

Sunday as a day of worship seems to be old-fashioned.

Moral standards require a superintendent who can contact young people with an understanding of their needs and, how to meet them. One who can visit women's prisons with the ability to show the prisoner that now is her opportunity for rehabilitation, and help her to get re-established when she is released.

Very fine preventive work can be done by Police women. It isn't easy to persuade men that women can do this work. We can only persist and when we win, prove that the results more than justify the expense.

A Superintendent of Moral Standards can co-operate with trained social workers in every field to combat the evils rampant today – partly at least caused by the lowering of almost all moral standards.

Wholesome recreations are a great necessity. Good clean sport, happy social gatherings where beverage alcohol is never served, and where some of the hymns the boys have learned at home are sung.

Where plans for a better world, when this time of war and ravage is over, are talked of.

Let our young folk know that is what we are expecting of them.

I can report little more than my share in the work with the girls of Mt. View Home. I sincerely recommend a younger Superintendent, one who can do the things suggested and more. (Source: 1942 L.C.W. Year Book, p. 53)

1943 Report by Mrs. J.B. Sibbald, Convenor

This is a living subject at present, and we hope for many reforms. The appointing of two police women will be a great forward step at this time, when so many girls are in need of the kind of help that just such a woman can give. A full-time matron at the City Hall is also greatly needed.

With respect to delinquent boys and girls, there is a vital need for a government correctional institution. At present there is no such institution for boys in Alberta, and most delinquent boys are placed on farms. Boys of later 'teen ages, such as those who have recently been sent to jail, would not stay on a farm, even if the farmer could be found who would be able to cope with the job. Chief Justice W.C. Ives, in passing sentence on 'teen age boys recently, said, "Boys like you, if the proper surroundings were furnished, and we were enabled to put you in those surroundings, could be taught to be splendid, efficient citizens." That applies to girls as well. A petition for such a Home for boys was sent by the Alberta Council of Child and Family Welfare to Premier Aberhart in 1939, and reaffirmed in 1942. This Home would be for the incorrigible boy, which is about one percent of the total number of delinquent boys.

The only building used for Protestant girls is Mount View Social Service Home. This Home has 26 beds, and is expected to service both Alberta and Saskatchewan. In the same way, the Home of the Good Shepherd at Edmonton accommodates the delinquent Catholic girls of Alberta.

There should be vocational training schools for both boys and girls, where trades other than farming and domestic labor are offered to those who are not interested in academic education. For girls, particularly, leaving these Homes to go into work, boarding homes should be available where there would be a supervised home life, provided by a responsible housemother.

If there were fewer delinquent parents, there would be fewer delinquent children. All forms of misconduct, both by juveniles and adults, now seem to be intensified due to the war.

If mothers who have to provide for their families were given a better allowance, they could stay at home and look after their children. The amount now given them will not pay for rent, food, clothing, school books, medicine, and the hundred and one incidentals cropping up in a home. A great deal needs to be done here. A mother who has to go out to work cannot look after the health and morals of her children properly.

We are expecting a great forward movement through the findings of the Committee which was set up at a Province-wide conference held in Edmonton last week, for the purpose of studying Provincial Acts dealing with child welfare and juvenile delinquency. (Source: 1943 L.C.W. Year Book, p. 41)

1944 Report by Mrs. J.B. Sibbald, Convener

That there is an effort being made to help readjust the lives that have gotten off to the wrong start is evidenced in the report of Mountview Social Service School for 'teen age girls.

This School is sponsored by the United Church of Canada, the girls being wards of the Alberta and Saskatchewan Governments.

There are nine such schools in Canada. Many more are needed.

Fifty-five girls were cared for in 1943. Sixteen transients and five unmarried mothers were given sanctuary. Of the five babies born all were adopted into carefully selected homes, while the mothers have been able to re-establish themselves in their home communities.

Ten of the fifty-five girls required and received hospitalization.

The girls are taught housework, cooking and sewing. There is a first class school teacher on the staff. Grades five to eleven are taught.

Their studies include needlework and basketry, the latter instruction being given by Mr. Ricks from the Blind Institute. Instruction in P.T. and folk dancing and First Aid are a part of their training.

The object is to rehabilitate the young folk in an environment as nearly normal as possible, and to create a normal home-like atmosphere. There is a Canadian Girls in Training leader, sports and shows, also Church attendance.

Drink and immorality in the homes play a large part and is the reason young girls and boys find themselves at an early age familiar with what is called the seamy side of life.

Authentic findings show that the use of alcohol is responsible for from seventy to ninety per cent of venereal infection.

Delinquency has increased the last few years due in part to the feverish, uncertain state of mind in war time, and partly to the desire of those who make large profits from beverage alcohol, who care little at what cost their profits are made, to increase these profits. My report is largely of girls as that is the work I am familiar with.

We have long fought for equal moral standards, let us endeavour to keep the standards high. It will require much thought and work and prayer to do this. (Source: 1944 L.C.W. Year Book, p. 35)

1946 Report by Martha L. Sibbald, Convener

No standard should ever be let down. Many of our boys and girls have seen moral standards sink very low during the war years.

The aftermath of war finds us with moral and social conditions at a low ebb. A thousand divorces a day, exclusive of Sunday, in the United States last year. A thousand major crimes committed by juveniles in Toronto in the past year. Many factors enter into the unhappy broken homes, and into the making of juvenile delinquents, such as crowded rooms, unemployment and salaries too low to provide the decencies of life.

Juvenile delinquency is an expression we hear too often. It is a disease that cannot be cured unless the root of the trouble is found and treated. The young children and youth in many families have not had the opportunity for family life. Fathers have been away to the war, and mothers have been working. It will not always be easy to reconstruct home life. The families have grown apart. War creates conditions that will take time and great patience to overcome.

Judge Parker, of Toronto, said recently, "Numerous beverage rooms have become incubators of crime."

In Alberta last year there was well over 26 million dollars spent in drink – that was three times as much money as the Provincial Government set aside for public welfare, charitable grants, hospitals, asylums, and gaols all put together. There will be broken homes, juvenile delinquency and lowered moral standards as long as this enemy drink is with us. L.D. Whitehead, in his book called "Jesus and Ourselves," says: "He would have been not interested, but passionately concerned, that there are people starving – concerned about unemployment – about our slums – people living herded together like animals. He was interested in housing, He knew that every home should have a room to which members of the family could withdraw to be quiet and pray." Surely He would be passionately concerned about the fact that in so many towns and cities today there is no place for young people to meet that has an uplifting rather than a degrading influence.

Our challenge today is to be concerned enough to do all in our power to raise the moral standards out of the dust. (Source: 1946 L.C.W. Year Book, p. 31)

Addendum D

Laws and Resolutions Committee: Proposed, Protested, Changed; A Veritable Social History

THE FOLLOWING is excerpted and edited from "How Leading Ladies Led" – a speech given by Marjorie Norris at the Glenbow Museum's *Untold Stories* series on November 18, 1995, after *A Leaven of Ladies* was published.

Mrs. Harold W. Riley – Convenor of Laws 1913–1933

Born in 1888, in St. Mary's Ontario, Alpha Maude Keen was the youngest daughter in a family of seven girls and two boys. As a very young woman she came west in 1903 to teach at the Nose Creek school on the northern outskirts of Calgary, after having taken her normal school training in Ontario at the London School of Pedagogy. The reasons why Maude Keen came west were common to others at the time. She had a relative (her sister May Spense) already living in Calgary; and, she came because of her health.

Even if her health was not robust, she certainly proved strong in will and in disciplinary fortitude. In the days when unruly pupils delighted in running off the schoolmarm, she survived. Romance, ended her stay there when she married Harold William Riley, eleven years her senior, in 1907 and moved to Edmonton because Harold was now Deputy Provincial Secretary to the new Province of Alberta. Then, when the University of Alberta came into being in 1908, he was named

Registrar. While in the capitol city Maude Riley became a member of the Local Council of Women. While there she also began lifelong friendships with two of Alberta's "Famous Five" – Henrietta Muir Edwards and Emily Murphy. The Rileys returned to Calgary in 1910 accompanied by their first born, a daughter, Maude Harriet. Within two years Maude Riley's stratagem proved a determining factor in the formation of Calgary's new Local Council of Women and within a few months she became its Laws Convener.

By 1913 Maude was in her mid twenties and the mother of two small children, her son Harold having been born in 1911. In 1916, the same year that their third child, Albert was born, Captain Harold Riley, Paymaster of the 137th Battalion, sailed for England where he was stationed until July of 1917. He then proceeded to France as Paymaster to the 2nd. Canadian Division Field Ambulances. Harold did not return to Calgary until 1919. Left with three small children to raise Maude, nevertheless emerged as a clubwoman par excellence, in part due to the support of her devoted maid, Bessie.

In Local Council's Committee of Officers hierarchy the Laws Convener spearheaded Local Council delegations when they met with the Mayor and other civic officials to ask for improvements in city legislation and services; and with the Premier and Cabinet when lobbying those reforms which only the Province could grant. The convenership was a high profile position, at times comparable to the office of president, but more enduring. The Local Council presidency usually rotated every two years, whereas the chairmanship of a committee promised greater longevity, time to persevere, time to recycle petitions, (their own special causes included) until such were addressed or finally abandoned, with a clear conscience.

There is evidence that Maude Riley took her position of Laws Convenor very seriously and managed that office efficiently, respectful of procedure. The 1925 Local Council Yearbook contains an impressive summary of 71 petitions asked for since the Council's inception in 1912. In it Maude Riley meticulously notes whether each petition was granted, partially granted, denied, or postponed. Thirty-eight of the 71 resolutions were presented to the Government of Alberta because that was where most legislative authority lay. Initially resolutions were presented directly to the Lieutenant-Governor-in-Council by the Local Council Laws Convener, then in 1916 through the Provincial Council of Women Law Committee, and in 1919 through the Provincial Executive of the National Council of Women, of which Mrs. O.C. Edwards was President. After the death of Mrs. Edwards in November of 1931, the Calgary Local Council nominated Mrs. Riley for the position. She became President of the Provincial Executive in 1932.

The parting of the ways occurred in the fall of 1933. On September 28, the Calgary Council on Child and Family Welfare, which was not an affiliate of Local Council although Mrs. Riley was President, passed a "clean literature" resolution. It asked for restrictions on the publication of salacious details from court cases and newspaper accounts to prevent injury to public morals, especially those of young readers. At the October 20 regular meeting Mrs. Riley presented the clean literature resolution to the Calgary Local Council, spoke to the resolution and moved for endorsation. It passed. The minutes of the November 17 regular meeting of the Local Council reveal the aftermath:

> Letter from Mrs. Harold Riley tendering her resignation as Convenor of Laws, same to take effect immediately, & thanking the members for loyalty and support and sending good wishes to the Council. Reason of resignation "Difference of opinion arising out of her dual position on the local council and the provincial body." Accepted with regret.

Towards the end of that very long meeting there was a fence mending attempt:

> Re resignation of Mrs. Harold Riley as Convener of Laws. The President stated that there had not been at any time a question of Mrs. Riley's dual position. Mrs. H.J. Akitt paid a glowing tribute to the work accomplished by Mrs. Riley for nearly 21 years Convener of Laws and moved – That Mrs Riley's resignation be not accepted. Seconded by Mrs. E. Hirst, motion was lost.
>
> Mrs. W. Blatchford stated that she was sure Mrs. Riley would not reconsider her resignation and moved – That we accept it with regret. This was seconded and carried.
>
> It was agreed that a letter of appreciation of her services on the Council would be sent to Mrs. Riley.

The next day the *Calgary Herald*, reported Mrs. Riley as saying that "Henceforth she would devote her energies to the presidency of the provincial executive of the National Council of Women."

That November 17 meeting re-convened after listening to the guest speaker, Mayor Davison, a candidate for re-election. The agenda still required the vetting of nominees for the 1934 executive. At this juncture names could be withdrawn prior to the list being sent to the affiliated societies, each of whom could add their own names. The President appointed three members as scrutineers of the 62 nominations to the 28 member executive. There were two for the office of President – Mrs. F.G. Grevett and Mrs. Harold Riley, and four for the now vacant Laws convenership – Miss Helen Steeves, Mrs. McCallum, Mrs. H.J. Akitt and Mrs. Guy Johnson. Two months later, at the January 22, 1934 Annual Meeting Mrs. F.G. Grevett was unanimously elected President, and members chose Miss Helen Steeves, a lawyer by profession, as Convener of Laws.

For Mrs. Riley, there was balm in Gilead: At the January 22 Annual Meeting Banquet held in the Elizabethan room of the Hudson's Bay Company, Mrs. H.J. Collins, Convener of Public Health, presented a basket of tulips and daffodils to Mrs. Riley, on behalf of the Local Council, and expressed the Council's gratitude to her for her untiring services as Convenor of Laws for nearly 21 years.

Mrs. Riley responded, saying it had only been through the love, trust and co-operation given by members that she had been enabled to carry on.

Maude Riley received honors in her lifetime. By 1919 she was one of three Canadian Women to receive the King of Belgium's Medialle de la Reine Elizabeth for outstanding service to the Belgian War Relief cause. For her other good works she received the 1935 King George V Coronation award. In 1946 she became the first woman to receive the Calgary Junior Chamber of Commerce Annual Citizenship award. Maude Riley died on July 13, 1962, four months before this daunting activist was to receive an Honorary Doctorate at the University of Alberta's Fall Convocation.

More than eleven years earlier (January 31, 1951), the Calgary Local Council of Women President, Mrs. Lillian Clarke, had submitted a request to Dr. Fred McNally, Chancellor of the University of Alberta, asking for the granting of an Honorary Doctorate to Mrs. Riley. It read:

> Through great interest of the Women's Organizations in Calgary and Provincial districts, I have been instructed to write to you asking recommendation of an Honorary Degree to one of our most outstanding women in voluntary service work, to the city of Calgary and the Province of Alberta.
>
> In the name of Mrs. Harold W. Riley (Maude), twenty-eight years President of the Alberta Child and Family Welfare Council.

There are no words to express what tremendous efforts this lady has performed in action and service to humanity without thought of reward. Mrs. Riley is advancing in years, so we, the women of the Council and other Societies with private citizens, feel that the time is at hand to ask for the honors that are duly hers.

Through the forty-five year of voluntary service and still in action with enormous experience, knowledge and wisdom yet to offer.

Enclosed you will find a copy, itemized briefly, of her life during the years we have known her, of which I anticipate will give you the foundations and beliefs she stands for.

Dr. McNally, I am rushing this letter to you, hoping we still have time to present this to the Faculty, through you. We trust that we are not too late for this term and I will forward petition names at an early date.

The 1920s

1912–25 Report by Mrs. Harold Riley, Convenor

In presenting my final report as Convenor of Laws for the Calgary Local Council of Women for the year ending January 29th, 1925, may I sketch briefly the petitions that have been asked for by this Council since it was first formed in 1912, and pressed for by your convenor and her committee during her term of office, ever since its first formation.

May I divide these petitions into three sections, specifying what progress has been made in each.

- CIVIC: That is, those presented to the Mayor, Commissioners, and members of the City Council; a total of 25.
- PROVINCIAL: Those presented to the Lieutenant-Governor-in-Council, first by your convenor direct, then

in 1916 through the Provincial Law Committee, and later, in 1919, through the Provincial Executive of the National Council of Women; a total of 38.

- FEDERAL: Those presented to the Governor-General-in-Council, through the National Council of Women; a total of 12; making an aggregate total of 73 petitions, which were as follows:

MUNICIPAL PETITIONS

(1)   No. 1 was in March, 1913, asking the Mayor, Commissioners, and members of the City Council, to make provision in a new City Charter for women to be eligible to sit on the School Board – Granted.

(2)   Police Matron – Granted.

(3)   Police women on the force; promised by chief but never given. Financial reasons given as the cause.

(4)   Nurses' Home – Separate building for nurses in the Calgary General Hospital – Granted.

(5)   Eight-hour day for nurses in the Calgary General Hospital – Granted.

(6)   That the registration be kept of all rooming houses willing to accommodate young boys and girls living in the city, and from time to time these places be properly inspected. Legislative committee of the city council thought it would be difficult to inspect rooms in private homes.

(7)   The municipality to provide every mother, if she so desires, with free hospital treatment at the birth of her child. Granted December, 1919, by Calgary, in semi-private wards. Last year restricted only to indigent mothers.

(8)   Chinese laundries shall not keep open to the public longer than other laundries. Granted under the Factory Act.

(9)   That we ask all employers for chamber and laundry work to furnish rubber gloves for the doing of this work. Partially granted by the Board of Health.

(10) Ringing of the curfew bell; passed by plebiscite. But Mayor Webster has declared same not feasible in the City of Calgary.

(11) That we petition the Mayor and Commissioners in the City Council of Calgary, at the approaching session of the Legislature, to have the city charter amended, so as to give them the power to pass a curfew by-law when and how they see fit, without the presentation of a petition. Signed by 25 per cent of the ratepayers voting at the last municipal election. – Granted.

(12) That a conference be arranged to ascertain if the early closing of drug stores was giving the best service to the sick of Calgary.

(13) That the Local Council urge upon the proper authorities the necessity for instruction in the rudiments of nursing in grade schools, to both boys and girls.

(14) That the Mayor and Commissioners have all cars belonging to the Health Department plainly marked as such, in accordance with city by-laws, and also that the health nurses wear some uniform which could be easily distinguished, and that such nurses entering houses where infectious diseases are, wear gowns for protection. Granted, all but the uniforms.

(15) That the Mayor, Commissioners, and members of the City Council pass a by-law compelling theatres and dance halls to employ a matron during all performances.

(16) That the City Council of Calgary operate the dance pavilions in parks, owned or controlled by the city. Granted and later cancelled for financial reasons by the Mayor and Commissioners.

(17) That the City Council pass a by-law whereby persons knowingly offering for sale animals or carcasses which are diseased and which have been killed, other than according to rules and regulations governing the slaughtering of ani-

mals for domestic purposes, be punished. Laws governing this be enforced by local inspector.

(18) That under the supervision of the Health Board, classes be instituted for the purpose of giving instruction in home nursing. Granted.

(19) That the Health Department take steps to formulate plans for the registration of classified helpers for homes in times of sickness, so that the general public requiring the services of a nurse can obtain the necessary assistance within their means. Partially granted.

(20) That all bread sold in the city should be properly wrapped before it left the bakeshop. Granted, but not strictly enforced.

(21) Seats be placed behind the counters in stores for the use of the clerks. Granted under the Factory Act.

(22) That the City Council of Calgary have the dance hall by-law amended so as to prevent the admittance of children under 18 years of age at a public dance. Granted by by-law.

(23) That infants in arms be not allowed at moving picture performances. City Council has no power to grant this request.

(24) That the City Council establish:

    (a) A Civic Clinic for children of pre-school age and babies;

    (b) A Civic Bureau for pre-natal and post-natal care.

These two resolutions came in from the Child Welfare Association in July, 1917, with the request for the Council's endorsation. This was readily given, and during the fall of 1922 the Local Council co-operated with the Child Welfare Association in pressing for this petition, with the result that we have the nucleus of a real city pre-school age clinic, but we must not forget that it is only in the making, and that eternal vigilance is the price of liberty.

On September 9th, 1922, it was unanimously passed at a general meeting of the Local Council of Women, that the Civic

Clinic for pre-school age and babies should include the following services:

- A provincial nurse and two civic nurses;
- A part-time specialist in children's diseases;
- A part-time eyes, ear, nose and throat specialist;
- A part-time dentist;
- A half-time orthopedic nurse and a part-time orthopedic doctor.

Granted by the Mayor, Commissioners and members of the City Council on October 2nd , 1922.

(25)   That the City Council prohibit the employment of white girls in Chinese laundries, restaurants. Your convenor took this matter up with Mayor Webster. Alberta has Act covering girls and women employed in restaurants and laundries, consequently there is no means of keeping track of such employees. Chief Ritchie estimates that there are approximately 20 to 25.

PROVINCIAL PETITIONS

(1)   The first petition to be presented was praying the Lieutenant-Governor-in-Council to establish an industrial school for delinquent girls.

(2)   An industrial school for delinquent boys.

The government has been unable to grant these requests on account of lack of finances, but they will be asked for every year until granted.

(3)   A detention home for women of confirmed evil habits. Still being asked for.

(4)   Care of destitute old people. Covered by Provincial statute.

(5)   Care of mental defectives. There is a home at present at Red Deer, but it is totally inadequate to accommodate all that need it.

(6) Franchise for women presented in 1915 and again in 1916, along with representatives of other organizations. Granted on the same basis as to men. Alberta the first province to promise the franchise to women.

(7) Amendment to the Marriage Law, asking that issuance of marriage licenses shall be by the Clerks of the Supreme and District Courts of the various Judicial Courts of Alberta. Not granted.

(8) Amendment to the Married Women's Home Protection Act, so that it would not be necessary for a married woman to file a caveat to prevent her home being sold, but to require that the married woman's consent must be given in writing before said property can be sold, transferred or mortgaged. This petition was granted later, and became known as The Dower Act.

(9) Equal Parental Control. Granted.

(10) Re. compulsory reporting of gonorrhea and syphillis as ordinary contagious diseases. Partially granted.

(11) Re. suppression of red-light district. Granted; up to public opinion and police to enforce the law.

(12) Re. inflammation of the eyes of the new-born, namely, compulsory treatment to prevent blindness. Granted.

(13) Mother's pensions asked for pensions to all needy mothers. Granted to widowed mothers and mothers whose husbands are in the insane asylums. Provincial executive still asking for pensions to deserted mothers, and also those mothers whose husbands are incapacitated by tuberculosis, etc.

(14) Partnership rights of a wife in her husband's estate. Still under discussion. Women, as yet, have not been able to agree on a definite concrete law. She has, at the present time, the protection given by

    (a) The Married Women's Relief Act;

    (b) The Devolution of Estates Act.

(15) The reading of a portion of the authorized version of the Bible and one prayer be given daily in the public and high schools of Alberta without comment.

(16) That the laws re. the duty of parent to child, and the penalties imposed, if neglected, be published in pamphlet form or in some other satisfactory way, and be distributed throughout the province as widely as possible by the proper authorities. Granted; law enforced by the Department of Neglected Children.

(17) That all marriage licenses be dispensed at the Court House only to responsible parties, and each day the names be published in the daily papers. Granted all but the publishing of the names.

(18) That when the fatherhood of a child born out of wedlock is proved, the father be made to support the child. Granted.

(19) That we petition the Legislature to establish a sanatorium for nervous diseases, and those temporarily deranged. Not granted on account of finances.

(20) To supply intensive training, which can easily be commercialized, in the proposed Institute of Technology for girls leaving school at the age of fifteen years and upwards, in the following: Millinery, dressmaking, tailoring, house assistants, laundry work, etc. Those successfully taking the diplomas by the Provincial Government entitling them to take course and passing the prescribed examination to be granted positions as skilled work women in the branch for which the diploma is given. Agreed to by the Minister of Education.

(21) Home for Incurables. Partially granted by the hospital at Macleod.

(22) Government care of indigent poor. Each municipality compelled to provide for its own poor.

(23) Custodial care of the mentally defective.

(24) That scientific truths about drugs and narcotics be taught in the public and high schools beginning in Grade III. Government not in favor of adding to the curriculum.

(25) That women be appointed on all boards and commissions where all women and children are concerned. Granted.

(26) That all divorces granted in Alberta be registered the same as births, marriages and deaths. Granted.

(27) Amendment to the Dower Act to include (a) the furniture. As it is now the man cannot will away his home, but he can will away his furniture. (b) The protection of the widow from her husband's heirs in the same way as a man is protected from his creditors. Granted.

(28) Court of Domestic Relations. Provincial Executive is still pressing for this petition.

(29) Re. Rural Nursing. Resolved that the Provincial Executive of the National Council of Women recommend to the Provincial Government the formation of an order of Nursing Housekeepers, the course to consist of five months in one of the agricultural schools of the province, embracing dietetics, household administration, elementary cooking, and four months' training in one of the municipal hospitals. These Nursing Housekeepers shall be for three months engaged in district nursing, in order that their efficiency in nursing be observed. These nurses shall not be allowed to work in the city until they have served three years in the rural districts. Steps being taken to grant this request.

Taken under consideration by the government, which is investigating with what progress and success similar legislation has met with in Saskatchewan.

(30) That the Provincial Government make it an offense to register, with his female companion, as man and wife, when they are not married. This was passed by the House of

Commons and thrown out by the Senate. The National Council will again press for it through the federal house. A provincial act along this line would be ultra vires.

(31) That whereas a wife's interest in the deceased husband's estate is protected by Dower and Married Woman's Relief Act, and whereas all legal responsibilities of parents for the maintenance of their minor children ceases upon the death of the parent; resolved, that the Provincial Government be asked to secure for minor children an interest in their deceased parent's estates for their maintenance until the age of sixteen years. Under consideration by the government.

(32) The Lord's Prayer. The school ordinance provides for the reading of the Lord's Prayer, and the councils and affiliated organizations are asked to see to it that this provision of the school ordinance is carried out and that the Lord's Prayer is repeated every day in each school in the province.

(33) Standardized Hospitals. The idea was not to enlarge the scope of the hospital or to make any added expense, but to work for greater efficiency; for example, in a city like Calgary, a competent pathologist, duly qualified, should be on the job all the year round. Great strides have been recently made by the government in standardizing hospitals along these lines.

(34) That we petition the Lieutenant-Governor-in-Council to have the schedule of doctors' fees issued by the Provincial Minister of Health, just as the schedule of lawyers' fees is issued by the Attorney-General in his Rules of Court. Granted, and the same has been published in pamphlet form for distribution.

(35) Strict enforcement of this law against traffic in drugs, especially with regard to young people. Again being pressed.

(36) Re. censorship of moving pictures, asking for the following amendment:

The said board shall not approve of any film or slide depicting scenes of an immoral or obscene nature, or which indicate or suggest lewdness or indecency or marital infidelity, or showing the details of murder, robbery, or criminal assault, or depicting criminals as heroic characters, and the board shall refuse to approve any other picture which said board may consider injurious to public morals, suggestive of evil to the minds of children or against the public welfare.

In the hands of the Provincial Executive to again present to government.

(37) That we petition the executive of the National Council to petition the Lieutenant-Governor-in-Council to appoint, throughout the country, honorary members, especially women, on the censor board as a vigilant committee, such members to have the right of entering any theatre, moving picture or otherwise, at all times, and report any thing which they deem objectionable to the board of provincial censors.

The reason your convener had for introducing this motion into the Calgary Local Council was that while it was true there were two women on the provincial board of censors, yet these women were stationed at Edmonton, and while the films were censored before they were released, yet the billboards, vaudeville, etc., were not, and the idea was to make safe for the boy and girl ALL theatres and even concerts throughout the province; hence the need of these honorary members as a vigilant committee. This petition was unanimously endorsed by the Provincial Executive, and will be presented by them when the delegation meets the government on February 4th.

(38) In this connection it was also decided by the Provincial Executive to ask the Lieutenant-Governor-in-

Council to [extend] the provincial censor board power over billboards and vaudeville.

Petitions 37 and 38 are still being considered by the government.

FEDERAL PETITIONS

(1)   It is significant that the first petition to the Governor-General-in-Council was that praying that the sentence of Mrs. Jennie Hawks, who was sentenced to be hanged for the murder of her husband under great provocation, be commuted. This was taken up direct with the Minister of Justice, your convener, and granted.

The remaining petitions have been sent to the National Council of Women to deal with.

(2)   That a woman or girl connected with a house of ill-fame, who has paid the penalty or fine impose by the courts, be given this protection – that any man knowing the life these women have lived, and approaching them after they have served their sentence, be given a term in jail, or fined, as the court sees fit.
(3)   That we ask the Dominion Government to force all railways in the Dominion to furnish a properly equipped coach for the comfort of mothers traveling with infants in arms or young children, and in view of the fact that accommodation is provided for men wishing to smoke, that if sacrifice has to be made, that the man and not the mothers and children, make the sacrifice. That on through trains a matron be employed for the care and protection of young women and children.
(5)   That the exhibition of deformed and freak children be prohibited.

(6) That we most earnestly petition the National Council of Women to take steps to prevent the exhibition of trained animals in any theatre or place of public amusement owing to the cruelty necessary in training.

(7) That divorce in Alberta be granted to a wife for the same cause as is now granted to the husband. Granted.

(8) That family desertion be made an extraditable offence. Granted.

(9) That we urge upon the proper authorities the question of heavier punishments being meted out to

    (a) Men who criminally assault or entice little girls under the age of consent;

    (b) Fathers who are so inhuman as to commit indecent attacks on their own young daughters;

    (c) Men who have been proven guilty of immoral practices on young boys;

    (d) In the opinion of this Council, nothing short of surgical treatment for such proven moral perverts;

    (e) If such punishment is not allowed by law, we, therefore, request the National Council of Women to petition the federal government to have the same enacted. These have been referred by the National Council of Women to Dr. Ritchie England for action.

(Source: 1925–26 L.C.W. Year Book, p. 64–71)

The 1930s

Mrs. Harold W. Riley, Convenor

I beg to present the report of the Committee on Laws for the year ending January 30th, 1933.

First with regard to municipal petitions: The Council has considered the petition "that where the property is in the husband's or wife's name then the wife or husband should automatically be placed upon the voters' list to vote on money by-laws."

Considerable discussion pro and con has taken place in the Council on this subject but the same will be dealt with by your committee at the next regular meeting of the newly appointed executive.

Now with regard to Provincial petitions: A delegation waited on the Provincial Executive of the National Council of Women in the Executive Council room of the Parliament Buildings, Edmonton, on Friday, January 27th, at 3 p.m. The members of the cabinet were all present except the Hon. Irene Parlby, and the Hon. George Hoadley who was ill in the east. The delegation from the Provincial Executive included representatives from the Calgary, Edmonton, and Medicine Hat Local Councils, the Provincial I.O.D.E., and the Provincial W.C.T.U. Mrs. Harold Riley, the Provincial President, presented the petitions and was assisted by representatives of each of the affiliated organizations. The petitions were as follows:

(1)   To designate the space in the Parliament buildings that will be given to the Memorial to the late Mrs. O.C. Edwards that the Government has given permission to the women of Alberta to place there.

The Premier stated that whatever space the women chose as the most desirable for the placing of the memorial to the Late Mrs. O.C. Edwards, the same would be agreeable to the Government.

(2)   That annual medical examination of all school children in Alberta be made compulsory.

Replying to the Premier's letter of January 25 of last year in which ways and means were spoken of in connection with the annual medical inspection of school children, we respectfully suggested for the consideration of the Government the feasibility of having the outlying areas mapped out into districts and that graduate medical students do field work from May 15th to June 30th, each graduate to have a sixth year medical student as his assistant. In this way medical supervision of all school children and pre-school children could be accomplished with little costs to Districts and Government.

The Premier replied that this request involved the University authorities also. We pointed out that graduates in Home Economics had to do post graduate work in hospitals; graduates in Law had to be articled for one year, so why not the medical graduates do field work for six weeks? The Premier promised that the Government would give our request careful consideration but advised us that the Government was economizing in every way possible.

(3)   That in the opening exercises of the Public and High Schools it should be made compulsory as part of these exercises to make a public recognition of God.

Both the Minister of Education and the Premier said that at the present time our request was optional with the School Boards, and they did not see any way of granting our request at present.

(4)   That there is need for provincial regulations as to the administration of punishment in the Schools, the kind of punishment and by whom administered.

It was pointed out that while the Provincial Executive was anxious to have discipline in the schools, yet it was felt that sarcasm and nagging were very detrimental to children, especially the sensitive ones.

The Minister of Education said if the Provincial Executive would write an article embodying our ideas that he would be pleased to send a copy of it to all the schools in the Province.

(5)   That there should be some recognition by Statute of the Wife's labor in the home. Why have the recommendations of the Advisory Committee on Community Property Rights, appointed by the Government in 1925, that reported on this subject not been put into effect by the Government?

Mrs. Riley drew the Premier's attention to clause (g) of this committee's report. It read:

That the Alberta Dower Act be amended along the lines of the Manitoba Dower Act so as to insure to the wife one half of the surplus over after a forced sale of the 'homestead' under mortgage, and so as to include in the definition of the word homestead under the act, in a city, town, or village six lots or one acre where no registered plan exists, and outside of a city, town or village 320 acres.

The Premier said he would check up on this recommendation from the Advisory Committee, and advise us further of the Government's decision.

(6)   That there should be provision for the legitimate child in the Father's Estate outside of the Intestacy Act.

The President pointed out to the Premier how dear this petition was to the heart of the Late Mrs. O.C. Edwards, and pointed out that a wife and mother might have no cognizance of any illegitimate children yet if he died with a judgment against him for the maintenance of these children, then this judgment became first claim on the estate regardless of the amount of the estate, or the claims of his lawful wife and children. Moreover, after satisfying the law as to the amount a man should leave his wife it was pointed out that a man was not compelled to leave anything to his children, and could will the remainder of his estate to anyone whomever he chose.

While recognizing that injustices might occur, the Premier said that he believed most men made their wives the executor of their estate, and he felt to grant our request that an injustice might be done to wives, except in big estates.

(7) That the age of Juveniles as to boys be raised to eighteen years as at present for girls.

The Attorney-General spoke of the parole system that was in force in the Province, and said if the age were raised to eighteen years for boys it would necessitate spending considerable money on an industrial school and the Government while recognizing the desirability of the request was unable to grant it at present due to lack of finances.

(8) That reckless drivers not holding Liability Insurance or having other assets, in case of an accident, be prohibited from driving until they have made restitution; and that Taxi Companies be compelled to carry Liability Insurance.

The Government is drafting a bill along these lines for presentation at this session of the Legislature. So this petition will be fully granted.

(9) That the Flag be shown and the National anthem played at all Picture Houses throughout the Province.

This petition came from the I.O.D.E., and was presented last year. The Premier was in sympathy with the request, and said he had given instructions to the Chief Censor to get in touch with the various moving picture operators to the end that this request would be complied with as fully as possible. He promised a fuller report on this matter.

(10) That the application for marriage be accompanied by a medical certificate or certificates certifying that both contracting parties are free from venereal disease.

The Premier said that this test might prove embarrassing for those who wished to get married. However the delegation pointed out that those who applied for life insurance had to submit to it and no objection was raised. The Government promised to look into the matter and see what could be done to grant our request.

(11) That bicycles be required to have larger license plates and numbers that can be easily read, if such is feasible.

The Government pointed out that this is purely a matter for the city.

(12)   While appreciating economic conditions, we believe that in the interests of women, capable women should be appointed to fill the vacant office of Woman Police Magistrate in Calgary and in Edmonton.

The Premier stated that this was purely a case of finances and as soon as finances permitted the Government would appoint Women Police Magistrates again. The Attorney-General stated that Mrs. Murphy was still a police magistrate and while not on full time duty, she was called when needed and paid accordingly.

(13)   That our school textbooks contain more information regarding Narcotics.

This resolution came from the annual meeting of the Provincial W.C.T.U. The Minister promised that this would be done when a new text book on Hygiene was gotten out.

(14)   As many instances have been brought to our attention of women who, not understanding their rights in the "Dower Act," have been influenced to sign away their dower rights, and depriving in consequence not only themselves but their family of a home, have become a charge on the community in which they live – we therefore petition the Government to see if legislation cannot be devised that will further prevent and protect wives from signing away their Dower Rights without getting adequate compensation for the same.

The President pointed out that if the Government put into force the recommendation of the Advisory Committee on Community Property Rights as spoken of in Petition 5, then it would cover this petition also.

(15)   That a greater measure of protection be given to those whose furniture is liable to seizure for non-payment of rent, in order that housekeeping may be carried on.

The Government will consider this request and report on same.

(16)   That the Government accede to the request of the Provincial W.C.T.U. re the prohibiting in Alberta of liquor advertising both direct and indirect.

This resolution came also from the Provincial W.C.T.U.

The Government said that if they were going to deal at this session with the petitions re the sale of beer, etc., then no action would be taken on this request, but if it did not deal with these petitions, then it would deal with this request. In the meantime the Premier promised consideration.

(17)   That the Government state its reasons for amending clause 6 of the Child Welfare Act, with regard to the ages at which boys may be licensed to peddle or sell papers.

The Attorney-General, Mr. Lymburn, stated that the Act as amended prohibited any female from peddling or selling papers, and also any boy under the age of 12 from so doing, and compelled boys between the ages of 12 and 14 to have a written consent of their parents.

(18)   That the Provincial Department of Health establish Clinics and other methods for the dissemination of scientific and reliable information on Family Limitation.

The President pointed out that in asking for this request the Provincial Executive did not wish to interfere with or dictate to anyone. They were asking that the Clinics and information be for married people only and that to every one their watchword was "Let your conscience be your guide"

The Premier stated that at the last conference between the Provinces and the Federal Government, the question had been discussed. There was the question of the Criminal Code to be considered, but it was felt that these clinics would be in the interests of the common good and therefore would not contravene the Criminal Code. In conclusion the Premier stated the Alberta Government was sympathetic,

232 / THE DO-GOODERS

and some action would be taken within the year to grant this request.

And so the conference ended: The Provincial Executive felt that it had been a very successful one, and it would not be fair to close this report without an appreciation for the patient, kindly, and sympathetic hearing, that was given the various petitions by the Premier and Cabinet. We may not get all we ask for, but we always do get something. True progress is often slow – but never forget that delegations are worthwhile, for "Eternal Vigilance is the price of Liberty." (Source: 1933 L.C.W. Souvenir Year Book, p. 20–23)

The 1940s

Mrs. Ruth Gorman, Convenor

My work this year consisted largely in submitting a brief to the Royal Commission appointed to investigate Welfare. This brief was as follows. [Editor: The remainder of this report is a quote of the brief.]

MAY IT PLEASE THE COMMISSION:
The Local Council of Women of Calgary, Alberta, wish to present the following brief to the judicial commission investigating welfare conditions in Alberta.

The Local Council of Women of Calgary is not a welfare or a charitable organization. The Council is composed of elected representatives from nearly twenty different women's clubs of Calgary. These clubs, which elect representatives to the Council, consist of various women's political clubs, of women's clubs from many different religious denominations, and of clubs which are of a welfare and charitable nature. Besides these groups, we have represented on the Council, clubs which have a special or common purpose, such as the Business and

Professional Womens Club, the Home Economics Club, the Old Age Pensioners Society, the Y.W.C.A., the Canadian Ukrainian Society, and the University Women's Club. These clubs are united in the Council for the purpose of improving the condition and lives of all the women in Calgary and Alberta. Naturally, welfare conditions are of primary interest to all women. The Local Council of Women of Calgary feel that although they have affiliated societies who do welfare and charity work in the council, that the council itself is not a welfare or charitable organization. Because of this fact, the council has neither the experience or the knowledge which would allow it to criticize welfare administration in this province, and we are in no way attempting to criticize the administration.

However, for some time the Council have been dissatisfied with the procedure by which an adoption is granted in Alberta. The procedure by which an adoption is granted in Alberta is governed by section 87 (1) and 87 (a) of the Child Welfare Act. Adoption is a matter which concerns not only those occupied in welfare work, but touches upon the legal rights of all individuals. Because it touches the legal rights of all individuals, and especially those of women and children, the Council feels it should present this brief to this Judicial Commission.

Now we are quite aware that we are asking for a change to be made in legislation regarding welfare rather than criticizing or asking for a change in the administration of welfare. We have listed our objections to the procedure by which an adoption in Alberta is granted, but before we present our objections to the Welfare Act as it now stands, and the amendments we would like the Legislature to make to the Welfare Act, I would like to point out to the Judicial Commission why they should hear and consider the matter.

This Judicial Commission was appointed under the Public Enquiries Act, Chapter 139 Revised Statutes of Alberta 1942. By that act any judicial commission which is properly appointed may (quote) "Enquire into and concerning any matter within the jurisdiction of the Legislative Assembly." An amendment to the Welfare Act would most certainly come within the meaning of that section. By the appointment of the Judicial Commission which was announced in the Alberta Gazette, the Commission was appointed to investigate specific speeches, articles, etc. which were made in Alberta concerning welfare, and by section 2 could, and I quote "investigate any other specific charge which may be disclosed or submitted to the Commission relating to the Child Welfare Branch of the Department of Public Welfare, which in the opinion of the Commission properly comes within the scope of the Commission's investigation." So it would seem that this Commission can, at its discretion, consider a brief which criticizes the present laws governing welfare in this province, and especially when it concerns the actions of the Welfare Commission in the matter of adoptions.

It is very important that the Commission use its discretionary powers, and consider our brief. We are not asking the Judicial Commission to alter the Law. We realize that that is quite beyond their power. We are only asking them, respectfully to choose to hear our charge that the law regarding adoptions is an unjust law. If after hearing our brief the Commission feels it has any merit, we are asking them to recommend to the Legislature that the law be changed in that matter. We only too well realize that no recommendation is going to change the law. That requires an act of the Legislature itself, but there have been many changes made in law in Canada because of the recommendation of various judicial commissions.

It is important this judicial commission consider recommendations regarding the laws governing welfare, because the laws which govern the administration of welfare are the foundation on which good welfare administration is built. If the laws are not good, the administration can never be good. Constantly groups will be dissatisfied with it and criticizing it.

Now, if the Commission will choose to hear our criticisms of the Welfare Act, they are as follows:

Under the Welfare Act, Section 87 (1) of the Child Welfare Act, Chapter 8, 1944 Statutes of Alberta, an adoption was granted in the following manner. The prospective parent filed a petition with the Clerk of the Court saying he wished to adopt a child. Notice of this petition was given to the Welfare Commission. The prospective parents and the Welfare Commission then appeared before a judge of the district court in chambers. The judge ascertained if the prospective parents were fit and worthy parents for a child and listened to what the Welfare Commission had to say regarding its investigation of the prospective parents and child. After having heard both sides the judge then gave his decision. I may further add that as the act then stood, no order for adoption could be given by a judge unless the Welfare Board was either present or signified their approval by not contesting the adoption. Plenty of time was given to the Welfare Commission to investigate the adoption. In other words, as the law previously stood, the procedure for adoption was that of an ordinary trial, with both parties appearing, the judge hearing all the evidence, and making a decision.

Last year parliament amended the Child Welfare Act, and this procedure of granting adoptions was done away with and a new procedure under an amended 87 (1) and 87 (1) (a) became law.

These sections read:

Any adult person being the full age of twenty-one years, wishing to adopt an unmarried minor as his child, may apply to the Commission, which shall submit his petition for an Order of adoption to a Judge within sixty days of the receipt thereof, and no Order of adoption shall be made unless the petition is presented to the Judge by the Commission.

The applicant for adoption shall be entitled to be heard either personally or by counsel on an application to the Judge.

At the time this Act was passed, the Calgary Local Council and the Alberta Bar Association protested vigorously against this passage, and some efforts were made by the government to modify the act from its original proposal as a bill. We appreciate the efforts of Mr. Manning and his government to co-operate with us, but we are not satisfied with the act in its present form, and our reasons are four in number.

1. It is wrong in principle because it bars the individual from a direct use of the courts. The act does guarantee him the right to use the court through another person, namely the Welfare Commission, but that is wrong in principle and being wrong in principle, it could be wrong in practice. We will presume a case where the Commission, either through error or omission should fail to file the petition within the sixty days period. What right then has the parent who wishes to adopt a child? If the prospective parent is aware of his legal rights he could bring a court action to make the Commission bring his adoption petition before the court. This would require time and effort on the part of the prospective parent, who, through no error of his own, finds his application for adoption not before the court. We must remember this person who may have this extra burden placed upon him is the prospective parent who is volunteering to adopt a child, and thus relieve the government of quite a financial responsibility. This is what might happen to a person who is aware of his rights and willing to fight for them when the Commission, through either error or omission, fails to file a petition.

Now let us consider the case of a prospective parent who, through ignorance, considers the whole matter settled when the Commission gave its decision, and who is not aware of his legal right to make the Commission bring his petition into court within sixty days. Such a prospective parent might think that the Commission's decision is final and go no further with his adoption. There is nothing in the Act which requires the Commission to tell the prospective parent that its decision is not final and that he will have a hearing in court. I know it is a necessary presumption that we are all presumed to know the law, but the nature of the act makes it almost a family and personal matter, rather than a legal matter, and being such, it is inclined to throw the parents off their guard regarding their legal rights. Also the fact that the individual cannot himself apply to the courts, but first must apply to the Commission, will tend to cause the parent to be lax into looking into the law concerning this matter.

Now I am not saying such things do take place, but as the Act now reads, such things could take place.

2. The Welfare Commission, by the Act, is given the first decision to make in the matter of granting an adoption. This Commission may, by its unfavorable attitude and decision, discourage a timid individual, who would feel that since the Commission had turned down his application, he had no chance of succeeding, and he might go no further. There is nothing in the Act requiring the Commission to record its reasons for turning down an application, and it would not be recorded until it got into court, which, if the prospective parent were discouraged, might be never. Furthermore, there is nothing in the Act requiring the Welfare Commission to have either special welfare training or judicial training to equip them to make such decisions. They are merely appointed by the political party in power. There is nothing to require any records of the Commission's first decision and report and they could, if they so desired, turn down an application because of political prejudice, and no one would be the wiser. I am not saying they would ever do this, but I am saying that such things could be possible under the Act as it now stands.

3. The Act does not say that no adoption shall be granted unless the prospective parent appears before a judge. I feel an adoption is certainly where both the Welfare Board and the prospective parent should have to appear before the judge before any adoption is granted. Previously the prospective parent made the application, and so appeared, and as the Act previously stood, no adoption could be granted unless the Welfare Commission were represented. The Act now says (quote) "The applicant for adoption shall be entitled to be heard either personally or by counsel on application of the judge." I understand that the present procedure is that when the petition is filed with the judge by the Welfare Commission the judge notifies the prospective foster parent to that effect. I am very glad that this is done, but we feel the order to appear should be stated in the Act, not done because of the judicial fairness of a judge.

4. Let us assume parent "A" wishes to adopt a child "B," and presents himself before the Child Welfare Commission for that purpose. Now if 10 days later parent "C" , who also wishes to adopt child "B," appears before the Welfare Commission for that purpose, it would be possible, as the laws presently stand, for the Child Welfare to launch parent "C's" application for adoption to the courts before parent "A's," and thus defeat parent "A's" application. Thus the Child Welfare Commission are in a position to decide whose application shall be heard, and even granted. Heretofore, parent "A" could launch his own application for child "B" and it would be dealt with and disposed of first. As the law now stands, "A's" application would be useless regarding child "B," who he might have a very special reason for wanting, and no remedy at all is left to him. The net result is the Child Welfare Commission has decided who will adopt child "B," and this is a judicial function.

These are four reasons for objecting to the Act as it now stands. This amendment is very recent, and I imagine few hardships have, as yet, resulted from it. The cases I suggest are all purely imaginary, but are also all possible in fact under the present amendment.

We hope the Commission will examine the objection contained herein and consider the damage which they may do to future welfare administration if this amended Act is left on the Stature Book.

The Local Council feel that the Act should never have been amended, and that there was nothing wrong with the procedure in adoptions in the Act as it stood in 1944.

Adoption is a very important phase of child welfare work, and it is submitted that the courts and their personnel are trained and equipped to make the important decisions pertaining to an adoption. Not only are the judges trained and equipped, but the judges hold their position for life, and under no circumstance could political pressure be brought to bear on them. Judges are the proper authorities to hear the first evidence and all the evidence in granting an adoption.

Individual access to the courts is one of the most cherished rights of British law, and it is submitted that Section 87 (1) and 87 (1a) of the Child Welfare Act, as it now stands, is an infringement on this right.

The Council respectfully asks this Commission to recommend that in the interest of welfare in this province that the amendment to Section 87 (1) and 87 (1a) be withdrawn and that Section 87 (1) of the Child Welfare Act 1944 be returned. (Source: 1949 L.C.W. Year Book, p. 31, 33, 35, 37, 39)

The 1950s

Mrs. J.C. (Ruth) Gorman, Convenor

One of the functions of a Local Council of Women is to assure that women in our community have adequate rights and protection under our system of law. There is a greater need today than there was in the past for an active women's council. In the past the responsibility for good government rested on the men's shoulders. Today it rests squarely on ours.

Very few women can make a study of conditions in their community; very few can present to their electors a list of their needs. Yet that is their responsibility. Through the Council we attempt to meet this responsibility. We do this by investigating problems and injustices in the community presented by our affiliated societies, then passing resolutions. These resolutions are presented to our 26 women's societies in Calgary, and then to our over 60 societies in Alberta, and finally to thousands of women across Canada. With these endorsations we give it to our lawmakers. It is reassuring how often the Legislature welcomes these suggestions and acts on them.

As your Convenor of Laws it is my duty to advise and present these suggested reforms. This year there are five.

RESOLUTION 1

Effect of the Agricultural Stability regulation of March 1958 was to raise the floor price of butter 6 cents a pound, with the result there was a higher price to the consumer, and the purchase of margarine increased one million pounds per month.

WHEREAS the preference of Canadian consumers has been established on the basis of price and taste, and

WHEREAS the discriminatory ban on colored margarine no longer serves its purpose as a protective measure for a Canadian industry,

BE IT RESOLVED that the color ban be lifted.

RESOLUTION 2

WHEREAS Calgary's Council of Women do earnestly desire the native Indian to enjoy and exercise his franchise; and

WHEREAS there are on the law books of this country laws that enable him to vote, but certain restrictive clauses in the law place the Indian in danger of being removed from his home on the Reserve if he exercises his franchise:

BE IT RESOLVED that these restrictive clauses be removed from the Indian Act so that he may vote without fear of forced removal from the Reserve.

RESOLUTION 3

WHEREAS there is an increased demand for employment among women of the over-40 age group; and

WHEREAS, due to the "marriage gap" many women lack needed skills to fill available jobs; and

WHEREAS active and mature women can make a contribution to such professions as teaching, social service, librarians, etc., in which there is an acute shortage:

BE IT RESOLVED that a special training and education program especially designed for older workers be set up by the Departments of Education and Labor.

RESOLUTION 4

WHEREAS it is brought to the attention of the Calgary Council of Women that little effort is being made to rehabilitate women prisoners in Fort Saskatchewan jail; and

WHEREAS it would be to the moral and financial benefit of all citizens for women prisoners to re-fit themselves for community living:

BE IT RESOLVED that the governments provide a compulsory training and vocational program for women prisoners, with segregation and special treatment for alcoholics and morally unfit.

RESOLUTION 5

RESOLVED that the Federal Government reconsider amending the Canadian Estates Tax Act to exempt from death duties property, real or personal, that was acquired, such as jointly-owned property occupied by the couple at the time of the husband's death, and pensions based on employment and made payable to the widow. These should be exempt in recognition of the wife's past unpaid contribution in acquiring family assets.

I suggest that, in the coming year, all resolutions be completed and handed to affiliate societies by January; and that between then and March when they must be voted on, affiliates can request that a knowledgeable speaker be provided to explain the subject matter to their members. In this way, endorsation of resolutions by affiliate societies would be based on complete understanding of the problem. (Source: 1959 L.C.W. Year Book, p. 29, 31)

The 1960s

Mrs. E.R. Bolton – Resolutions Chairman

Although there has been, during the year, a lively interest and discussion of a number of possible subjects for resolution, only four Resolutions have, in fact, emanated from Calgary Local Council of Women this year, as follows:

(1)   A request for amendment of the Income Tax Act to allow the deduction as personal expenses of a working mother the cost of baby-sitters or other household help made necessary by her absence at work. This Resolution, passed at our 1967 Annual Meeting, has been approved by the Alberta Provincial Council, and is very similar to another also approved by Provincial Council, both having now

gone forward to National Council of Women for adoption and action.

(2)   A request that increased accommodation to be made available to technical school students in Southern Alberta, to avoid the incidence of forced school drop-outs. This Resolution, passed as an Emergency at our 1967 Annual Meeting, was presented to Alberta Provincial Council, but has been returned to us for further study, particularly for more detailed background material.

(3)   A request that the City enact a by-law making it mandatory that apartment projects provide not only adequate parking for tenants but also proportionate areas for lawns and planting. This Resolution was passed in principle at our Annual Meeting in 1967, but tabled for further study as to the wording. Formal wording has not yet been agreed upon, however with permission of the Executive some effective action has been taken on the basis of this Resolution. In the meantime it is still under study, and consideration is now being given to include another factor in it. It is possible a new Resolution will be presented to the Annual Meeting.

(4)   A request for the establishment of Forensic Clinics in Alberta. This Resolution was approved at the October Executive meeting, and immediately circulated by mail to all affiliates. It has now been presented to and adopted by Alberta Provincial Council who will be taking it before the appropriate Cabinet Minister.

During this year, also, seven Resolutions from National Council of Women were circulated and studied, as well as two Resolutions from Provincial Council.

The following are some of the subjects which have been under discussion during the year, and are still under study which may culminate in the proposal of a Resolution at a future date:

(a)   The need for more Day Care Centres in Calgary. It is
to be noted that in November, 1967, at a meeting of Alberta
Provincial Council, an Emergency Resolution regarding
Day Care Centres was adopted, and in view of this it may
well be that there is now no need for a further resolution on
this subject.
(b)   Land use in Calgary, particularly the preservation of
park areas near water; also the question of land fill versus a
proper fertilizer plant.
(c)   The training of personnel to use the breathalyzer at
Calgary.
(d)   The suggestion that seats on the School Board be
increased to nine.
(e)   A study as to the effect of the present law as to Old
Age Security Pension and Old Age income tax exemption,
and the question of whether Canadian citizenship should be
a requirement.

I believe that in the making of Resolutions and putting them
forward for action lies the great power and the main reason for
existence of our Local Council of Women. In the hope of
increasing and making even more effective the very considerable strength of a Local Council in this respect, I have two suggestions to make:

I would strongly urge that the "emergency" procedure be
used ONLY when there is really an emergency. Mrs. Van
Ginkel, National Chairman of Resolutions, says: "The emergency resolution is not the best means of formulating N.C.W.
(or L.C.W.) policy, because there is insufficient time for study
of the background material and for formulation of a well-
informed opinion. It is important that we are able to act via the
"emergency resolution" in order to take care of rapidly changing events. But some of the resolutions presented as emergencies could have been foreseen." In other words, there are very
few real emergencies, and in most cases there is ample time to

collect material, and to analyze and define the issue specifically and to present a well-informed opinion.

May I say, as a newcomer to Local Council, how very impressed I am by the sincerity and enthusiasm of its members, and its intelligent approach towards the changes, corrections and general social improvements it advocates. It is certainly a very important and effective group of women whose work should go far towards making this community a better place to work and live in. I hope that 1968 and all the years to follow will bring to its members much satisfaction in meaningful work. (Source: 1968–69 L.C.W. Hand Book, p. 16–17)

The 1970s

Acting Chairman Anne Van Heteren

Due to an increased civic and business workload, Mary Ellen Johnson was forced to resign the Chairmanship of the Resolutions Committee, but remained on the Committee as member and legal advisor. Another committee member, Anne Van Heteren, became acting Chairman.

The two much discussed Resolutions of the past year dealt with topics that were foremost in the public mind and were examined on the Federal, Provincial as well as Civic level.

(1)   Day Care. In its insistence on QUALITY Day Care, LC.W. voted a token financial contribution to the pilot Bowness-Montgomery Day Care Centre. A brief was sent to the "Day Care Study" of the City of Calgary.

(2)   Education. A request was sent – via the "Moir Commission" – to the Provincial government to request the Federal government to revoke Bill 41, which provides for a 2 year teaching period, income tax free, for teachers from other countries.

The Resolutions brought before the 1971 Annual Meeting are mainly dealing with "environment" issues:

(3)   Federal Government. A request that L.C.W. goes on public record as fully supporting the 1968 legislation that bans supersonic flights over Canadian territories, thus rules out regular commercial SST flights.

(4)   Federal Government. A request that L.C.W. send its written support to the Federal Government in its quest to protect the West Coast and coastal waters from pollution, which is inevitable if an oil tanker route is opened in this area.

(5)   Calgary City Council. A request that that the Calgary City Council and Calgary Regional Planning Council seriously consider the construction of bicycle lanes, for commuting as well as for pleasure; reasoning that not only is the use of the bicycle a healthy exercise, it would also prevent much pollution and should therefore be encouraged.

(6)   Calgary City Council. A request that L.C.W. take whatever action needed to preserve the natural green belt around Calgary. Furthermore, that L.C.W. support the Calgary Planning Department in its attempts to prevent fragmentation of the green belt, pending the completion of the Comprehensive Study by the City of future City needs.

(7)   Calgary City Council. A request that L.C.W. request Calgary City Council to withhold decision on the use of the James Short School site, pending an investigation into the feasibility of developing a park on this site, or a park combining with a Civic Cultural Centre.

(8)   Calgary City Council. A request that L.C.W. support efforts to obtain the original site of Fort Calgary for the city's centennial's celebrations in 1975, reasoning that the preservation of the historical heritage of Calgary for future generations is more important than presently planned commercial development.

(9)   Provincial Government. A most important request on behalf of the working women of Alberta (and those who

intend to work) to the Provincial Government of Alberta, regarding revision of the Alberta Labor Act, 1955, amended to 1968.

The requested revisions are mainly based on "Bill 83" of the Ontario Legislature, 1970: "WOMEN'S EQUAL EMPLOYMENT OPPORTUNITY ACT," thus providing for the women of Alberta similar laws the women of Ontario enjoy.

The 10th Resolution was to deal with the Battered Child Syndrome; however, due to various legal entanglements, the Resolutions Committee was unable to have this Resolution prepared for the Annual Meeting. We hope to have it available for the next session. (Source: 1970–71 L.C.W. Hand Book, p. 16–17)

Addendum E

Tributes

Madame Alvina Rouleau, President 1895–1897

IT IS WITH THE DEEPEST regret that we have to announce the death of Madame Rouleau, which sad event took place at the Holy Cross Hospital on Monday Afternoon at 3:30 o'clock.

The deceased lady was one of the first residents of Calgary and we are safe in saying that to all, high, low, rich and poor, she was always a true friend to help those in wants, trouble or need of any kind and was in consequence held in the highest esteem and in fact beloved by all who knew her. Her sad demise will leave a blank impossible to fill as no one knows half the charitable and kindly work done by her. It was chiefly owing to her exertions that the noble institution in which she died (The Holy Cross Hospital) was founded by her and her name was constantly associated with worthy deeds. Her memory will ever live in the recollection of those with whom she came in contact.

Madame Rouleau has lived in the North West the greater part of her married life and was at Battleford at the time of the Rebellion from which place she had a most wonderful escape from the Indians.

The sincerest sympathy of the community is with her sorrowing husband Mr. Justice Rouleau and children in their irreparable loss. Although the deceased lady has been ill for a considerable time the sad news was a great shock to her many friends.

Brilliant sociality, a true friend, a model mother, a devoted wife, noble hearted, a ready helper to those in need, all that can be said of few and in saying this, it is not more than is due to this most estimable lady.

> My friend, thy friend
> Best friend, dear friend,
> Glory and peace be with you now and evermore.

(Source: "The Late Madame Rouleau" *The Albertan*, May 29, 1901, p. 1)

Georgina Newhall, Convenor of the Economics Committee 1913–1919 and Founder of the Consumers' League

For several years, in its economic and literary life, Calgary has been deprived of the valuable services of Mrs. Newhall, as a result of her lingering illness, and now has sustained a great loss in the removal by death of this outstanding worker and highly esteemed citizen.

In her youth Mrs. Newhall enjoyed the distinction of being the first woman stenographer in Canada. She studied secretarial work in Toronto and later held important positions in the offices of Wills, Gordon and Sampson, barristers and solicitors, afterward becoming secretary to the well known newspaperman, J.W. Bengough, who was at that time court reporter.

Along literary lines Mrs. Newhall early on demonstrated her talent, being one of the pioneer writers in Canada to take charge of a woman's page, that of the Mail and Empire. She also contributed frequently to the columns of Saturday Night. Her name occupies an honored place in "Scottish-Canadian Anthologies" published thirty years ago by the Caledonian Society of Toronto.

Throughout her life she continued to write poems, articles on the Scottish bards, on economics, and various phases of women's work. She contributed to a number of Canadian and American magazines – was a member of the Calgary branch of the Authors' Association, the Mount Royal Educational Club and also served a number of years on the Board of the Public Library.

When the women of Alberta were working to secure the franchise, Mrs. Newhall was one of the leaders in that campaign – successful in 1915 – winning for the women of Alberta the right to cast their ballot.

As a thinker and writer along lines of economics and food conservation the late Mrs. Newhall showed marked initiative. She was for many years convenor of the committee on economics in the Local Council of Women. During the war she worked out and gave to the public many useful schemes for the production and conservation of foods. At that time she stimulated the work of conserving meat for the soldiers by substituting fish for the civilian population of this province. In this connection she discovered that Lesser Slave Lake was leased to a firm in Chicago, whose facilities were so inadequate that there was considerable mismanagement and an enormous waste. She discovered also that the fish were shipped to Chicago, then back to Alberta and classified "fresh." Through her efforts this state of affairs was brought to the attention of the government authorities and a decided improvement brought about in the trade in white fish.

Just previous to the war Mrs. Newhall organized the Public Market on Fourth street east – a farmers' market – which was a decided boon to Calgarians, where they could trade at first hand with the producers. She was always keenly interested in conditions affecting the home, in laws and problems relating to women and children, as well as in child welfare work.

Although a Canadian, born Georgina Fraser, at Galt, Ontario, of Scottish parents, Mrs. Newhall was an active worker in the American Women's Club of this city, being eligible through her marriage to a citizen of the United States. Part of her married life was spent in that country, where she was also prominent in community work. When a resident of the city of

Toledo, Ohio, she was an enthusiastic supporter of the Shakespearian Club, and founded the Women's Civic League in that city. In Canton, Ohio, she was a prominent worker in women's organizations.

A woman of lofty ideals and high character, absolutely devoid of self-seeking, devoted to her home and family, the late Mrs. Newhall leaves to mourn her passing two sons, V.A. of this city, Harold W. of West Newton, Mass., and five grandchildren, her husband E.P. Newhall of the C.N.R. staff, having predeceased her five years ago. (Source: "Tribute to Late Mrs. G. Newhall," November 19, 1932, *Calgary Herald*, p. 17)

Mrs. H.G.H. Glass, President 1922–23

Dedicated to the memory of the late H.G.H. Glass, by the Calgary Local Council of Women, as a token of affection, esteem and sincere gratitude for her untiring efforts on behalf of the social and community life of this city.

While President in 1923, Mrs. Glass sponsored the publication of the Council's first Year Book.

Not the friend of a chosen few, but of all who were privileged to know her, showing a genuine sympathy and concern for those less fortunate. A lady at all times, possessing a wonderful personality, she disliked deceit and vulgarity, but found keen enjoyment in good clean fun. An ideal wife and mother, beloved by her husband and family, a woman whose word was her bond, open and above board, four-square in all her dealings.

Many in Calgary and elsewhere will feel the loss of her presence, wise council and guidance, yet the inculcations of her ideals will always remain, leaving their impress for good.

Some day we may again be greeted with her smile, her happy laugh, and feel the warm clasp of her hand when we have reached "Our Journey's End."

During Mrs. Glass's residence in Calgary she was jointly responsible for the founding of a number of women's organizations, being a member of the Y.W.C.A. Board, first President of the Women's Canadian Club, President of the Local Council of Women. As President of the latter organization, she was responsible for a number of reforms beneficial to the women and children of this city.

Keenly interested in the civic life of the city, she took an active part in the formation of the Calgary Women's Civic Association, and was elected its first President. Mrs. Glass was also a member of the Mount Royal Educational Club from its inception.

Born in London, Ontario, on the 26th of July, 1873, her maiden name was Jessie Ann Isabelle Smith; her father was Alexander Smith, of Glasgow, Scotland, while her mother was a grand-daughter of the Macgillivarys of Gaelong Willa, Inverness. She married Herbert George Glass, of London, Ontario, November 19th, 1892, coming to Calgary in the year 1906.

Died at Penticton, B.C., October 1st, 1937.

Mrs. Glass was a member of St. Stephen's Anglican Church, Calgary. She was buried from St. Saviour's Anglican Church, Penticton, leaving to mourn her loss her husband, a daughter, Mrs. James G. Porter, Ottawa, Ontario, and a son, Lester Smith Glass, Brazil. (Source: 1938 L.C.W. Year Book, p. 13)

Mrs. W.A. Geddes, President 1924–25

For many years prominent in women's organizations in the city, Mrs. W.A. Geddes, Past President of the Local Council of Women, was called "Home" on August 17th, 1938, at the age of 79 years.

Daughter of the late Judge Boyd, of the Supreme Court of Ontario, and Mrs. Boyd, Mrs. Geddes came to Calgary with her husband in 1907, and resided here until the time of her death.

Mrs. Geddes was a member of St. Stephen's Anglican Church, Past President of the Calgary Diocesan Board of the Women's Auxiliary, Past President of the Local Council of Women, Past President of the Women's Canadian Club, and President of the Lend-a-Hand Society, which position she held for 18 years, until the time of her death.

While serving many other good causes, it is perhaps as organizer of the Lend-a-Hand Society that Mrs. Geddes will be long and lovingly remembered. It was in the autumn of 1921 that Mrs. Geddes learned that several parochial missionaries were having a real struggle to make ends meet, owing to the early frost of that year which had destroyed many vegetable gardens and ruined promising potato crops. More than one missionary had to thaw out the solidly frozen vegetables in order to secure food for his family, and sickness had made conditions even worse. In an endeavor to help, Mrs. Geddes called several Calgary women together, told them the story, with the result that the Society was formed. Under her leadership the efforts of the Lend-a-Hand Society, in their 18 years of service, has been along the same lines, to help those who help themselves, and to endeavor to make life more cheerful for the underprivileged, and the record of the Society is one of Christian principles put into practice, - a helping hand extended wherever possible.

The Lend-a-Hand Society was affiliated with the Local Council all these years and was in complete accord with its aims and objects.

The "Home Call" of Mrs. Geddes, eagerly looked for by herself, was a great loss to her many friends and Calgarians at large. A truly Christian character in every sense of the world, her life was devoted to good works, and she has long since heard the words of her Lord and Master, "Well done, good and faithful servant," and has entered into her reward. (Source: Emily L. Akitt, 1939 L.C.W. Year Book, p. 18)

Mrs. G.W. Kerby, President 1917

Mrs. G.W. Kerby was born in Toronto, the daughter of Rev. James Spenser, M.A., who was for some time a professor of Victoria College, and later editor of the Christian Guardian. She graduated from the Toronto Normal School, and later became principal of a large public school in Paris, Ontario. In 1888 she married George W. Kerby and with him served in the pastorate of the Methodist Church in Woodstock, Hamilton, St. Catharines, Brantford, and Montreal. Answering the call of the west in 1903, they arrived in Calgary with their two children, Spenser and Helen.

Dr. and Mrs. Kerby took charge of the Central Methodist (now United) Church for eight years. Here they developed church activities to meet the needs of a rapidly increasing population. Feeling a need of a residential school to take care of the educational needs of the young city and province, they set about the organization necessary, and later were prevailed upon to accept the responsibility of becoming the principals of Mount Royal College. Through depression and wartime and more depression they piloted the College to greater usefulness as a Junior College in affiliation with the University of Alberta. Thousands of students there are who remember Mrs. Kerby as a counselor, a good friend, and a jolly, happy, scintillating conversationalist.

Possessed by the spirit of the Master, the pioneer enthusiasm of her Loyalist ancestors, great vigor of mind and body, Mrs. Kerby on her arrival in the foothill city of Calgary soon realized that here many things should be organized.

With the idea that service to humanity has many facets, she went to work, in the church and out, organizing and holding out the welcoming and helping hand to all who came within her reach.

Were a detailed account of her many activities possible, we would find that she responded to the needs of mankind – as an

individual, a group, the church and the state with an understanding sympathy, and organizing ability possessed by few. To
those who knew here intimately, her outstanding characteristic
was her selflessness.

Largely through the efforts of Mrs. Kerby the Y.W.C.A. came
into being, and throughout the years that followed she worked
incessantly for a greater and better "Y." As a charter member and
president of the Local Council of Women, and as first vice-president of the National Council of Women, she sought for better
social, economic, cultural, and political conditions for women.
As a charter member and one time president of the Women's
Canadian Club, she sought to interest women in world-wide
affairs. She was in the forefront of those who fought for and
secured the suffrage for women in Alberta and the Dominion.
She was an active member in the Women's Civic Organization
and a member of the Women's Research Club.

The Mount Royal College Educational Club was born of
her spirit and for fifteen years she was its guiding light, arousing interest in cultural and world affairs.

The following lines epitomized her ideal of a Women's
Club:

A Woman's Club
What is a woman's club? No idle place
Wherein to chatter of the last new play
Or whisper of a sister gone astray
Or strip with cruel gossip every trace
Of sweetness from some life borne down with strife.
'Tis not a place where fashion reigns supreme,
Where lack of style is sin beyond redeem.
Where outward garb is more than inward life.
No room is there for careless jest or sneer,
Or meaning glances with dire purpose cast
To cause some soul to blush in fear.
All these are what a woman's club is not:

What is a woman's club? A meeting ground
For those of purpose, great and broad and strong,
Whose aim is in the stars, who ever long
To make the patient listening world resound
With sweeter music, purer, freer tones;
A place where kindly lifting words are said'
Where kindlier deeds are done, where hearts are fed,
Where wealth of brain for poverty atones,
Where hand grasps hand and soul finds touch with soul;
Where victors in the race for fame and power
Look backward even in their triumph hour
To beckon others to the shining goal.
This is a woman's club – a haven fair,
Where toilers drop an hour their load of care.
(NATIONAL REPUBLIC)

A civic reception had been arranged for the date of their golden wedding on October 11th, when the citizens of Calgary were to pay tribute to Dr. and Mrs. Kerby as citizens who had from the early days of the city become the very warp and woof of its religious, educational, social and cultural fabric.

On October 3rd, 1938, Emily Spenser Kerby answered the Great Call, leaving to mourn her absence her husband, George W. Kerby, B.A., D.D., L.L.D.; her daughter, Mrs. A.J. Cowan of Vancouver; a son, H. Spencer Kerby, Group Commander, London, England; a granddaughter and three grandsons.

She was "a haven fair, where toilers drop an hour their load of care." (Source: M.L. Carrick, 1939 L.C.W. Year Book, p. 15–17)

Mrs. C.R. (Harriet) Edwards, Health Committee Convener

Mrs. Edwards was born in New Dundee, Ontario, and grew up in Kitchener. A daughter of U.E.L. (United Empire Loyalist) stock she possessed that same commendable zeal for progress which compelled her early forebears to erect the first school house in Waterloo County, Ontario. Fragile in physique, dynamic in energy, consumed with a zeal for the welfare of childhood, she confronted obstacles and opposition that might well have quelled a less indomitable spirit. Mrs. Edwards was a capable housewife, an excellent mother, a woman of ideals and a complete honesty of purpose.

The first woman in Canada to sit on a Commerce Board by appointment of the Calgary City Council in 1919, Mrs. Edwards represented the Consumers in the investigation into the high cost of living in the City. Some of her criticisms and recommendations are worth noting. "It is necessary for the employers to first set a standard of honesty for themselves, after which they may demand honesty from their employees." "If honesty and genuine gratitude were the net profits of Canada's four years of suffering and of Canadian soldiers efforts, we would not today be needing a board to determine what should be a fair basis of profit."

As the founder and first president of the Normal Practice Mother's Club in 1915, she became a member of the Local Council Executive.

There in a larger sphere her alertness to public welfare resulted in her appointment to the convenorship of the Health Committee, serving nine years in this capacity.

First she waged almost a single-handed fight for purer City water, facing opposition and even ridicule, with courage and the determination to secure what she knew to be a large factor in safeguarding public health.

In that capacity she was largely instrumental in having enforced a number of civic measures, safeguarding the health of Calgarians, such as the covering of cooked foods in market stalls and a requisite standard of health for those handling them.

During the year 1927 a series of five health lectures were arranged and given by members of the Local Medical

Association. In 1928 Mrs. Edwards advocated the registration of Blood Donors for transfusions to hospitals. At that time too, this health worker was tireless in her public agitation concerning the prevalence and increase of goiter in the City, especially among school children. For facts concerning this malady, its numerous and insidious effects, remedial treatment etc., Mrs. Edwards received valuable information and assistance from the late Dr. Richie of Cochrane, also from the late Dr. Sheppard, Dean of Medicine at McGill University. In recognition of these outstanding campaigns and other protective measures for which she was largely responsible, Mrs. Edwards was nominated to National Council of Women as Convenor of Health for the years 1925–26, 1926–27.

Mrs. Edwards never became weary in well-doing and her work will live after her a monument to her memory and an inspiration to others for nobler living. (Source: Alice L. Grevette, 1939 L.C.W. Year Book, p. 19)

Mrs. R.R. Jamieson, President 1912–1916

Alice Jane Jukes was born in New York City, on July 14, 1860 to Isabella and James Jukes.

She was of Puritan Stock, her maternal Grandfather was Jabz Duxbury, a direct descendant of Miles Standish. They had the same birthplace, Duxbury Hall, Lancashire, England. Her father, James Jukes, was also of English birth. Both of her parents came to America when in their early teens, met and married there.

During the American Civil War Mr. Jukes served with the Federal Forces, as a Naval Officer.

Alice Jukes lived in the United States until her marriage at Springfield Ohio, on March 8th, 1882, to Reuben Rupert Jamieson. They left immediately for Canada, and made their home in Toronto. As Mr. Jamieson was a British subject, resident in Canada, Mrs. Jamieson lost her identity as a United States citizen and became a British subject.

Their five children were born in Toronto – one died in infancy.

Mr. Jamieson was connected with the C.P.R. and the family moved from place to place in Canada as his work called for, and eventually they moved to Calgary in 1903.

Mrs. Jamieson was always keenly interested in Community affairs, taking active part in Church work, Hospital Aid and Musical Circles.

After Mr. Jamieson's election as Mayor of Calgary in 1908, Mrs. Jamieson's interests in public affairs broadened and Mayor Jamieson gave her great encouragement in her interest in the Welfare work in the young and growing city.

After Mr. Jamieson's death in 1911 – Mrs. Jamieson gave more and more of her time to public affairs. Through her work and concern in Children's Welfare, Mrs. Jamieson was appointed a Judge of the Juvenile Court in 1913. A Judge, or Commissioner of Juvenile Court at that time and probably still is, not a Civil Service Appointment, being a gratuitous service in the interest of Child Welfare rendered by the person so appointed.

In 1915 her appointment as a Justice of the Peace was Gazetted, and in 1916 Judge Jamieson was appointed a Police Magistrate.

The Magistrate of Police Court was a Civil Service appointment. Magistrate Jamieson's work in this connection was principally concerned with cases where women were involved in the charges, and in taking evidence, and where necessary, making commitments to Mental Hospitals, of which unfortunately there are many such cases, both of women and men.

Another function of Magistrate Jamieson towards public welfare was presiding over Truancy Court, held under the auspices of the Calgary School Board. This she did from its inception up to the time of her retirement from the Police Court

Bench in 1931.

Magistrate Jamieson's many activities in Calgary included work in the Women's Hospital Aid of the General Hospital. Being one of the organizers of the Y.W.C.A. she was a very active member of the Board of Managers, for many years.

She was also active in forming a Local Council of Women and was the first President of the Council.

Magistrate Jamieson was a charter member of the Calgary Women's Musical Club and the Mount Royal Educational Club. During World War I she was very active in Red Cross Work and was given a Life Membership in recognition of that Service.

Magistrate Jamieson's particular interests were in Children's Welfare work; Women's Rights; the Franchise for Women; Labor and working conditions for women.

Her last act in the interest of public welfare was seeing the need of, and starting the move to establish, the School Patrols. It was Magistrate Jamieson that brought the need of their urgency to the notice of the Chief of Police, David Richie.

First President of Calgary Local Council of Women, and Life Member of Calgary Local Council of Women.[31]

Rest in Peace. (Source: Hand written tribute by her Local Council friend Alice Grevett for the 1950 L.C.W. Year Book)

Mrs. F.G. (Alice) Grevett, President 1933–34 and 1938

She was not, as she said, a "violent" feminist, but she had forever the interests of women at heart. She was keenly aware of injustice, whether political, economic or legal and she worked with a will to improve women's condition.

She was born in Cambridgeshire, England, and after her marriage in 1905, came to Calgary with her husband shepherding 150 emigrants under the auspices of the Church Army.[32] In 1907 she was appointed Matron of the Victoria School on the Peigan Reserve and later of the Indian Reservation School at

Sarcee where her husband was Principal. They did conscientious work there for some years before moving into Calgary.

In the city she became interested in the W.C.T.U. which was not merely concerned with the problem of liquor but in many other areas. She served as a Canadian representative at a Convention in Grand Rapids, Michigan. She was also an enthusiastic member of the Calgary Local Council of Women, was its President in the 1930's and for four years was Vice-President of the National Association which is an indication of her ability to make far-reaching decisions. Her work in community affairs led her to run for the City Council in 1940[33] as she had run for the School Board years earlier. That she didn't make it did not stop her work however. She had been awarded the Coronation Medal in 1937 to recognize her worth to her community and to Canada. (Source: From the original 1975 L.C.W. History project)

The 1960s

Mrs. Ethel Johnson (Mrs. Ralph H. Johnson)

This issue of our Handbook is dedicated to ETHEL MARGARET JOHNSON, who successfully produced its five predecessors, but died before she could build on the groundwork she had laid for this one. With the *Albertan*'s kind permission we reprint here that paper's editorial comment at the time of Mrs. Johnson's passing. It sums up for us and the community her wide range of concerns and valuable contribution to society.

> When we said the other day that "Calgary has been extremely fortunate in the calibre of its school boards," we were thinking of people like Mrs. Ethel Johnson, who died on Tuesday. Mrs. Johnson served on the Calgary Public School Board for 12 years, and her interest in and devotion to education never flagged during that period.

Her worth as a trustee was undoubtedly enhanced, moreover, by her interest in public affairs in general. She was active both in politics (she began a second term as president of the Alberta Women's Liberal Association recently), in community affairs (she had served on the executive of the Scarboro Community Association for six years), and in the mobilization of others of her sex (she was a life member of the Calgary Council of Women and president of the Alberta Council of Women).

She was, in short, proof that women can make a significant contribution to the organization and betterment of society, and can find their reward in public appreciation and esteem as well as in the satisfaction of work well done. Mrs. Johnson's energy, dedication and wise counsel will be missed in many areas of local and provincial activity.

The *Calgary Herald*, February 19, 1996, on page 28 captioned its account "Deceased Member Honored By Council." It read:

The women didn't wear black, but each heart was mourning for its friend, adviser and leader – Mrs. Ethel Johnson.

The late provincial president of the Local Council of Women whose funeral was held today, died suddenly in her home Wednesday, two days before the annual meeting of the Calgary club.

At the meeting Friday, Mrs. Oscar Stonewall expressed the sentiments of the entire group in a short eulogy to the memory of Mrs. Johnson.

"In her mind a thirst for knowledge, in her heart desire to serve, in her mind an open book." said Mrs. Stonewall.

In addition to her work with the council, Mrs. Johnson was a public school board member for 12 years, Alberta Women's Liberal Association President, a member of the Business and Professional Women's Club, a member of the Alberta School Trustees' Association and an active community worker.

She brought dignity and prestige to the Council of Women and left a legacy to strengthen spirit with education, said Mrs. Stonewall.

Mrs. Johnson herself had been enrolled in a UAC extension course to increase her own educational qualifications.

Shortly before noon, during their meeting, the members of the L.C.W. paused to join the children of Calgary schools in paying tribute to Mrs. Johnson.

(Source: 1966–67 L.C.W. Hand Book, p. 1)

Addendum F

Life Members

1975 Life Members of the National Council of Women

NATIONAL LIFE MEMBERSHIPS could be awarded to members who rendered valuable service to Council of Women and the community; at the discretion, and approval of, the Executive Committee.

- Dr. Ruth Gorman
- Mrs. Russell Clark
- Mrs. Oscar Stonewall
- Mrs. Harry Johnson
- Mrs. Mary Dover
- Mrs. K.F. MacLennan
- Mrs. T.A. Crowe
- Mrs. C.G. Crosland

Ruth Gorman BA, LLB, LLD, OC, Convenor of Laws 1942–1965

I am a native Calgarian who grew up in a Mount Royal Home. My father was M.B. Peacock, a prominent partner in R.B. Bennett's law firm, my mother was a concert pianist, and I was their only child. You might say I grew up in a world of privilege, but I was also expected to follow in the family tradition and become a lawyer.

Upon graduating in law from the University of Alberta in 1940, and while taking my articles in my father's law firm in Calgary, I was asked to be the Local Council's Convenor of Laws. I was the first such Convenor for Local Council who was actually a lawyer willing to take on an unpaid, time-consuming job which entailed a long-term commitment. There were, of course, very few women lawyers around. As I recall, only one other woman practiced law in Calgary when I did.

When I told my mother about my intention to accept, she recommended against it. To my further amazement, she announced that years before, for a very brief time, she had been a Local Council Convenor of Laws. This absolutely amazed me. My mother had a university degree, but it was in the field of music and her knowledge of law was almost nil. She was loaded with charm and great commonsense, but I couldn't see how she could advise other women on their needs in the field of legal rights. Her explanation was simple. She said, "I just came home and asked your father and he told me what to do." Since my father was an able lawyer, the system worked fine. But in earlier days, that was actually how L.C.W. worked. Women who had been denied experience in the world of government leaned on the advice of supportive husbands to achieve their reforms.

I was to stay on as Convenor for another twenty-three years, part of that time serving also as the National Council of Women's Honorary Convenor of Laws. They were very rewarding years indeed, not only because of the fine women I met and worked with, but for what we were able to achieve.

There were exciting women on Local Council. Some were young women concerned for the future of their sons and daughters. Our Council membership consisted of two elected or appointed members from each of our affiliate clubs, so they were already concerned women prepared to be active in their communities. Later, when I became chairman of the Nominating Committee, we inaugurated the policy of inviting women from the community who had special interests and training in the fields of health, education, etc. to serve on our various study committees. Often they became so interested in Council's achievements that they would join us as an individual member, and so we were able to expand and enlarge our interests in women's problems even beyond that of our affiliated clubs' specific interest.

The procedure followed when my Laws Committee or a club proposed the endorsement of a reform was that we would first study it in the Laws Committee to determine if the proposal was possible, compatible with Council's purpose and likely to be supported by a majority of the affiliates. Since there were strong differences among church groups themselves, as well as within political groups, it was a sensitive and time-consuming job, but worth it. When a resolution received the support of Local Council's membership, it meant that it was backed by a very vocal proportion of Calgary women. Calgary's City Council respected us so much that we were allowed to hold meetings without charge in City Hall's council chambers when they were not being used by the aldermen. My experience was that politicians on all levels of government gave careful consideration to our well-analyzed and thoroughly backed demands when I presented them on behalf of L.C.W.

The legal reforms we considered and backed were, I am afraid, never carefully recorded by me except in our minutes, and L.C.W.'s minutes have blanks in them. This was due to the fact that we had no club house, and executive members including secretaries, changed frequently, as changes occurred in affiliate membership. Fires, moves, death and illness also caused breaks in a permanent and continuous record being handed on. For my part, I never had extra time to allocate to keeping a personal account of my experiences. Local Council always had many and varied legal projects going on at the same time. So it was a relief to be done with one project, whether we succeeded or failed, because there were always others we would have to deal with immediately in various stages of study, passage or implementation. Taking the required time to record the sequence was not a prime object. We were all volunteers and all women serving not just in one field but in several. I must now apologize for any omissions due to my own imperfect memory of past events.

By the time I became the first trained lawyer who reviewed and recommended legal changes for the Local Council of Women, the nature of Calgary had changed. We were now a large city, beginning to gain both population and financial growth through the petroleum industry's growth. The whole nature of government had changed. Local Council had never really been a money-raising organization, and we found the mothering role, through which we had improved our community for so many, was now largely under government control. If we wished reforms in these fields, we were referred to the various departments of health, welfare and education at the appropriate provincial or national level. These departments were manned by civil servants who would alter or consider our proposal but not too often act on our recommendations, preferring instead that they come only from their own departments. The fact that we represented a healthy portion of voters was of little interest to them.

Women's roles in our communities had begun to change, especially after World War II. More women were full-time workers and therefore less able to be active in club activities. Also, more women held either advisory or elected positions. True, we now had new societies like the business and professional women's auxiliaries, auxiliaries to unions (the Women's Typographical Union), and fewer private church groups or charitable organizations. The women's auxiliaries to the political parties were often busy establishing themselves in an effort to obtain representation on their party's own executive and stand for elected office.

However, despite these changes, the CLCW found many times they could still serve the communities well. Often the male-dominated political parties turned a deaf ear to their own women members. As an alternative, these women could then unite with other women from political parties affiliated with

Local Council to lobby for desired improvements, working through Council to goad governments in areas where reform was felt to be needed.

My own very first effort at legal reform as their Convenor of Laws, I think, was what converted me for the next twenty years to work with Local Council. Council members and other Alberta women had been instrumental in passing the province's Dower Act, an act which recognized the wife's right to a voice in the disposal of the family's home, and requires the spouse's consent by affidavit before the home can be sold out from under the other person. As the law then read, if the husband sold without the wife's consent, her only recovery was against her own husband. This claim was all too frequently useless, as he had left the country, and thus the wife found herself and her children penniless and on the street. The law could be amended so the wife could recover her share from the purchaser, who had often, in connivance with the husband, just paid the money over to him. I had watched a case in the courts like this, so as their Convenor of Laws, I persuaded Local Council to ask the provincial government for a change in law. Mr. Aberhart had been newly elected to government by a tremendous landslide, so I, inexperienced as I was, took it upon myself, once I had the L.C.W. affiliates' backing, to visit him personally and recommend this change. I emphasized that all persons who had no monetary intent for prosecuting their wife would approve of its passage. To my amazement, he personally agreed to present it at the Legislature, and to my consternation, he even suggested I become his attorney-general as he was having some difficulty finding one! I explained that I really had a husband and small baby to care for, but I remember realizing how powerful was L.C.W., and how valuable to the community and women of Calgary, and for the next twenty years I gladly served as their Laws chairman. As a result the Dower Act was later amended, and today women have an enforceable legal right in their own home.

However, in my first years with Local Council, we nearly did part company, and this was over the matter of us being determined that the City should provide public toilets. The resolution had found its way into L.C.W. from farm women's groups who came to the city to shop. Each year L.C.W. would endorse this resolution, and as Convenor of Laws, I was sent before our City Council to request it. My appearances were always met with some raunchy jokes, and invariably the resolution was turned down. The city was not going to get into the business of financing public toilets. I finally told L.C.W. I just couldn't waste my time or theirs on more appearances promoting this. However, despite our failure in this issue, as a result of the publicity we gave the matter, department stores eventually saw it expedient to put in more public toilets. Putting a slightly different complexion on the matter, a law was passed saying wherever women were employed in the same building with men, separate toilets should be available for them, so I guess it wasn't a total loss.

In my time, especially at the local level, many resolutions we passed had to be presented to boards, and I usually fell into the job. It was our president, Mrs. Alberta Clark, and I who had to appear before the Public Utilities Board to argue for skim milk for Calgary. The unions, the dairy industry, and the dairy men all appeared with the high-priced, most able lawyers in town opposing it, but our plea that skim milk was as nutritious but lower in price and should be available for growing children won our point. This is just another recollection of our ongoing efforts in presenting resolutions and preparing written briefs which I presented to government advisory boards and commissions for the protection of the public at large.

In the field of crime law, we became concerned over the different treatment of women from men. We agitated for and got one-way vision mirrors to enable women to identify their attackers without fear of reprisal. Women were added to the police force too. We took note of the poorer treatment that women received in jails in comparison to men. One of our presidents, Jessie Hutchison, and Grace Johnson, Assistant Convenor of Laws, made a personal inspection of the jails and reported on the conditions they saw. Women prisoners' complaints were often negated by the women authorities, and the women prisoners were afraid to testify. We therefore took tape recorded evidence from them and presented that to the government on their behalf.

L.C.W. was certainly outstanding in its promotion of tolerance in this city. We had all political parties as members, and we had the majority of different religious denominations. Furthermore, we had as executive members at various times, a Native woman, Daisey Crowchild, representing native Indian school children, and from a Baptist church a very fine African-Canadian woman, Mrs. Stella King, who was honored with a life membership in L.C.W., and the Jewish women's clubs had at that time a representative at our meetings. In a practical way, we practiced tolerance, and we knew it worked. As is explained in Lilian MacLennan's detailed history, we had participated in 1951 in the first promoting of the brotherhood banquets. Before I came on the scene, that great friend of the Indians, John Laurie, could count on L.C.W. to endorse the Indian's requests for improvements to their conditions, and such requests were sent frequently to Ottawa. When I became the Indian Association of Alberta's volunteer lawyer, CLCW was most active in backing up my three-year Hobbema legal trial which allowed treaty Indians to remain on their reserves. When I went to Ottawa, I carried the great support of not only Calgary's L.C.W. but of local councils across Canada in my request for the removal of the compulsory Franchise section from the Indian Act. Such removal would then allow our Indians to vote without losing their homes and treaty status as Indians.

It was L.C.W. with its community conscience which worked for the establishment of much-needed centres for two disadvantaged groups in Calgary. Along with their affiliates, Local Council persevered in establishing the Indian Friendship Centre, and it was a vice-president, Grace Johnson, who devoted the last years of her life to running it for them until it eventually moved from renting an old house to the fine centre we have now. The L.C.W. also promoted understanding and tolerance for the physically disabled citizens of Calgary and were of unbelievable assistance in helping me get the first centre for this group. Later, with their backing again, I appeared before the school board and demanded we create a form of public schooling for disabled children, children limited to schooling by correspondence because of their crippled bodies, not their minds.

The women seemed to be very understanding of injustices to such groups, no doubt remembering their earlier battles to obtain fairness in law and status themselves. (Source: Autobiography prepared for *A Leaven of Ladies*)

1975 Life Members of the Calgary Local Council of Women

Section 3 of the Local Council of Women By-Laws allowed a maximum of 3 life memberships a year. The honor, for which only members who had rendered signal service to The Council qualified, was awarded on the recommendation of the L.C.W. Executive Committee at the Annual Meeting. The required $25 could be contributed by an affiliate, or others.

- Mrs. J.F. (Cynthia) Aikenhead
- Mrs. Mary Beattie
- Mrs. Chris Crum
- Mrs. Russell (Alberta) Clark

- Mrs. A.A. (Flo) Frawley
- Mrs. Donald Fleming
- Mrs. Frank (Aileen) Fish
- Dr. Ruth Gorman
- Mrs. C.H. (Beth) Hoar
- Mrs. C. Hollingworth
- Mrs. C. Irving
- Mrs. Harry (Grace) Johnson
- Mrs. B.D. Barbara Langridge
- Mrs. J.C. Jean Leslie
- Mrs. A. (Millie) Luft
- Mrs. Mrs. K.F. (Lillian) MacLennan
- Mrs. H.G. McCullough
- Mrs. A. Putnik
- Mrs. H.K. (Frances) Roessingh
- Mrs. W.H. Ross
- Mrs. G.L. Somerville
- Mrs. Oscar (Grace) Stonewall
- Mrs. A.D. (Mary) Winspear
- Mrs. Edith Crowe
- Mrs. Addison Wilson
- Mrs. C.G. (Mabel) Crosland

Grace Stonewall, President of C.L.C.W. 1959–1963

Among the present honorary life members, my Local Council connection seems to go back the farthest. My mother, Dorothy Little, joined the Calgary Local Council of Women in the 1930s. It was she who encouraged me to attend one of the meetings. I did so in 1949.

Let me begin by saying that I am a native Calgarian, born in 1922 at the Holy Cross Hospital, the seventh and last child of Methodist parents, Mr. and Mrs. David Little. My heritage was British – an English mother and a Scottish father with a few drops of Irish blood in his veins. As a young man "with sand in his shoes" he left the old country to seek his fortune in America. After a brief stay in Philadelphia, he travelled to the far West, to Washington State. While there he sent for his British sweetheart, Dorothy Dixon, and my parents began married life in the United States. A few years and one child later, they decided that Canada's British values were better suited to raising a family, so they moved north in 1907 to take up land near Rimbey, Alberta. After a time farming, they moved to Calgary, where father went into the draying and real estate business, then bought out the Crown Coal Co., changing its name to the David Little Coal Co. Mother was his office manager and bookkeeper until his death, then stayed on to help my brother, Andrew, who took over the business.

While faithfully carrying out her family and business obligations, my mother made time for church and lodge work, community service, women's lobby organizations, and campaign work for the Conservative Association, which she joined immediately after women got the federal vote in 1918. She became my role model.

Mother was a woman with a strong social conscience who began her philanthropic work with the Ladies' Orange Benevolent Association (LOBA) in 1916.

There she gave decades of dedicated service. Soon after joining she organized and supervised Lodge tag days, which raised funds for a motherless children's home at Olds run by the Reverend George Woods and his wife Annie. This old country couple – practicing Christians they truly were – gave most of their limited personal resources to providing a loving, decent home atmosphere for children rendered motherless by death, illness or abandonment at a time when the fathers were fighting World War I. When the Woods home relocated to the western edge of Calgary in the former Bethel Sanatorium at Bowness, my mother became the first Board member and through that association became a close friend of Mrs. Annie Woods. She served on the Board until her death.

My mother's first contact with the Calgary Local Council of Women was probably through her friend and President at the time, Mrs. F.G. Grevett, who thought the work would interest her. It did. Mother served on committees (Immigration being one) and held the office of vice-president. Later on, when I was married with a young family of three girls (now, by the way, all graduates of the University of Calgary), she suggested that the CLCW would probably interest me because I already belonged to an affiliate, the Crystal Chapter LOBA. My earliest recollection of a Local Council Meeting, which I likely attended in 1949, was that it was held in the old YWCA and John Laurie was the guest speaker. He had been one of my favorite teachers at Crescent Heights High School and was on that day speaking about his work as Secretary of the Alberta Indian Association. Thus began my 40-year membership in the Local Council.

When I first joined the Calgary Local Council of Women as an individual member, the organization was flagging. The President, Mrs. Lillian Clarke, realized that a re-organization was required, so she scheduled a "George Washington Tea" at Central United Church in hope that others would undertake executive roles. Among those who came was another Mrs. Clark – Mrs. Russell Clark – who had come to Calgary from Regina, where she had been a leading Local Council of Women officer. Alberta Clark proved to be the organization's revitalizing force, able to energize others. Alberta served as our president for four years, from 1951 until 1955, and in 1961 was elected a vice-president of the National Council of Women of Canada, one of the few Calgary women to be so recognized nationally. When she was president, the first Calgary branch of the Council of Christians and Jews formed, and the Council of Women sponsored the celebratory banquet that was judged such a success that it was declared an annual event. A few years later, in 1959, during the presidency of Jessie Hutchison, ten new affiliates affiliated, bringing the total to 25. One of these, the Friends of the Indians Society, with professional advice of our Convenor of Laws, Dr. Ruth Gorman (herself a lawyer), undertook a special study of the Indian Act. Their particular concern was that when an Indian voted, certain restrictive clauses in the Indian Act, if applied, would result in the loss of that person's home on the reserve. A resolution requesting the removal of the appropriate restrictive clauses was prepared for circulation to our affiliates. I also supported Dr. Gorman in her campaigns to establish an Indian rest and information center and to save the cupola from Calgary's first high school, James Short. Probably my longest commitment, though, was to the acquisition of land for Nose Hill Park. For many years I represented the Calgary Local Council of Women there, working on committees to ensure that what is now Canada's largest urban park would remain in its natural state.

I became an affiliate representative to Local Council through active participation in politics. In the post World War II period of the late 1940s, I worked on a campaign to send Conservative candidate Colonel Douglas Harkness to Ottawa. Partly through our friendship, I spent many active years in the Calgary Women's Progressive Conservative Association. After I was designated the Association's representative to the Council of Women, I became so interested in Local Council's work that I went on to serve as its president for four years (from 1959 to 1963) during a period of growth and extensive involvement with community and various levels of government. We started the custom of inviting the mayor's wife to serve as our honorary president. In this capacity, Mrs. Don MacKay, Mrs. Harry Hays and Mrs. Jack Leslie graciously hosted our annual teas in their homes. Jean Leslie had also been one of our Local Council vice-presidents before her husband became mayor. I remember Mrs. Grant MacEwan presented me with my honorary life membership in the National Council of Women during her husband's mayorship. In retrospect our community profile was particularly high in those years. As a long-time member it seems to me that this organization moves in cycles. It flourishes and fades but manages to survive.

My other community service included two terms as a member of the first University of Calgary Senate, the presidency of Mount Royal College Auxiliary, and five years on the City of Calgary Library Board. My lifetime church affiliation has been Rosedale United.

My husband, Oscar, always gave me full support because he felt women could do anything if given the opportunity. Now that he has retired from the position of Credit Manager of the *Calgary Herald*, I share his athletic interests – the Calgary Outdoor Hiking and Skating Club, the Calgary Senior Skaters, and Canadian and American Elder Hostels. (Source: Autobiography prepared for *A Leaven of Ladies*)

Group Photo of nineteen Honorary Life Members taken at the 1967 Annual Meeting at the Highlander Hotel. Photo courtesy of Glenbow Archives, L.C.W. fonds, M5841/NID-1.

Front row (left to right): Mrs. W.H. Ross, Mme. Olga Valda, Mrs. T.W. Keler, Mrs. T.E. Black, Mrs. C.J. Hollingsworth, Mrs. Jack Leslie, Mrs. H.B. Johnson, Mrs. F.E. Fish, and Mrs. A.C. Luft.

Back Row (left to right): Mrs. A.A. Frawley, Mrs. Russell Clark. Mrs. C.S. Irving, Mrs. H.G. McCullough, Mrs. A.D. Winspear, Mrs. C.R. Hoar, Mrs. K.F. MacLennan, Mrs. D.C. Fleming, Mrs. G.L. Somerville, and Mrs. Oscar Stonewall.

Missing were Dr. Ruth Gorman, Mrs. Anne Putnik, Mrs. Cris Crum, and Mrs. J.R. King.

Addendum G

Members and Affiliates Who Took Part in Community Improvement: A Veritable Who's Who of Calgary Decade by Decade

1895

Calgary Local Council of Women Table Officers

- President – Madame Rouleau
- Vice Presidents:
  - Mrs. J.A. Lougheed
  - Mrs. J.D. Lafferty
  - Mrs. Amos Rowe
  - Mrs. J.R. Costigan
- Corresponding Secretary – Mrs. George MacDonald
- Recording Secretary – Mrs. Horace Harvey
- Treasurer – Mrs. D.W. Marsh

Affiliated Societies

CHURCH SOCIETIES

- St. Mary's Church Ladies' Aid Society (Catholic)
  President: Mrs. Costello
- Methodist Church Ladies' Aid Society
  President: Mrs. Buchanan

Formed in 1885 with Mrs. W.H. Cushing as president

- Church of the Redeemer Women's Guild (Anglican)
  President: Mrs. Lindsay
- Church of the Redeemer Women's Missionary Society
  President: Mrs. W.L. Bernard
- Knox Church Women's Aid Society (Presbyterian)
  President: Mrs. Herdman
  Formed in 1885 with Mrs. Herdman, wife of Reverend Herdman as president.
- Knox Church Christian Endeavour Society
  Representative: Mrs. Thom

PHILANTHROPIC

- Calgary General Hospital Society
  President: Mrs. Jean Pinkham
  The Society was formed in 1890 by Mrs. Pinkham, the wife of Anglican bishop Rev. Cyprian Pinkham. She served as President for 11 years. The Society's name changed over the years to the Girls' Hospital Aid Society and then to the Children's Hospital Aid Society.
- Women's Christian Temperance Union
  President: Mrs. L.A. Clarke
  Calgary's first W.C.T.U. formed in 1886 during an organizing tour of the West by Mrs. Letitia Youmans, the first president of the Dominion W.C.T.U. who also organized branches at Morley and Regina. In October of 1904 the W.C.T.U. of the Northwest Territories was formed with Mrs. Craig of Olds as President and Mrs. McKinney of Claresholm as Secretary
  The WCTU's goal was prohibition of alcohol and temperance education, and its motto: "Agitate – Educate – Legislate." As a badge of loyalty its members wore a white ribbon; and took its pledge of abstinence which read: "I hereby solemnly promise, God helping

me, to abstain from all alcoholic liquors and beverages, whether distilled, fermented, or malted; from opium in all its forms, and to employ all proper means to discourage the use of and traffic in the same. (Source: *Woman's Century – Special Number*, Vol. 6, No. 9, p. 173, published 1918.)

- Women's Christian Union
President: Mrs. Amos Rowe
The Women's Christian Union, which formed circa 1888, was a charity which became a cornerstone of the Calgary Relief Society.

- The Aberdeen Society
President: Mrs. Barwis
The Calgary Branch of the Aberdeen Society formed in October, 1894. It was undenominational and its purpose was to distribute periodicals, religious and secular magazines, illustrated papers, etc., among the bachelors and scattered families on the prairies of Manitoba and the North West Territories. During its first year materials were sent to Springbank, Fort Saskatchewan, High River, Olds and Nose Creek. (Source: *Calgary Daily Herald*, Nov. 25, 1895, p. 1)

EDUCATIONAL

- Convent of the Sacred Heart (Catholic)
President: Mrs. Prince

1912

Calgary Local Council of Women Table Officers

- President – Mrs. R.R. Jamieson
- First Vice President – Mrs. G.W. Kerby
- Second Vice President – Mrs. E.A. Cruikshank

- Third Vice President – Mrs. William Pearce
- Fourth Vice President – Mrs. P.J. Nolan
- Recording Secretary – Miss Burns
- Corresponding Secretary – Mrs. H.G. Glass
- Assistant Corresponding Secretary – Mrs. F.S. Jacobs
- Treasurer – Mrs. P.S. Woodhall

Standing Committees

- Home Economics Committee – Mrs. E.P. Newhall
- Press Committee – Mrs. Clarihew (convenor)
- Legislative Committee – Mrs. Harold Riley
- Billboard and Printing Censor – Mrs. Conway
- Feeble-minded children and aged and poor Committee – Mrs. F.D. Beveridge
- Civic and Public Health Committee – Miss Hayden
- Immigration Committee – Mrs. W.D. Spence

Affiliated Societies

CHURCH SOCIETIES

- Ladies' Aid, Protestant Cathedral
- Ladies' Aid, St. Stephen's Church
- Ladies' Aid, Crescent Heights Methodist Church
- Ladies' Aid, Wesley Methodist Church
- Ladies' Aid Trinity Methodist Church
- Ladies' Aid, Victoria (Central) Methodist Church
- Ladies' Aid West End Methodist Church
- Ladies' Aid Grace Presbyterian Church
- Ladies' Aid Knox Presbyterian Church
- Ladies' Aid St. Paul's Presbyterian Church
- Ladies' Aid Olivet Baptist Church
- Ladies' Westbourne Baptist Church
- Ladies' Aid Hillhurst Baptist Church

- Ladies' Aid First Baptist Church.
- Extension Society, Roman Catholic Church
- Children of Mary Society (Roman Catholic)
- Missionary Societies
- Women's Guild Church of the Redeemer (Anglican) Formed in 1899
- Trinity Methodist Church
- St. Paul's Presbyterian Church
- Knox Presbyterian Church
- First Baptist Church
- Hillhurst Baptist Church
- Westbourne Baptist Church
- Heath Baptist Church

OTHERS

- Daughters of the Empire (I.O.D.E.)
  The I.O.D.E. is a patriotic and philanthropic organization, has as its motto "One flag, one crown, one Empire." It formed during the Boer War to supply comforts for Canadian soldiers. Calgary's first chapter formed later, in October of 1909, when Senator and Lady Lougheed hosted the founding meeting at their stately home, Beaulieu. The chapter was given the name Colonel MacLeod, to honor the distinguished local soldier and to symbolize its interest in "the welfare of the soldiers of the empire." The 31 founding members elected Mrs. Pinkham, the wife of Anglican Bishop, as their Regent.
- Calgary Women's Canadian Club
  Formed January 19, 1911
  Fifty-two members signed as charter members of the Woman's Canadian Club of Calgary at the organization meeting in the Y.W.C.A. parlors Saturday afternoon. The number assembled was unexpectedly large. And the enthusiasm manifested was a favorable augury for the

future of the new club. The gathering was also representative of almost every district of the city and the discussions were at all times democratic. During the first year the club will be officered by Mrs. C.A. Stuart, president; Miss Martin first Vice-president; Mrs. Pinkham, second vice-president; Mrs. Wm. Carson, third vice-president; Mrs. T. Moffat, fourth vice president; Miss Jean Grant, literary correspondent; Mrs. Cross, treasurer; Mrs. A.A. Moore, secretary; and an executive committee of eight. The purpose of the club: to foster patriotism by encouraging the study of the institutions, history, arts, literature, and resources of Canada, and to unite Canadians in such work for the welfare and progress of the Dominion as may be desirable and expedient Ref: "Woman's Canadian Club Has Fifty-Two Members" (Source: *Morning Albertan*, Jan. 23, 1911, p. 4)

- American Women's Club
  American born Calgary women launched their organization quite informally at the home of Mrs. Edgar Anderson, on March 29, 1912. On April 4, six days later, over seventy members convened at the Unity Hall where they appointed Georgina Newhall convener of their bylaws and constitution committee. "American women or wives of American men are eligible for membership in the club, the idea being to include in the membership roll especially those women who are excluded from membership in several clubs in the city by reason of the patriotic aims of these, and to avoid any possibility of overlapping with these. The club aim will be to make residence in Calgary as pleasant as possible for American newcomers, and to improve conditions wherever desirable." (Source: *Morning Albertan*, April 5, 1912, p. 4)

- Central W.C.T.U. (Women's Christian Temperance Union)

By 1904 there were eight more branches in Alberta, and by 1912 the number had grown to 43, all overseen by a joint Alberta-Saskatchewan Provincial Committee of Officers.

- Crescent Heights W.C.T.U.
- West End W.C.T.U.
- Y.W.C.A. (Young Women's Christian Association)
  In July 1907, a meeting was held in Knox Presbyterian Church to consider the advisability of organizing a young Women's Christian Association. Miss Little, General Secretary of the Dominion, gave an address on association work, after which a Y.W.C.A. committee was formed, with Mrs. G.W. Kerby as convenor. An advisory board was selected, consisting of Hon. W.H. Cushing, Thos. Underwood, Judge Stuart, W.G. Hunt, R.J. Hutchings and C.W. Rowley. The ladies laid before this board their plans to collect money to furnish a home for the girls. Mrs. Underwood was unanimously chosen president of the association. Undaunted by difficulties, in November a house was rented at 222 Fifteenth avenue west which accommodated some fourteen girls. Miss Adra Luton was appointed general secretary, and under her efficient management at the close of the year the books showed a good balance on the right side. (Source: 1915 Calgary Club Woman's Blue Book, p. 43–44)
- Naomi Mothers' Society
  The main purpose of this well known interdenominational society was to offer mothers guidance in exemplary parenting.
- Welland Union
- Young Women's Club
- Young Women's Benevolent Society
  The President of this small, informal charitable group was Mrs. J.H. Woods. Its purpose was to aid other charitable causes, and its one requirement was that every

member had to be a conscientious working member, willing to attend meetings regularly and punctually.

- Presbyterian Home Social Service
- Women's Hostel
  The Women's Hostel joined on December 16, 1912. A Board managed the hostel, which was a large home used as a temporary boarding house for Old Country women newly arrived in the city. Able to accommodate two dozen women, it was soon too small to meet the need.
- Women's Hospital Aid Society
- Society for the Prevention of Tuberculosis
  Over eighty members joined Calgary's anti-tuberculosis society when it formed at a meeting held at the YMCA on November 16, 1911. Patrons were Hon. R.L. Borden, A.L. Sifton, Senator Lougheed, Honorary President R.B. Bennett and Honorary Vice Presidents Hon. W.H. Cushing and Mr. T.M. Tweedie. Mr. A. Price was elected President, Mayor Mitchell, First Vice President, Dr. Anderson, Second Vice President, and Mrs. C.A. Stuart, third. Recording secretary, Mrs. J.H. Hanna, Corresponding secretary Mrs. Harold Riley, treasurer Mrs. W.T.D. Lathwell.

  The object of the organization was to erect buildings for the care of the sick and to educate the public as to the prevention and cure of the disease and to secure grants from the provincial and dominion governments to aid in the work. (Source: *News Telegram*, Nov. 17, 1911, p. 10)

PROFESSIONAL

- Women's Press Club
  The ten month old Calgary Women's Press Club, whose president Mrs. F.S. Jacobs was corresponding secretary on the new Calgary Local Council, joined at the outset. "This rather exclusive professional group of talented

writers and journalists, a few of whom were members of the Canadian Women's Press Club, began with only seven members and grew slowly. What they lacked in numbers they made up in endeavor, including a study of Canadian women writers, the commemoration of Dickens' Centennial Anniversary, and special invitations to contemporary women writers and to women eminent in other fields." (Source: *A Leaven of Ladies*, 63–64)

- Calgary Women Teachers' Association
- Graduate Nurses' Association
- Business Women's Club
 "The first of the kind in western Canada, and somewhat different in purpose from many of the self-supporting women's organizations," it was organized in 1912. "They are working to secure a rest room downtown for women; public lavatories in all parts of the city for women; to clean up dirty office blocks; to insist on seats for women in department stores and shops; to improve the ventilation, lighting and sanitation in industrial and commercial buildings of all kinds; to assist in the solution of the housing problem for working women; to prevent overcrowding; to maintain the wage standard of various lines of work; and to improve the moral conditions of the city as far as possible. 'They are doing it!' – The history of the club may be summed up in these four words."
 (Source: "Three Thousand Club Women," *The Western Standard – Opportunity Number*, June 12, 1913)
- Alberta Women's Association
 With the establishment of a university in Calgary, the Calgary branch of the Alberta Women's Association, a unique and pretentious organization of university women has accomplished considerable to stimulate interest in higher education.
 About sixty graduates of Canadian, American and British universities, and the wives of members of the sen-

ate and board of governors of Calgary University constitute the membership.

The association is active in all advanced educational
movements, and has provided several valuable university
and high school scholarships. (Source: The Calgary
Women's Press Club Issue of the *Western Standard*, June
12, 1913)

- Consumers League
  The first in Canada, it formed in late May of 1913 and
  joined the Council of Women on September 19, 1913.
  Its aims were to investigate the increasing cost of living,
  and to counteract the same by any legitimate means
  within their power; to study and teach the principles of
  cooperation in connection with home economics. And
  to watch, influence and promote civic legislation in connection with either of the foregoing clauses.

CULTURAL

- Calgary Women's Musical Club
- Calgary Women's Literary Society
  It formed in 1906 and its membership was limited to 35,
  with a waiting list. Members' dues were given to a charitable cause.
- Women's Alliance Unitarian Church.
  Its members believed in the unity of God and the
  humanity of Jesus, in contrast to belief in the Trinity and
  the deity of Christ. By 1913 there were only ten such
  societies in all of Canada and among these the Calgary
  Alliance, which formed in 1910, was the third largest. It
  was the entrepreneurial ladies of this society who
  launched the first "Made in Calgary" show in April
  1913, to raise money for their new church building

1920

Calgary Local Council of Women Table Officers

- President – Mrs. P.S. Woodhall
- First Vice President – Mrs. H. G. Glass
- Second Vice President – Mrs. S. Houlton
- Third Vice President – Mrs. MacWilliams
- Fourth Vice President – Mrs. W.A. Geddes
- Recording Secretary – Mrs. H. Akitt
- Corresponding Secretary – Mrs. R.C. Marshall
- Assistant Corresponding Secretary – Mrs. Dingman
- Treasurer – Miss McKimmey

Standing Committees

- Law – Mrs. Harold Riley
- Immigration – Mrs. G.W. Kerby
- Conservation – Mrs. C.E. Fenkell.
- Taxation – Mrs. J. Hall
- Employment of Women – Mrs. Glassford
- National Recreation – Mrs. F. Davis
- Education – Mrs. B. Stavert
- Public Health – Mrs. Edwards
- Citizenship – Mrs. R.R. Jamieson
- Finance Committee – Mrs. Nelson

Affiliated Societies

- Associated Consumers
- American Women's Club. President: Mrs. Savage
- First Baptist Church Ladies' Aid. President: Mrs. W.T. Johnston
- Bankview Presbyterian Ladies' Aid. President: Mrs. Elder

- Olivet Baptist Church Ladies' Aid. President: Mrs. J.O. Trotter
- Central Methodist Church Ladies' Aid. President: Mrs. Boynton.
- Crescent Heights Ladies' Aid
- Central Methodist Ladies Aid
- Crescent Heights Methodist Church Ladies' Aid
  President: Mrs. Mrs. J.E. Bull
- Central Committee Mothers' Union (forerunner of Home and School)
- Church of Christ Missionary Society
- Canadian Business Women's Club
- Crescent Heights Women's Auxiliary
- Connaught School Mothers' Club and Art League
- Calgary Graduate Nurses' Association
- Central W.C.T.U.
  President: Mrs. Aird
- Elbow Park Mothers' Club
- Housekeepers' Association.
  President: Miss H.J. Manning
- Hillhurst W.C.T.U.
  President: Mrs. J.J. Dunn
- Hebrew Church Ladies' Aid.
  President: Mrs. J.A. Guttman
- Jewish Benevolent Society
- Knox Church Missionary Society
  President: Mrs. J.L. Rowe
- Knox Church Ladies' Aid
  President: Mrs. C.A. Stewart
- Normal Practice School Mothers' Club
  President: Mrs. C.R. Edwards
- Pro-Cathedral Mothers' Union
  President: Mrs. Mrs. Tansley
- Pro-Cathedral Woman's Auxiliary
- Samaritan Club (joined in 1920)

- St. Marks' Guild
  President: Mrs. Powell
- St. Marks Woman's Auxiliary
  President: President, Mrs. Grevett
- St. Stephens Mothers' Union
  President: Mrs. Willis James
- St. Pauls' Presbyterian Church Ladies' Aid
  President: Mrs. J.P. Ross
- Sunalta Mothers' Club
  President: Mrs. Sutherland
- Tubercular Hospital Women's Auxiliary
- The Friday Club
- Unity Club
  President: Miss Coutts
- Victoria Church Ladies' Aid
  President: Mrs. Richardson
- West Calgary Methodist Ladies' Aid
  President: Mrs. Ovans
- Women's Musical Club
- Women's Canadian Club
- Wesley Methodist Ladies' Aid
  President: Mrs. J.R. McNab
- Working Women's Association
- West End W.C.T.U.
- Women's Social Service Club
  President: Mrs. J. Hall
- Women's Press Club
  President: Miss MacGregor
- Women's Institute
  Its motto was "For home and Country" and it was initial-
  ly a rural women's organization. The first Calgary branch
  formed in March of 1918, with Mrs. J.F. Price as presi-
  dent. Over the years it became a valuable link between
  city and rural homemakers.
- Women's Alliance Unitarian Church

1930

Calgary Local Council of Women Table Officers

- President – Mrs. H.J. Robie
- First Vice President – Mrs. Guy Johnson
- Second Vice President – Mrs. F.G. Grevett
- Third Vice President – Mrs. R.L. Freeman
- Fourth Vice President – Mrs. E.G. Hartshorn
- Recording Secretary – Mrs. A.E. Hope
- Corresponding Secretary – Mrs. A. Blight
- Assistant Corresponding Secretary – Mrs. R.A. Pearson
- Treasurer – Mrs. F.A. Sage

Standing Committees

- Applied Art – Mrs. W. Motherwell
- Citizenship – Mrs. A. MacWilliams
- Education – Mrs. W.H. Blatchford
- Employment of Women – Mrs. John Drummond
- Equal Moral Standards – Mrs. G. McElroy
- Film and Printed Matter – Mrs. Ceredig Evans
- Housing and Town Planning – Mrs. M. Millard
- Immigration – Mrs. W.S. Woods
- Household Economics – Mrs. M.N. Whitely
- Laws – Mrs. Harold Riley
- League of Nations – Mrs. Wm. Carson
- Natural Resources – Mrs. E. Hirst
- National Recreation – Mrs. F. Soper
- Public Health – Mrs. H.J. Collins

Affiliated Societies

- American Women's Club
- Armistice Chapter I.O.D.E.

- Anti-Tuberculosis Society
- Amba Yahangin Chapter I.O.D.E.
- Calgary Arts and Crafts Club
- First Baptist Ladies' Aid
- Bankview Scarboro Ladies' Aid
- Connaught P.T.A.
- Central United Church Ladies' Aid
- Central Church of Christ Ladies' Aid
- Col. Russel Boyle Chapter I.O.D.E.
  In 1934 there were 11 chapters in Calgary. Their objectives encompassed Canadianization of the foreign born, maintaining a fresh air camp, relief work, assistance to the blind, and the promotion of education by scholarships
- Canadian Women's Club
- Catholic Women's League
  Originally the Faithful Companions of Jesus which formed circa 1889.
- Council of Jewish Women
- Central W.C.T.U.
- Cliff Bungalow P.T.A.
- Col. Walker Chapter I.O.D.E.
- Earl Grey P.T.A.
- Hillhurst W.C.T.U.
- Hebrew Ladies' Aid
- Hillhurst United Ladies' Aid
- Humane Society
- King George P.T.A.
- Knox United Church Ladies' Aid
- Lend a Hand Society
  The Society initially was formed by Mrs. W.A. Geddes in the fall of 1921 The aims of the Lend a Hand Society were to help those who help themselves and to make life more cheerful for the underprivileged.
- Military Chapter I.O.D.E.

- Mount Royal P.T.A.
- McDougall P.T.A.
- Ramsay P.T.A.
- Royal Scots Chapter I.O.D.E.
- St. Andrews Presbyterian Ladies' Aid
- Sacred Heart Ladies' Aid
- St. Josephs Altar Society
- St. Ann's Altar Society
- St. Vincent de Paul Society
- Social Service Home
- United Social Service
- Victoria P.T.A.
- Women's Institute
- West End W.C.T.U.
- Women's Liberal Club
- Wesley United Ladies' Aid
- Women's Hostel
- Women's Labor League
- Y.W.C.A. Board
- Y.M.C.A. Ladies' Auxiliary

1940

Calgary Local Council of Women Table Officers

- President – Mrs. E. Hirst
- First Vice President – Mrs. A. Whyte
- Second Vice President – H.M. McCallum
- Third Vice-President – Mrs. W. Rothwell
- Fourth Vice President – Mrs. Joseph Shaw
- Recording Secretary – Mrs. F. Walker
- Treasurer – Mrs. W. Duncan

Standing Committees

- Arts and Letters – Mrs. Kate Martin
- Citizenship – Mrs. A.E. Pearson
- Cinema and Printed Matter – Mrs. A.E. Boyce
- Economics – Miss Vera McKim
- Education – Miss Mary Willison
- Housing and Town Planning – Mrs. Fred White
- League of Nations – Mrs. Fairy Walker
- Laws – Mrs. Eileen Lannon
- Mental Hygiene – Dr. Clara Christie
- Natural Resources – Mrs. G.T. Jackson
- Public Health – Dr. Lola McLatchie
- Soldiers, Sailors and Airmen – Mrs. M. McElroy
- Trades and Professions – Mrs. F.S. Ditto
- Immigration – Mrs. N. Price
- Moral Standards – Mrs. B. Sibbald
- Child Welfare – Mrs. Jean McDonald

Affiliated Societies

- Calgary Branch of Women's Institute
- Calgary Branch of Business and Professional Club
- Co-operative Commonwealth Federation (C.C.F.) Women's Club
  Now known as the New Democratic Party (N.D.P.), the C.C.F. was a democratic socialist party, founded at Calgary in 1932 by members of farm, labor and socialist parties under the leadership of J.S. Woodsworth. The New Democratic Party, was founded in 1961 at a convention in Ottawa
- Calgary Section of Jewish Women
- Earl Grey Home and School Association
- Hadassah Chapter of Jewish Women
- Ladies' Aid of First Baptist Church

- Lend-a-Hand Society
- Langevin Junior High Home and School Association
- Langevin & Bridgehead Handicrafts Guild
- Ramsay Home and School Association
- Scarboro Ladies' Aid
- Soroptimist Club
- St. Paul's Ladies' Aid
- United Church Social Service
- University Women's Club
  Originally the Alberta Woman's Association, it joined the Local Council in 1931.
- Unemployed Women's Association
  Joined the Local Council in 1931.
- West End W.C.T.U.
- Wesley Women's Association
- Women's Section of Dominion Labor Party
- Women's International League for Peace and Freedom
  Joined the Local Council in 1931
- Women's Labor League
- Women's Section Ukrainian Labor Temple Association
- Y.M.C.A. Men's Board
- Y.W.C.A.

1950

Calgary Local Council of Women Table Officers

- President – Mrs. H.F. Clarke
- Vice Presidents:
  - Mrs. D.F. Kpbylnyk
  - Mrs. K. Clennan
  - Mrs. William Rothwell
  - Mrs. Thomas Mowbray
- Recording Secretary – Mrs. E.C. Cameron
- Corresponding Secretary – Mrs. F.G.S. Grevett

- Assistant – Mrs. Hugh Ryan
- Treasurer – Mrs. Wallace Neale

Standing Committees

- Arts and Letters – Miss Katherine Martin
- Child Welfare – Mrs. Russell Clark
- Citizenship – Mrs. A. Hall
- Education – Miss M. Willison
- Economics and Taxation – Mrs. Joseph Grabowski
- Laws – Mrs. John Gorman
- Public Health – Mrs. Hugh Ryan
- Natural resources – Mrs. Ervin Hirst
- Trades and Professions – to be appointed
- Soldiers, Sailors and Airmen – to be appointed
- United Nations – Mrs. James Zimmerman
- Immigration and Morals Standards – to be appointed.

Affiliated Societies

- Women's Council Mountview Social Service Home
  The only training school for Protestant delinquent girls
  in the Province of Alberta is operated under a local board
  by the Board of Evangelism and Social Service of the
  United Church of Canada.

  The girls, whose ages range from 13 to 17 ½ years, are
  admitted into the home as wards of the Provincial
  Government of Alberta, and are committed by the
  Juvenile Courts. They usually remain for 6 months to
  one and one half years and are on the honor system.
  They attend school and are taught housework and cook-
  ing. Unmarried mothers are also cared for, but they are
  usually private cases.
- National Council of Jewish Women
- National Security Association

- St. Vladimir's Ladies' Ukrainian Church
- Women's Institute
- Auxiliary to Grace Hospital
- University Women's Club
- Hillhurst Baptist Missionary Circle

1960

Calgary Local Council of Women Table Officers

- Honorary President – Mrs. Harry Hayes
- Honorary Vice-President – Alderman Mary Dover
- Past President – Mrs. A. Russell Hutchison
- President – Mrs. Grace Stonewall
- First Vice President – Mrs. Ralph Johnson, Chairman of Finance Committee
- Second Vice President – Mrs. A.A. Frawley, in charge of arranging executive meetings
- Third Vice President – Mrs. Frank Fish
- Fourth Vice President – Mrs. K.F. MacLennan
- Treasurer – Mrs. Russell Clark
- Recording Secretary – Mrs. Robert Wilson
- Corresponding Secretary – Mrs. Addison E. Wilson
- Courtesy Secretary – Mrs. S.C. Harrington

Standing Committees

- Arts and Letters – Mrs. Frank Fish
- Economics – Mrs. K.F. MacLennan
- Education – Mrs. Felix Leew
- Health – Dr. Agnes O'Neil, City Hall Health Department and Dr. Hoy, City Hall Dental Department
- Laws – Mrs. J.C. Gorman
- Nutrition and Food – Mrs. G.L. Somerville
- Press, Radio & T.V. – Mrs. A.A. Frawley

- Safety Council – Mrs. Russell Clark
- Trades & Labour – Mrs. A.A. Frawley
- Welfare – Mrs H.J. Follinsbee and Mrs. W.D. Mair
- International Affairs – Mrs. C. Richard Hoar

Affiliated Societies

- Alberta Association of Registered Nurses
  President: Miss Jean Cumming
  Representative: Miss E.M. Hagerman
  Members: 887
  Aims: Better Patient Care & Community Service.
- American Women's Club
  President: Mrs. B.C. Day
  Members: 250
  Aims: Social, Service & Education.
- Business & Professional Women's Club
  President: Mrs. James McRobb
  Representative: Mrs. J. Bridger
  Members: 120
  Aims: Encourage co-operation among business and professional women. Improve status, extend educational opportunities.
- Calgary Activettes
  President: Mrs. A.C. Levitt
  Representatives: Mrs. Harry Johnson, Mrs. C. Irving
  Members: 50
  Aims: Auxiliary to Active Club; aid to underprivileged children.
- Calgary Association for Retarded Children
  President: Mrs. H.J. Follensbee.
  Representative: Mrs. W. Meikle
  Members: 165
  Aims: Teach retarded children to be self supporting members of society.

- Calgary Liberal Women's Association
  President: Mrs. F.P. Hussey
  Representatives: Mrs. Ralph Johnson, Mrs. W.H. Ross
  Members: 150
  Aims: The cause of Liberalism; selection and election of
      candidates.
- Calgary North Women's Liberal Association
  President: Miss Natalie Chapman
  Representative: Mrs. S.C. Harrington
  Members: 100
  Aims: The cause of Liberalism; selection and election of
      candidates.
- Calgary Women's Conservative Association
  President: Mrs. E.R. Tavender
  Representatives: Mrs. A.A. Frawley, Mrs. Eric James
  Members: 400
  Aims: To work for Conservative Party to better the con-
      ditions of all people.
- Canadian Association of Consumers, Calgary Branch
  President: Mrs. K.F. MacLennan
  Members: 250
  Aims: To study consumer problems; make recommenda-
      tions for solution to Government, trade and
      industry; publicize matters of consumer interest;
      secure opinions.
- Columbian Ladies
  President: Mrs. Joe Comessotti
  Representative: Mrs. Joe Comessotti
  Members: 40
  Aims: Auxiliary to Knights of Columbis
- First Baptist Church Women's Organization
  President: Mrs. David Wilson
  Representative: Mrs. F.B. Cummings
  Members: 350

Aims: Spiritual and Social Welfare of Church and Community; Christian Fellowship; home and foreign mission support.

- Friends of the Indian Society
President: Mr. W.B. Gallup
Representative: Mrs. W.R. Shearer
Members: 75
Aims: To encourage Indians to improve themselves; to assist them in any possible way.
- Grace Hospital Ladies Auxiliary
President: Mrs. G. Rhodes
Representative: Mrs. T.W. Kelter
Members: 25
Aims: Provide needed service and equipment for hospital.
- Hillhurst Baptist Mission Circle
President: Mrs. H.P. Saunders
Representative: Mrs. R. Binnion
Members: 38
Aims: Support and study of home and foreign Missions.
- Holy Cross Ladies Auxiliary
President: Mrs. Addison Wilson
Representative: Mrs. C.D. Lemmon
Members: 200
Aims: To render service to hospital and patients; to provide specialized equipment.
- Ladies Auxiliary to National Union of Public Employees
President: Mrs. M.G. Mitchell
Representatives: Mrs. W. LeBar, Mrs. Evelyn Brunton
Members: 35
Aims: Philanthropic Service; Emphasis on youth 16 to 20 age group.
- Ladies Club Hounsfield Heights and Briar Hill
President: Mrs. F.J. Desreux
Representative: Mrs. F. Conduit

Members: 200

Aims: Community Service.

- National Council of Jewish Women

  President: Mrs. Harry Cohen.

  Representative: Mrs. Cecil Alexander

  Members: 300

  Aims: Opportunity for Jewish Women to work together for broader concept of faith and humanity. Projects: education, community service, international welfare.

- National Social Security Study Group

  President: Mrs. J.A. Mc Donald

  Representatives: Mrs. L.G. Clark and Mrs. Mary Beattie

  Aims: Study National Social Security problems with view to action.

- Quota Club

  President: Miss Violet Haines

  Representatives: Mrs. G.L. Somerville, Mrs. J.H. Hillier

  Members: 20

  Aims: Advancing ideals of righteousness, justice, and mutual understanding.

- Rehabilitation Society of Calgary

  President: Mr. William Ireland

  Representative: Mrs. John Gorman

  Members: 300

  Aims: Social Adjustment, Mental Health, employment assistance for physically handicapped persons.

- St. Vladimer's Womens Auxiliary

  President: Mrs. M. Kowal

  Representative: Mrs. Stephen Putnik

  Members: 50

  Aims: Service to Church and Community

- Star & Crescent Ladies Orange Benevolent Association

  President: Mrs. Harry LeVesconte

Representatives: Mrs. W. Hinchelwood, Mrs. Clarence Hollingworth.

Members: 75

Aims: Community Welfare Work; Project: Support two 4-Bed Wards at Woods Christian Home.

- University Women's Club

President: Mrs. Ronald Wyer

Representatives: Mrs. G.K. Sheane and Mrs. J.L. Haw

Aims: To stimulate intellectual activity, friendship, participation in public affairs, advancement of arts, science and literature.

- Women's Institute

President: Mrs. W.J. Ockley

Representative: Mrs. Earl Wilson

Members: 30

Aims: Community Service; World Wide Friendships.

- Young Women's Christian Association

President: Mrs. McLean Jones

Representatives: Mrs. J.C. Orman, Mrs. F.G. Wetherall

Members: 4786

Aims: To build a fellowship of Women and Girls devoted to the task of realizing in our common life those ideals of personal and social living to which we are committed by our Faith.

1970

Calgary Local Council of Women Table Officers

- President – Mrs. B.D. Langridge
- Vice Presidents:
  - Mrs. J. Van Heteren
  - Mrs. J.M. Johnson
- Past President – Mrs. A.C. Luft
- Corresponding Secretary – Mrs. J. Anderson

- Recording Secretary – Mrs. J.H. Waite
- Treasurer – Mrs. J.G. Mills
- Publicity – Mrs. H.K. Roessingh
- Telephone Secretary – Mrs. T.A. Crowe
- Courtesy Secretary – Mrs. R.G.S. Currie
- Archives – Mrs. Harry Johnson

Standing Committees

- Arts and Letters – Mrs. J. VanHeteren
- Citizenship – Miss Barbara Scott
- Education – Mrs. Joni Chorny
- Health and Welfare – Mrs. H. A. Swinton
- Planning – Mrs. Grace Martens
- International Affairs – Mrs. F.C. Engbaum
- Laws and Resolutions – Mrs. J. Van Heteren
- Radio, T.V. Films – Mrs. J. Aikenhead
- Social – Mrs. K. Vine
- Membership – Mrs. S. (Marjorie) Norris

Affiliated Societies

- Calgary Activettes
  President: Mrs. F.J. (Gena) Capune
  Representative: Mrs. H.M. (Valerie) Turnbull
- Calgary Business and Professional Women
  President: Miss Jean Casselman
  Representatives: Mrs. J.M. (Mary Ellen) Johnson and
  Mrs. D.E.A. (Virginia) McKay
- Calgary Home Economics Association
  President: Mrs. Jackie Betts
  Representatives: Mrs. Edith Wilcock and Mrs. Marjorie
  Lawrence

- Calgary Jaycettes
  President: Mrs. W. (Joan Sumner)
  Representative: Mrs. Walter (Gay) Cross
- Calgary Liberal Women's Association
  President: Mrs. U. Guichon
  Representatives: Mrs. W.H. Ross and Mrs. F.E. Wright
- Calgary Women's Conservative Association
  President: Mrs. E. Sutherland
  Representatives: Mrs. R.G.S. Currie, Mrs. Oscar (Grace) Stonewall and alternate Mrs. E.W.M. James
- Canadian Save the Children Fund (CANSAVE)
  President: Mrs. C.G. Crosland
  The Fund helps needy children throughout the world. It does respond in emergency and disaster situations, but is chiefly concerned with long range programs which enable destitute children and families to help themselves. In 1971 the Calgary branch raised almost $9000.
- Catholic Women's League
  President: Mrs. R.A. Wilcox
  Representative: Mrs. J.P Ziebart
- Faculty Women's Club – University of Calgary
  President: Mrs. A.E.D. Schonfield
  Representatives: Mrs. Stanley (Marjorie) Norris and Mrs. Joni Chorny
- First Baptist Church Women's Organization
  President: Mrs. Austin Torrell
  Representatives: Mrs. K.F. MacLennan and Miss Belle Beveridge
- Grace Hospital Ladies' Auxiliary
  President: Mrs. G. Corrie Broer
  Representatives: Mrs. J.G. (Rhoda) Mills and Mrs. R.T. (Vi) Robinson
- Hadassah Council
  President: Mrs. Burt Promislow
  Representative: Mrs. Jack Smolensky

- Hillhurst Baptist Mission Circle
  President: Mrs. Roselle Harris
  Representative: Mrs. Alan Hilton
- Holy Cross Hospital Ladies' Auxiliary
  President: Mrs. C.G. Crosland
- National Council of Jewish Women, Calgary Section
  President: Mrs. Leonard Fox
  Representatives: Mrs. Dina Spindel and Mrs. H. Belzberg
- North Calgary Business and Professional Women's Club
  President: Miss Grace Tench.
  Representative: Miss Jean Hutchison
- Quota Club
  President: Mrs. I.D. (Jessie) Douglas
  Representatives: Mrs. F.E. Burnard and Mrs. Marguerite Durwin
- Rosedale United Church Women
  President: Mrs. Vern Winters
  Representatives: Mrs. J. Hergert and Miss Helen Morrison
- Salvation Army Children's Village
  Captain: Marguerite Lloyd
- Social Credit Women's Auxiliary Calgary Council (SCWA)
  President: Mrs. Chris Barker
  Representatives: Mrs. Olive Lowry and Mrs. Louise Bulger
  The SWCA is composed of a number of auxiliaries in the city. Its main objective during 1971 was to encourage the auxiliaries to donate books of Canadian and Social Credit history to schools and libraries. The major project was the presentation of the biography of William Aberhart and the early history of the Social Credit movement to the Aberhart Foundation, Historical library and Archives.

- Soroptimist Club of Calgary
  President: Mrs. Scott Duguid
  Representative: Mrs. Isobel Beveridge
- St. Vladimir's Women's Auxiliary
  President: Mrs. P. Petrasuk
  Representatives: Mrs. H.C. Mekitiak and Mrs. M. Kurczaba
- St. David's United Church Women
  President: Mrs. J. James
  Representative Mrs. Josephine Prescott
- Star & Crescent L.O.B.A
  President: Mrs. G. Miller
  Representatives: Mrs. T.A. Crowe and Mrs. J.C. (Joan) Hollingworth
- Calgary U.N.I.C.E.F.
  Chairman: Mrs. Mrs. Peter J. Huber
  Representative: Mrs. Barbara Langridge
  The Committee report of 1972 noted that 24 000 boxes were distributed to 183 schools and 43 youth groups at Halloween. The coins collect amounted to $19 165.90 and the sale of Greeting Cards totaled $17 296.75.
- Calgary Presbyterial United Church Women
  President: Mrs. Addison Scratch
  Representative: Mrs. G.M. Tough
  The Presbyterial is comprised of members of each United Church in the city. Its concern is for the work and enrichment of the women within the church, their work in the community (in co-operation with other religious denominations, community organizations and service groups), and the support of mission work throughout Canada and foreign lands.
- The University Women's Club
  President: Mrs. H.P. Thornton
  Representatives: Mrs. J.A. Brown and Mrs. G.F. Woolcock

- The Voice of Women
  President: Mrs. Douglas Fitch
  Representative: Mrs. J. VanHeteren
- Young Women's Christian Association
  President: Miss Bevan Patterson
  Representative: Mrs. R. Tillman

1975

Calgary Local Council of Women Table Officers

- Honorary President – Muriel Kovitz
- Past President – Joni Chorny
- President – Gwen Thorssen
- Vice-Presidents:
  - Nora Lockerbie
  - Frances Roessingh
- Corresponding Secretary – Gunilla Mungen
- Treasurer – Evelyn Tough
- Recording Secretary – Dorothy Groves

Administrative Committee

- Publicity Convener – Norma Bicknell
- Telephone Secretary – Marg Ziebart
- Membership – Committee of Vice Presidents
- Courtesy Secretary – Betty Barker

Standing Committees

- Arts and Letters – Convener Lois Currie, Eileen Atkinson
- Citizenship – Convener Marjorie Norris, Barbara Scott
- Education – Convener Betty Shifflet, Eleanor Werry
- Health and Welfare – Christine Gilhooly

- International Affairs – Joan Onofrio
- Radio, T.V. and Films – Convener Ena Hertz, Flora Greenhalgh
- Economics – Grace Martens
- Public Safety – DoDe Chapman
- Laws and Resolutions – Joni Chorny
- Nutrition – Carol Diamond
- Social – Convener Irma Wright, Edith Crowe
- Conservation – Frances Roessingh
- Housing and Community Planning – Convener Sheila Grime, Mrs. Carl Youngren
- Status of Women – Convener Dr. E. Silverman, Christine Bell, Dorothy Groves

Affiliated Societies

- Calgary Activettes: Mrs. D. Snyde
- Calgary Home Economics Association: Nora Lockerbie
- Calgary Council of Social Credit Women's Auxiliary: Betty Barker
- Consumer's Association of Canada, Calgary Branch: Mrs. W.A. Thom
- The Calgary Birth Control Association: Gunilla Mungen
- University Women's Club of Calgary: Sheila Evans
- UNICEF Alberta: Faye Keevil
- CANSAVE: Mabel Crosland
- Catholic Women's League: Yolande Gagnon
- Calgary Presbyterial United Church Women: Irene E. Fitzsimmons
- Star and Crescent Lodge L.O.B.A: Edith Crowe
- Baptist Women of the First Baptist Church Calgary: Do De Chapman
- Calgary Presbyterial Women's Missionary Society Western Division

- Calgary Women's Progressive Conservative Association: Mrs. S.W. Olsen
- Family Life Education Council: Betty Shifflett
- Calgary Women's Liberal Association: Blanche Anderson
- C.N.I.B.: Miss C. McKellar
- Faculty Women's Club: Dorothy Groves
- Foothills Professional Business Women
- Holy Cross Auxiliary: Addie Marshall
- Elizabeth Fry Society of Alberta: Christine Bell
- Samaritans
- Soroptimist Club of Calgary: Emily Gilmour
- Women for Political Action
- Y.W.C.A.
- Calgary Women' Emergency Shelter: Susan Easton.

The following Emergency Resolution was presented by the University Women's Club of Calgary. "Be it resolved that every WOMAN be urged to write to her member of parliament, the Minister of Justice and the Prime Minister (reaffirming our Resolution of 1970) requesting removal of abortion from the Criminal Code." Presented by Sheila Evans, seconded by Betty Shifflett. Discussion followed. The need for this as an emergency resolution having been questioned and answered it was agreed to put it to the vote. Mrs. Gagnon asked that there be a record of those wishing to abstain or vote against this resolution. The vote by official ballot was 42 in favor, 19 against. Passed. The following names were recorded as wishing to show their vote: Margaret Ziebart, Yolande Gagnong (against – with the request that if any publicity is given to this motion "please make sure that our view is noted'). Irene Martin (same as Mrs. Gagnon), DoDe Chapman (voted against) and Blanche Anderson (abstained).

Notes

1   The editorial titled "The Voice of Women" read:

> The National Council of Women made a submission this week to the Royal Commission on Price Spreads. Claiming to speak for women generally, it said that "Women seek the right to choose a product on the basis of true value. . . . They do not want expensive giveaways and gimmicks. . . . Packaging products for their visual appeal without regard for intrinsic merit, comes close to deception." . . . We do not quarrel with the general attitude of the National Council of Women, but we do challenge its authority. It does not represent Canadian women. It is misnamed. It should call itself the National Council of Old-fashioned Sensible Women. (*The Morning Albertan*, November 19, 1958, p. 4.)

The then Calgary Coucil President penned a spirited defense of National Council to the *Albertan* editor that read in part:

> As to the brief submitted to the Royal Commission on Price Spreads, I suggest you sit down and study the whole brief. It is intensely interesting and enlightening. The sentence which you misquoted reads, "The enclosure of a product in a package planned and engineered to draw sales by the attractiveness or eye appeal of the package, without due and sufficient regard to fair value given therein, comes close to deception." Well doesn't it?
>   Have you ever watched a young mother with two or three tots hanging to her skirts, trying to engineer

her way through the market? Has she time to read the fine print on the pretty red packet? Or does she want to make a scene by quarrelling with Junior over the latest gimmick in the breakfast food package, which, by the way, is usually set well within Junior's sight and reach? Is this fair exploitation of the inexperienced and harried home maker? Who is there to teach her or protect her if old, sensible Council of Women doesn't take a hand?

You should be grateful there is enough moral indignation left in 700 000 women in Canada to be profoundly shocked by the brainwashing tactics and bland cynicism of the motivation analysts and methods used by the commercial propagandist. Should they be allowed to take advantage of the weaker instincts of the public, whether it is the harried young matron buying peace with a gimmick or the ambitious young man who motgages his future to buy a fish-tailed monster which blaring automobile advertisements assure him "three out of four" can afford?

Surely, marketing education for the young home maker is needed. We have just started, Mr. Editor, but never underestimate the power of the "old and sensible National Council of Women."

Mrs. A. Russell Hutchison
President, Calgary Council of Women

2   Alice Jamieson was recently widowed. Her husband, Reuben Rupert Jamieson, a two term mayor of Calgary (1909 and 1910), died at age 54 on May 30, 1911, at Burrard Sanitarium, Vancouver, where he was being treated for severe mental and physical breakdown attributed to overwork and the nerve-wracking strain of municipal administration during his mayoralty.

3   Press coverage of the Consumers' League market venture identified its Local Council origin, the civic indifference of the skeptical city council, and resignations attributable to competing factions within the League itself. By mid-December of 1919, the halcyon days were gone, and its very existence was at stake. When the amendment to close the market ended in a tie vote – six aldermen for and six against – Mayor Marshall cast the deciding vote, and the market was spared.

4   The minutes of the April 21, 1922 Local Council Meeting contain this account:

> Mrs. Akitt reported for the Memorial Tree Planting Campaign. Individual trees or a plot may be had in the Memorial Driveway from Hillhurst Bridge to St. Georges' Island, in memory of soldiers who fell in the late war or a spot in the city might be beautified as the Council's memorial. The Committee had enquired of Mr. Reader the approximate cost of seeding and planting a small section in Elbow Park which was in a very unsightly condition owing to the car-tracks being moved. Mr. Reader thought the City would do their share and hoped the Council would assist. As a memorial, the sum of $75 was suggested by the Committee, but a smaller sum would be acceptable. It was thought a Tea might be given to raise this money.
>
> The Council were of the opinion the residents of Elbow Park should be asked to assist in beautifying this spot and a Committee to see to this and other plans was named – Mrs. Stavert, Mrs. Nelson, Mrs. G. McKay, Mrs. Petrie, Mrs. Paddeu, & Mrs. Akitt.

5   See Addendum B: Laws and Resolutions Committee, The 1920s, 1912–25 Report by Mrs. Harold Riley, Convenor, Municipal Petitions, No. 24.

6   The St. Joseph's Altar Society, the St. Vincent de Paul
    Society, and the St. Ann's Altar Society also withdrew in
    1933 because of the passing of the family limitation resolu-
    tion.

7   The History Pageant consisted of a mock trial to determine
    if the Local Council had been a success. The attorney for
    the prosecution charged: "There are still no permanent
    woman police magistrates in Calgary, no women judges, no
    women on the board of the Bank of Canada, or on our
    library board." The attorney for the defense cited Local
    Council's role in the Married Women's Relief Act, the
    Dower Act, Mothers' Allowance and Equal Parental
    Rights, as well as local improvements like copper coinage,
    vacant lot gardens, wrapped bread, and covered meat. The
    judge ruled in favor of the Council. Other parts of the pag-
    eant depicted Emmeline Pankhurst's fight for suffrage, the
    need for greater vigilance in the matter of maternal mortal-
    ity, and hope for a future of health, happiness and peace.
    ("Banquet Followed by History Pageant," *Calgary Daily
    Herald*, January 27, 1939, p.16).

8   Millicent McElroy died on September 12, 1950. The next
    day's *Calgary Herald*, on page 18, featured a picture of her
    playing her cornet with. The words "A Personal Salute" and
    caption "Familiar Local Figure During Wartime Dies"
    headed the obituary:

    Mrs. George McElroy, 81, of 517 Underwood Block,
    who was a familiar figure at the C.P.R. station during
    two Great Wars, playing salutes on her cornet to
    departing and arriving servicemen, died Tuesday
    night in Calgary.
       Born in Crossgate, England, Mrs. McElroy first
    took up cornet-playing when she travelled Britain
    playing at meetings conducted by General William
    Booth, founder of the Salvation Army. Many years

later she played for the general's grandson, William Booth Clibbon, when he conducted Salvation Army meetings here.

Mrs. McElroy first started playing the cornet to entertain servicemen when the British troops returned home from the Boer War.

She and her husband moved to Calgary in 1911 from Britain and during the First Great War she met practically every troop train going through Calgary, playing her cornet either solo or standing with attending military bands.

During the Second Great War Mrs. McElroy was not able to meet every troop train but she was on hand for a good many departures and arrivals , again playing solo or accompanying a military musical aggregation. She once said that although she could not do a great deal for "the boys" she felt her station appearance was a personal salute to the men in uniform.

Mrs. McElroy was active in the Women's Auxiliary of the Canadian Legion, the W.C.T.U., the Local council of Women, and the child welfare movement.

She is survived by her husband George in Calgary; a daughter, Mrs. J.E. Patton of Calgary; a son, George Jr. of Calgary; 10 grandchildren and 11 great-grand-children.

Jacques funeral home is in charge of funeral arrangements which have not been completed."

9   The 1951 L.C.W. yearbook on page 23 named "Mayor D.H. Mackay in the Chair. Rev. Preston McLeod, Pastor of the Knox United Church, as guest speaker."

Other dignitaries attending included L.C.W.'s new president Mrs. Russell Clark; Mr. Cyrus B. Follmer, American Consul; Rabbi Elmner for the Jewish People; Father O'Day for the Catholic Church; Major Edna M. Burrows, Salvation Army; Chief Crowchild and Mr. John Lawrie, Scarcee Indians and Indian people; Mrs. Charles Walton and Mrs. H. Richardson, colored people; Mr. and Mrs. Cyril Howartz representing Jewish Associations; Mr. Ho Lem, Jr., Chinese; Mr. D.K. Kobylinyk, Ukrainian; and Mrs. Leona Flegal Patterson representing the Canadian Way of Life.

10 The following year she was elected president of the Provincial Council of Women where she served two terms. Then, in 1961, she was elected vice-president of the National Council.

11 In her Economics Convenor report on page 35 of the 1960 L.C.W. Year Book, Lillian identified the store as Loblaws and reported that, after the Provincial Government outlawed trading stamps, she wrote a letter of commendation to the Deputy Minister of Industry and Development, at Local Council's request. (See Addendum B: Laws and Resolutions Committee, The 1960s, Economics, Mrs. K.F. MacLennan, Convenor.

12 At the January 27, 1965, regular meeting of Local Council, members voted on "Resolution No. 2" – a resolution asking for a Judicial Inquiry into civic affairs. The result: 8 for, 4 against, and 10 abstaining. (Source: Minutes of the January 27, 1965, regular L.C.W. meeting, Glenbow archives, L.C.W. fonds M5841/31.

13 The anonymous angel was soon identified as geologist J. Richard Harris.

14 Prince's Island proved a temporary home, albeit for 18 years. A boom that went bust in the early 1980s demolished plans to build two fifty-storey office towers on the site. In June of 1991, the cupola returned to its original James Short School site where it became the centerpiece of the James Short Park at 4th. Avenue and Centre Street S.W.

15 An excerpt from the minutes of the September 28, 1960 L.C.W. meeting read in part: "The program for the afternoon, the panel on 'the Treatment of Women in Prison,' was presented with Mrs. John Gorman as moderator who introduced the Panel. Mrs. Harry Johnson, Miss Marjorie Larson, Mr. B.A. Baugh: The speakers all were careful to present the true facts as they found them. The Tape recording of two unseen Women Ex-Prisoners of Fort Saskatchewan Jail was most enlightening. Mrs. Gorman, and Mrs. Johnson, our conveners of laws, both presented their on the spot findings of conditions in Edmonton jails and Calgary. Miss Larsen and Mr. Baugh, both of the John Howard Society, verified these statements. The majority of the offences of women were not of a criminal nature but of a more social. Liquor, vagrancy, and prostitution. Liquor and vagrancy accounting for 50% of all convictions. The most tragic revelation was 70% of all inmates are Indian women."

16 An account published on the City page in the September 4, 1964, *Albertan* captioned "Indian Centre Paternalistic," read:

Calgary's Indian Centre – to open in October – is still drawing fire.

Some of it seems to be aimed at the Local Council of Women for setting up the venture.

Indian lawyer William Wuttunee said: "They were going to do it come Hell or high water and they did."

He objected to the paternalistic approach and doubted the Indian community is fully behind the scheme.

The L.C.W.'s Mrs. Grace Johnson said eight chiefs, five reserves and at least 2,000 Indians support the move. She claimed the L.C.W. had spent two years researching the need and getting the Indian people's opinion.

Earlier, she announced a year's lease had been signed for a three-storey frame house at 504 4th Ave. S.W. This is to become the Calgary Indian Friendship Society centre.

Bert Marcuse of the Calgary Family Service Bureau felt a centre would help Indian entry into the white community. But he felt it should be a temporary thing.

He also said there had been "a lot of stupid controversy" about the centre.

Dr. Tim Tyler of the Council of Community Services said conflict was so strong "all I got was recriminations when I raised a few questions."

He said the emphasis is away from buildings. And he had reservations about this sort of centre being promoted by non-Indians.

It could make the Indian more visible and trend away from integration, he said. But the centre could also help them identify their own aspirations.

Mrs. Johnson is chairman of the Indian Friendship Society's provisional board. Eventually, a majority of Indians is to take over.

Two grants of $5,000 – from the city and the province – are dependent on opening of the 16-room centre. It is to be staffed by Indians or descendants. Renovations are now under way.

Membership is open to anyone for $1.

17 See Addendum B: Laws and Resolutions Committee, The 1960s, Mrs. E.R. Boulton, Chairman.

18 The 1933 Local Council argued that daylight saving time was not needed in Calgary because we had long summer evenings, and extending the hours would be detrimental to

the health of children." 1941 L.C.W. Yearbook, Emily Atkitt's "History of the Local Council of Women" p. 37.

19 The Local Council strongly recommended Alberta Clark in a September 14, 1961, letter to city council. She was not appointed. The city's Nominating Committee recommended instead that Mr. A.E. Hookway and Mr. A.T. Baker be reappointed to the hospital board for a further two year term.

20 Mrs. Pat Waite served as Corresponding Secretary for two terms.

21 Mrs. R.R. Neve was chairman of the Nutrition Committee.

22 Ruth Gorman's critique was appropriate. The Local Council was in another periodic low.

23 Gwen Thorssen served as the first Chairman of the L.C.W. Status of Women Committee until she was elected Calgary Local Council's president in 1975.

24 The December 17, 1971, feisty letter from Mayor Rod Sykes to Grace Stonewall, chairman of the Special Historical Committee, read:

> Dear Mrs. Stonewall:
>
> I am not "unnecessarily bent" on destroying Rundle Lodge – and certainly I believe I have done more than most people to preserve and improve worthwhile amenities for the benefit of the community.
>
> The problems of this building are fairly simple; if it remains there, it prevents the development of a first-class senior citizen's home which was planned as a two-stage project; it is *not* an attractive building architecturally; and it has been rejected on historical grounds by Federal and Provincial authorities as well as locally by Heritage Park. Finally, the cost of restoring the building to meet building codes for public use is apparently excessive. I have seen no detailed esti-

mates, but the best assessment I could obtain a year or more ago was in the region of $100 000. Any benefit to the community – and I can see little or none – is far outweighed by the fact that there are many, many more urgent needs in a time of considerable hardship for many people.

You may recollect that a relatively small sum of money was apparently not forthcoming from the people who clamoured for preservation of the cupola from the James Short School. If that project, which I think has more merit than this one, cannot enlist public support in the only way that really counts – financially – then how do you think this will fare?

It seems to me that a responsibility attaches to the people who claim public funds for their projects – a responsibility to back up their ideas with justification, with work, and with money. It is easy to talk.
Sincerely,
Rod Sykes
Mayor

The opening paragraph of Grace Stonewall's September 30, 1971, letter likely proved irritating: "Why are you bent on unnecessarily destroying another of the few remaining bits of Calgary's history? We say 'unnecessarily' because Rundle Lodge is not on expensive land; it does not stand in the way of progress, or on land needed for more utilitarian purposes."

25 The *Calgary Herald* account of the June 21, 1992, official opening of the 1127 hectare park was captioned, "Nose Hill becomes Canada's largest urban park." – "Opening marks end of battle to save area from developers." During a brief on-site interview, I commented as follows: "This is a great heritage acquisition. And it's a glorious tribute to nature. After the year 2000, people are going to marvel that

such an open place exists, especially as the city grows." I was identified as "Marjorie Norris, who during the early '70s was president of the local Council of Women, a lobby of about 30 women's groups which began the fight to keep Nose Hill natural." A cabinet minister destined to become premier had this to say: "The only people weeping today are the developers. Isn't it so much better the way it is?" asked provincial Environment Minister Ralph Klein during the opening ceremonies. *Calgary Herald*, June 22, 1992, p. B1.

26 While on the ECA Public Advisory Committee (PAC), Margaret Buckmaster served as chairman of the Non-Renewable Resource Committee and chairman of the Resolutions Committee for four years. She resigned from the PAC in late 1976 on a matter of principle when the government of Alberta replaced it with a government-controlled Environment Council of Alberta.

27 Mrs. Drina Dranchuk was sentenced to die on the gallows on December 12th, 1934. The executive of the Calgary Local Council called an emergency meeting for October 19th at which time they voted unanimously to "petition the Government to commute the death sentence. The resolution they sent to their affiliates read:

> Resolved that we petition the Minister of Justice in view of the jury's recommendation to mercy, and in view also of the reasons herein set forth, to exercise clemency by commuting the sentence of death pronounced upon Mrs. Dina Dranchuk of St. Paul Alberta.
> Evidence submitted to the court showed that Mrs. Danchuk had been driven to desperation by her husband's most inhuman and brutal treatment over a long period of years, and it is reasonable to believe that this, combined with abject poverty and the

provocation which immediately preceded the crime, produced temporarily an abnormal condition of mind in the accused.

In pronouncing the sentence the judge showed that he was compelled to act in accordance with the law, which gave him no alternative to the sentence of death. But at the same time His Lordship showed evident sympathy with the jury's recommendation to mercy and pointed out that the sole right to exercise clemency rests with the Minister of Justice, in behalf of the Crown. (Glenbow Archives, L.C.W. Executive October 19, 1934, emergency meeting minutes, pp. 67–69)

28 Premier John Edward Brownlee resigned his office on July 10, 1934 after a sensational trial in which he was accused of seducing a government employee, Vivian Mac Millan. On June 30, the jury found the premier guilty and awarded $10 000 damages to Miss MacMillan and $5000 to her father, A.D. MacMillan of Edson. On appeal by the associate defence counsel, M.M. Porter K.C., the presiding judge, Acting Chief Justice W.C. Ives, dismissed the $15 000 damages for seduction and ordered the MacMillans to pay court costs. The MacMillans appealed Ives's ruling. On July 23, the executive of the L.C.W. met in the Albertan community room to deal with an emergency resolution proposal to amend the seduction law and contribute to the appeal campaign fund for the MacMillans. The *Calgary Daily Herald* of July 24th reported the meeting under the caption "Local Council Will Not Take Stand on Judgment Appeal." It read:

Decision to take no action concerning the McMillan-Brownlee case with special reference to the appeal for funds now being made, was rapidly reached on a motion presented by Mrs. R.R. Jamieson at an emergency meeting of the Local Council of Women executive held in the Albertan community room, Monday afternoon.

Against her personal conviction that it was not a subject for the council to consider, Mrs. F.G. Grevett explained that she had called the meeting at the behest of a strong element which felt it necessary that the council express itself on the subject as a group interesting itself in the protection of women and children. Mrs. A. Blight and Mrs. E. Hirst spoke in support of the motion.

Attention was drawn to the fact that monetary help could be given individually to the MacMillan appeal if anyone so desired by sending donations direct to Edmonton.

Suggestion was made that the Alberta laws concerning seduction were weak in that they allowed for confusion as that evidenced in the recent case. It was recognized, however, that until the court of appeal had brought in its decision it was both unnecessary and unwise to take up the matter of amendment.

29 The women were to use the books provided by the W.P.T.B. to record the prices of current purchases.

30 On Tuesday, July 4th, the city finance and budget committee endorsed acquisition of the land at the Bow-Elbow junction for the restoration of Fort Calgary as one of its two official centenary projects!

31 Mrs. Jamieson was presented with a life membership in the National Council of Women in 1934 by the then president, Alice Grevett, at the Local Council's annual banquet.

32 The Church Army in Canada trains and supplies full-time lay evangelists.

33 By November of 1940, the citizenry were preoccupied with the war. Both the *Calgary Herald* and the *Albertan* editorialized that "no useful purpose could be served at this time by staging a contest for the commissionership, the city council and the school board." There were no major issues and the $5500 allocated for the election costs would be better spent on the war effort. An election could be avoided by nominating only one candidate for each vacancy, i.e., City Commissioner; the seven aldermanic vacancies; and the three school board vacancies. The political status quo could be retained by nominating all of the five retiring aldermen and nominating one C.G.T.A. (Civic Government Taxpayers Association) and one Labor representative for the two remaining seats. The November 4th *Albertan* editorial ended with this admonition: "It is up to would-be candidates to decide if they will co-operate or place personal aspirations before the city's welfare."

Personal aspirations prevailed. Eleven candidates chose to run for alderman. The 22 percent voter turnout on the November 20th election set a record low. Alice Grevett, who ran as an Independent, received 654 votes, 354 votes behind newly elected alderman E.H. Starr, also an Independent.

34 Staff writer Carol Conway's timely report of the extent Council of Women's involvement in the Murdoch case appeared on page 6 of the April 30, 1974 edition of *The Calgary Herald*, under the heading "Calgary Council of Women." and caption "Test case helps promote cause." It read:

The Calgary Local Council of Women "put their money where their mouth was" when they took up the cause of Mrs. Irene Murdoch, deprived of an equal share in her husband's farm by a Supreme Court of Canada decision.

That money, for Mrs. Murdoch's legal costs, has now risen to the sum of $1,226. collected in just over one month – and has also won the acknowledgement of the National Council of Women.

National president, Mrs. Kay Armstrong, in Calgary Monday, pledged the support of the national council to any group which took a similar stand on an issue that affected the rights of women.

Mrs. Armstrong said the Calgary group had actually done something to further the work of the council in Canada rather than just talk about it.

Local president, Mrs. Joni Chorny, at the council's annual conference, at the Palliser Hotel, said the money, which was raised by public appeal, had come in from all parts of the country.

"The response has been unbelievable," Mrs. Chorny, re-elected for another year as president, told the conference.

In all the letters and phone calls I received there was not one note of discord. We even had letters from men, who said they supported what we were doing."

Mrs. Murdoch, who now lives in Turner Valley, was adopted by the council as a test case when she lost her appeal to get an equal share in the farm which she said she had invested in, and jointly worked for 25 years.

She was awarded $200 in monthly separation payments, while her estranged husband kept the land, farm buildings, house, furniture, car and all revenue from the farm and cattle.

"The Murdoch case showed great tragedy and a need for a change in the law," said Ruth Gorman, the conference's luncheon speaker.

Dr. Gorman, a Calgary lawyer, and a long-time member of the council, said that a change in the law about property rights in marriage had already been recommended by a provincial advisory group.

The Calgary Local council of Women was the first council in Alberta to endorse this recommendation, she added, although that proposal is still not yet law.

Dr. Gorman urged the council to press for a change in legislation, and at the same for each member to make sure that any property she and her husband owned was registered jointly.

The local conference took on a national aspect when Mrs. Armstrong officially launched Environment Day from the Palliser's penthouse dining room.

She said she felt it appropriate that such a day should be launched from Calgary, situated so near the Rockies, Canada's greatest heritage area.

Mrs. Armstrong outlined the national council's projects for the year which she said included legal reform which called for a unified family court system, and a very careful look at the environment and the population growth.

The council is also studying immigration to Canada, looking at it in the context of population settlement, ecology and human needs.

She said she wanted to see "equal weight" given to the views of women coming into Canada, and urged for Canadian women counsellors at ports of entry to talk to the women immigrants.

Mrs. Armstrong said she was also calling for instant deportation of any landed immigrant who gained a criminal record before citizenship, because "crime affects the whole community."

The conference was a chance for the receiving of some money, and a plea for for some more.

Miss Catherine Arthur, director of the Women's Bureau of Alberta, presented a cheque for $3600 to Mrs. Chorny, to underwrite a book, to be published next year, about the women of Calgary.

The book, prepared by the council, will feature all the women's organizations in the city, compiled from histories and information they provide.

The appeal for money came from Mrs. Chorny, who said, as her president's project, she wished to set up a foundation for women in Calgary who would like to become patrons of the local council. A donation of $100 will establish the donor as a patron.

Index